WITHDRAWN

Advances in
# THE STUDY OF BEHAVIOR
VOLUME 18

# Advances in
# THE STUDY OF BEHAVIOR

*Edited by*

JAY S. ROSENBLATT
*Institute of Animal Behavior*
*Rutgers University*
*Newark, New Jersey*

COLIN BEER
*Institute of Animal Behavior*
*Rutgers University*
*Newark, New Jersey*

MARIE-CLAIRE BUSNEL
*UER Biomédicale*
*Groupe Génétique et Comportemente*
*Faculté de Médecine Paris V*
*Paris, France*

PETER J. B. SLATER
*Department of Biology and Preclinical Medicine*
*University of St. Andrews*
*Fife, Scotland*

——————— VOLUME 18 ———————

ACADEMIC PRESS, INC.
**Harcourt Brace Jovanovich, Publishers**
San Diego   New York   Berkeley   Boston
London   Sydney   Tokyo   Toronto

COPYRIGHT © 1988 BY ACADEMIC PRESS, INC.
ALL RIGHTS RESERVED.
NO PART OF THIS PUBLICATION MAY BE REPRODUCED OR
TRANSMITTED IN ANY FORM OR BY ANY MEANS, ELECTRONIC
OR MECHANICAL, INCLUDING PHOTOCOPY, RECORDING, OR
ANY INFORMATION STORAGE AND RETRIEVAL SYSTEM, WITHOUT
PERMISSION IN WRITING FROM THE PUBLISHER.

ACADEMIC PRESS, INC.
1250 Sixth Avenue
San Diego, California 92101

*United Kingdom Edition published by*
ACADEMIC PRESS INC. (LONDON) LTD.
24-28 Oval Road, London NW1 7DX

LIBRARY OF CONGRESS CATALOG CARD NUMBER: 64-8031

ISBN 0-12-004518-4 (alk. paper)

PRINTED IN THE UNITED STATES OF AMERICA
88  89  90  91      9  8  7  6  5  4  3  2  1

# Contents

Contributors ................................................... vii
Preface ........................................................ ix

Song Learning in Zebra Finches (*Taeniopygia guttata*): Progress and Prospects
PETER J. B. SLATER, LUCY A. EALES, AND N. S. CLAYTON

| | |
|---|---|
| I. Introduction | 1 |
| II. Song Development in the Laboratory | 5 |
| III. Can Birds Produce Songs Heard after 65 Days? | 12 |
| IV. Can Birds Produce Songs Heard before 35 Days? | 15 |
| V. Is There an Own-Species Bias? | 22 |
| VI. How Do Zebra Finches Choose Their Song Tutors? | 25 |
| VII. Conclusion | 29 |
| References | 31 |

Behavioral Aspects of Sperm Competition in Birds
T. R. BIRKHEAD

| | |
|---|---|
| I. Introduction | 35 |
| II. Detecting Extrapair Paternity | 36 |
| III. Mechanism of Sperm Competition | 39 |
| IV. Case Studies | 58 |
| V. Conclusions and Directions for Future Research | 63 |
| References | 66 |

Neural Mechanisms of Perception and Motor Control
in a Weakly Electric Fish
WALTER HEILIGENBERG

| | |
|---|---|
| I. Introduction | 73 |
| II. The Mechanism of Electrolocation: "Seeing" Objects as Perturbations of Electric Fields | 74 |

| | | |
|---|---|---|
| III. | The Jamming Avoidance Response | 78 |
| IV. | The Neuronal Substrate for the Analysis of Phase and Amplitude Information | 82 |
| V. | The Ambiguity of Messages Encoded by Individual Neurons | 89 |
| VI. | The Improvisational Character of Neuronal Systems and Traces of Their Evolution | 93 |
| VII. | Developmental Considerations | 96 |
| | References | 96 |

## Behavioral Adaptations to Aquatic Life in Insects: An Example
### ANN CLOAREC

| | | |
|---|---|---|
| I. | Introduction | 99 |
| II. | Respiratory and Locomotory Adaptations to Aquatic Life | 101 |
| III. | Spatial Distribution | 114 |
| IV. | Time Budget of *Ranatra* | 123 |
| V. | Comparisons between Aquatic and Terrestrial Ambush Predators | 128 |
| VI. | Discussion | 145 |
| | References | 146 |

## The Circadian Organization of Behavior: Timekeeping in the Tsetse Fly, A Model System
### JOHN BRADY

| | | |
|---|---|---|
| I. | Introduction | 153 |
| II. | Bouting of Flight | 154 |
| III. | Activity Pattern in Nature: Temperature Effects | 157 |
| IV. | Diel Pattern of Activity in the Laboratory | 160 |
| V. | Circadian Rhythm in the Laboratory | 161 |
| VI. | Diel Pattern of Other Behaviors | 165 |
| VII. | Physiological Inputs That Affect the Diel Pattern of Behavior | 168 |
| VIII. | Changes in Responsiveness: Central or Peripheral? | 178 |
| IX. | The Overall Circadian Organization of Behavior | 182 |
| | References | 186 |

*Index* .......... 193

# Contributors

Numbers in parentheses indicate the pages on which the authors' contributions begin.

T.R. BIRKHEAD (35), *Zoology Department, The University, Sheffield, S10 2TN, England*

JOHN BRADY (153), *Department of Pure and Applied Biology, Imperial College of Science and Technology, London SW7 2AZ, England*

N. S. CLAYTON[1] (1), *Department of Biology and Preclinical Medicine, University of St. Andrews, Fife KY16 9TS, Scotland*

ANN CLOAREC (99), *Laboratoire d'Ethologie, CNRS UA 373, Université de Rennes I, Campus de Beaulieu, 35042 Rennes Cedex, France*

LUCY A. EALES (1), *Department of Biology and Preclinical Medicine, University of St. Andrews, Fife KY16 9TS, Scotland*

WALTER HEILIGENBERG (73), *Neurobiology Unit, Scripps Institution of Oceanography, University of California at San Diego, La Jolla, California 92093*

PETER J. B. SLATER (1), *Department of Biology and Preclinical Medicine, University of St. Andrews, Fife KY16 9TS, Scotland*

[1]Present address: Lehrstuhl für Verhaltenphysiologie, Universität Bielefeld, 4800 Bielefeld 1, West Germany.

# Preface

The aim of *Advances in the Study of Behavior* is to serve the increasing number of scientists who are engaged in the study of animal behavior by presenting their theoretical ideas and research to their colleagues and to those in neighboring fields. Since its inception in 1965, this publication has not changed its aim, to serve "... as a contribution to the development of cooperation and communication among scientists in our field." We acknowledge that in the interim new vigor has been given to traditional fields of animal behavior by their coalescence with closely related fields and by the closer relationship that now exists between those studying animal and human subjects. Scientists studying animal behavior now range from ecologists to evolutionary biologists, geneticists, endocrinologists, ethologists, comparative and developmental psychobiologists, and those doing research in the neurosciences. As the task of developing cooperation and communication among scientists whose skills and concepts necessarily differ in accordance with the diversity of phenomena that they study has become more difficult, the need to do so has become greater. The Editors and publisher of *Advances in the Study of Behavior* will continue to provide the means to meet this need by publishing critical reviews, by inviting extended presentations of significant research programs, by encouraging the writing of theoretical syntheses and reformulations of persistent problems, and by highlighting especially penetrating research that introduces important new concepts.

# Song Learning in Zebra Finches (*Taeniopygia guttata*): Progress and Prospects

Peter J. B. Slater, Lucy A. Eales, and N. S. Clayton[1]

DEPARTMENT OF BIOLOGY AND PRECLINICAL MEDICINE
UNIVERSITY OF ST. ANDREWS
FIFE, KY16 9TS SCOTLAND

## I. Introduction

Studies of song learning in birds have contributed substantially to our understanding of the processes of behavioral development. This is partly for the apparently trivial, but actually very important, reason that the sound spectrograph permits detailed and objective measurement and analysis of sounds in a way that is difficult for other behavior patterns. But work on song has also illustrated particularly well the subtlety of the interaction between the organism and its environment that takes place during ontogeny. While all studies on songbirds (Oscines) agree that the fine details of song are learned, they also show that birds will not learn just any sounds but are usually constrained in some way to learn those with particular features.

On detailed study, species differences in vocal development become striking. The songs of some Suboscines are relatively complex yet develop normally without the opportunity to copy (Kroodsma, 1984), and in other cases learning is known to play a key role in the ontogeny of very simple call notes (e.g., Mundinger, 1979). Thus the fact that song is a relatively long and complex utterance, which is often the only objective means of separating it from other sounds that birds produce, cannot be taken as the simple reason why song learning evolved. Even among the songbirds, exact developmental strategies are widely different, and the differences between close relatives are often sharp. For example, the number of different song phrases that individuals develop can range from one up to several thousand, and can even vary from 1 to 200 within a single genus (e.g., thrushes, *Turdus* spp., Ince and Slater, 1985). Species also range from those that only copy their own

---

[1]Present address: Lehrstuhl für Verhaltensphysiologie, Universität Bielefeld, Bielefeld, West Germany.

species to those that mimic others, from those that copy every detail with precision to those that commonly improvize and rearrange the sounds that they hear, and from those that only learn during a short period early in development to those that can modify their songs throughout life (see Slater, 1983, for a review).

These differences among species make it hard to generalize. They are doubtless related to differences in the function that song serves in each, which in turn depends on other aspects of their breeding biology. Catchpole (1982) and Slater (1981) have proposed that a key factor may be the extent to which song is used for mate attraction and for rival repulsion in different species. In many species it appears to have both of these roles, but they may vary in which is the more important, so that the form of song can only be a compromise. From this argument it is predicted that song adapted primarily as a mate attractant would be likely, through sexual selection, to become more varied and elaborate, would not necessarily be copied accurately, and might well be modified throughout life. On the other hand, songs used as signals between rival males would be short and discrete, with accurate copying allowing matched countersinging on territorial boundaries, and with learning before first breeding ensuring that territorial defense could be achieved as soon as a bird was mature.

Such variations caution against attempting to make broad generalizations about song learning as a whole, but ideas and theories may still have broad application even if details do not. Two such ideas are those of *auditory template* and *sensitive phase*, both of which have been influential in guiding thinking about the development of song.

The auditory template idea, developed by Konishi (e.g., 1965) and Marler (e.g., 1976), sees the constraints on what is learned as deriving from "active filtering of incoming sensory information" (Marler and Mundinger, 1971). Some sort of filtering clearly does go on, as most birds only produce a very small subset of the sounds that they hear, but subsequent work raises questions about the extent to which such filtering stems from the physical characteristics of the auditory system, as the expression *auditory template* might suggest. In a number of species, of which the zebra finch is one (Eales, 1985a), it has been found that young birds will not learn from loudspeakers or tape recordings and may also require visual as well as vocal interaction with tutors to learn song from them (e.g., nightingale, *Luscinia megarhynchos*, Todt *et al.*, 1979; indigo bunting, *Passerina cyanea*, Payne, 1981). Social factors may thus be of great importance. Indeed, even in those species where learning from tape recordings can occur, a wider range of sounds might be learned if social interaction were allowed (Baptista and Petrinovich, 1986), so that these experiments have not necessarily delineated the shape of the template. Furthermore, some species are known to produce a greater variety of sounds in subsong than they do in full song, indicating that at least part of the filtering is neither a sensory nor a motor constraint, but "an active culling process" (Marler and Peters, 1982a). It is also known that birds can learn, and respond to, the characteristics of songs that they do not sing at all (McGregor and Avery, 1986); here again auditory filtering does not explain the selection of those that are produced. Finally, and perhaps most obviously, characteristics of the syrinx may set limits: The remarkable range of species mimicked by the marsh warbler (*Acrocephalus palustris*) studied by Dowsett-Lemaire (1979) suggests that the only sounds it hears but does not reproduce are those too deep for its syrinx to master. These findings indicate that, while a useful aid to thought about song learning, the auditory template idea needs to be seen alongside several other possible filtering mechanisms which may contribute to the fact that adult birds often sing only a small proportion of the many sounds that they have heard during their lives.

The sensitive phase idea is one that is useful in discussing aspects of development (e.g., Bateson, 1979), but is particularly striking in some song examples where learning is limited to a comparatively brief period early in life (e.g., Kroodsma, 1978). We follow Immelmann and Suomi (1981) in referring to sensitive *phases* rather than *periods*. They argue against the word *period* on the grounds that its German meaning, like an alternative English one, is that of repetition at regular intervals and is clearly inappropriate. In addition, its American usage to refer to the *period* at the end of a sentence introduces an added complication: This suggests steplike starting and stopping and rather fixed duration. As we learn more about the processes involved it is clear that a more gradual onset and termination, which varies in both timing and duration according to experience, is a much more realistic description: The word *phase* is better matched to this conception. We return repeatedly to the topic of sensitive phases, as work on zebra finches has shed considerable light on them.

The zebra finch is one of the species most commonly used in laboratory studies of song learning. Among the practical reasons for this are that it is a widely available cagebird which breeds throughout the year in captivity, can easily be bred in a small cage, and has a generation time of 90 days or less. Furthermore, each adult male has only a single rather brief song, easing analysis and comparison with other individuals. This song usually starts with a few repeated introductory elements which are all of the same form, followed by repetitions of a single phrase of several different element types which are not themselves usually repeated within the phrase (Fig. 1). In captivity, the total number of elements in the song varies from 3 to 13 among individuals, although most have from 6 to 11 (Böhner, 1983: $n = 11$, mean = 8.6; Clayton, 1987b: $n = 15$, mean = 9.6). No tendency has been found for young males to be affected in their choice of song tutor by the number of elements in the tutor's song (Clayton, 1987b).

Given that birdsong and its development vary among species in ways that are likely to be related to other aspects of their breeding biology, it is worth

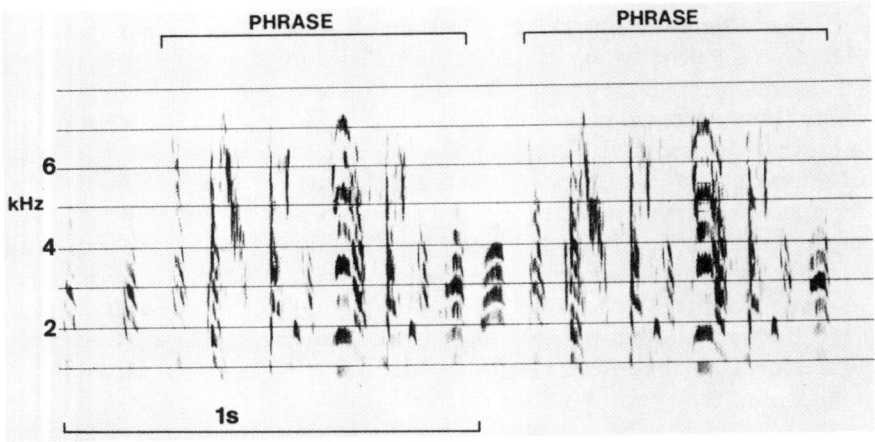

FIG. 1. Two song phrases from a male zebra finch. This particular bird puts a call note betweeen two successive phrases. For most birds, each phrase is composed of different elements and several identical phrases are usually sung in succession to form a song bout; the first phrase of each song bout is often preceded by several introductory elements which, in some songs, are similar to the first element of each song phrase. In this figure, and others showing sonagrams in this article, the noise band up to 500 Hz has been removed.

summarizing briefly what is known of the way of life of the zebra finch in the wild, where it occurs in Australia and the Lesser Sunda islands. It is an intensely sociable species, occurring in large flocks and breeding colonially in response to the rainfall which is essential if there is to be sufficient food for feeding chicks. In some parts of its range rain is unpredictable, explaining the readiness of the birds to breed at all times of year. As well as being unpredictable, conditions suitable for breeding are brief and transient; the stable, monogamous pair bond ensures rapid onset of reproduction when rain does occur. Only males sing, and the song appears not to have territorial function as they will tolerate other individuals very close to the nest. The song is rather quiet and is used both during courtship (directed song) and by solitary males (undirected). Although the postures adopted in these two contexts are rather different, the sounds produced are acoustically very similar (Sossinka and Böhner, 1980). Zebra finch song therefore seems largely to act as a signal between the sexes, although it is simple in structure and does not therefore fit easily into the scheme of song function proposed by Catchpole (1982) and Slater (1981) discussed above. Rather than being concerned primarily with mate attraction or rival repulsion, its major role may be in stimulating ovarian development including ovulation, a function song is known to possess in other species (Brockway, 1965; Kroodsma, 1976). Zebra finches also have several different call notes, one of which is sexually dimorphic and influenced by learning (Zann, 1985), but these are not discussed in detail here.

This review covers recent findings in song learning in zebra finches and brings them together with earlier studies of song learning in this species as well as recent physiological work on this species that is relevant to song development. Zebra finch song also affords excellent prospects for further advances in our understanding of principles of behavioral development; the review concludes by considering some of these remaining questions.

## II. Song Development in the Laboratory

In talking about song development, it is necessary to define the precise conditions giving rise to particular findings. In the wild, zebra finches are reared by both parents and stay with them until around 35 days of age, at which stage they join flocks of nonbreeding birds in the area of the breeding colony (Immelmann, 1962a, 1965). In line with this, in most of our laboratory experiments we cage the young birds with their parents until an average clutch age of 35 days and then separate them into groups. These are our standard conditions against which we can compare other experimental treatments. These conditions obviously do not match precisely the situation in the wild, nor could any experimental arrangement do so. This proviso must be borne in mind if attempts are made to interpret the results of laboratory experiments in functional terms.

Male zebra finches begin to sing at around 30 days of age, a few days before they become independent from their parents. However, the timing of this first song varies greatly among individuals: Captive males have been known to start as early as 25 days (Immelmann, 1962a) and may do so earlier (C. ten Cate, personal communication). Others have not been observed to sing until more than 40 days old. Wild birds, similarly, were observed by Immelmann (1962a) to begin to sing at 4 to 5 weeks.

Arnold (1975) has described song development in some detail. Singing appears first as subsong, which consists of quiet bursts of sound with variable structure produced at irregular intervals. The amount of singing at this stage varies considerably among individuals: Some birds sing rarely to begin with, whereas others sing frequently from the start (Eales, 1985a). These early singing bouts show little evidence of adult phrasing and contain many elements not found in the adult repertoire. By about 40 days, elements may be recognized which show some consistency of form. Although a high variability in both sequence and structure still remains, these elements may also resemble those used by the bird in its final song. The variability gradually reduces until, by about 60 days of age, almost all of the elements of the final song are present and may be given in sequences which are like those of the final song. Between this time and 80 days, song development is completed (Immelmann, 1969), although there may be a subsequent slight increase in tempo and song length, the song phrases becoming linked together into long repetitive sequences.

In this article we describe what is known about the song-learning system in zebra finches and suggest ways in which the timing, accuracy, and selectivity of learning is affected by the environment that the young bird experiences during its development. As with other songbirds, if normal song is to develop the young zebra finch needs to experience adult male song during a sensitive phase for song learning. In zebra finches this phase occurs during the first 3 months of life, in line with the early maturation of the species, and it ends at the time when the bird is likely to begin breeding. Initial work suggested that a young male raised by females alone and so denied a male from which to copy would still produce a species-typical song phrase, but one composed mainly of call notes (Price, 1979). However, as this article shows, recent evidence points to a more complex interaction between age and experience.

Song "learning" can be viewed as consisting of two stages. In addition to the process of memorization, in which sounds that are heard are stored, there is the process of motor development during which the young bird develops its own song by perfecting its motor output and matching it to sounds that it has heard. In some species these two processes are, or can be, at quite separate times. For example, Marler and Peters (1982b) have found that swamp sparrows (*Melospiza georgiana*) produce songs consisting of sounds which they heard several months earlier but have not practiced in the intervening period. However, in zebra finches memorization and song development overlap considerably in time; indeed, under our standard conditions most males begin to produce subsong before the sensitive phase for song learning has started, and this gradually changes into full song over the period in which memorization takes place.

In his original studies of song learning in zebra finches, Immelmann (1969) transferred single eggs to fresh Bengalese finch (*Lonchura striata* var. *domestica*) clutches of similar age. The young were reared by their foster parents in soundproof chambers and then moved into isolation at different ages to investigate the timing of song acquisition. Immelmann reported that males isolated after 80 days old produced a song which was identical with that of their foster father. Males isolated between Days 38 and 66 developed a song which consisted entirely of song elements copied from the foster father but was not identical in either the sequence of the elements or the length of the phrase. Males isolated before Day 40 developed a song containing some elements obviously derived from those of the foster father but differing in almost all other features (e.g., length, sequencing, and number of elements).

The songs of these males tended to be slow and uniform and thus were similar to the songs of males reared without a tutor.

From these results Immelmann concluded that various characteristics of zebra finch songs are acquired at different ages. First, the song elements of the tutor are memorized. This can be done before the young male begins to sing; one male reproduced some elements from its foster father although it was isolated at 25 days of age and did not begin subsong until 35 days old. Another male, isolated on Day 38, developed a song containing all the elements of the foster father's song phrase. For this bird, therefore, the acquisition of song elements must have already been completed at the time when subsong was just beginning. On the other hand, Immelmann concluded that the sequence of song elements, together with the length of song and its rhythm, are acquired much later, between Days 40 and 80, during the time that song output is developing.

To investigate whether song heard after adulthood has been reached has any influence, Immelmann put three males 80–90 days old, which had developed the song of their Bengalese finch foster father, in an aviary containing adult male zebra finches. He found only a few minor subsequent alterations in the songs of these birds and so concluded that the song phrase is more or less fixed once it is fully developed.

Immelmann also looked at the selectivity of song acquisition. He found that five out of seven cross-fostered birds developed a song which was identical to that of their foster father, despite the fact that they could hear and see other zebra finches in neighboring cages. The other two males produced a song which contained some zebra finch elements. In another experiment, eight cross-fostered males were raised in an aviary which also contained adult zebra finches. Five of these males were fed exclusively by their foster parents and imitated the song of the foster father, but the other three were also fed by a pair of adult zebra finches after fledging and developed a song which contained elements of both males, but with a preference for the zebra finch. Finally, three males raised only by females of their own species, but able to hear and see males, developed a species-specific song composed of elements copied from various different neighbors.

From these results Immelmann concluded that young zebra finches show a preference both for song of the right tonal quality (own-species bias) and for that of the individual that feeds them. His experiments dissociated the two and suggested that the latter influence was the stronger.

Immelmann's results might be taken to suggest that young males in the wild would develop songs which sound much like those used by their fathers. If learning is normally from the father, and copying is reasonably accurate but not perfect, songs would differ among males in ways that reflected their kinship. This could have an important influence on various aspects of social behavior (Treisman, 1978). For example, Slater and Clements (1981) suggested that females might use the similarity between the songs of related males as a cue in mate choice so as to achieve optimal outbreeding (cf. Bateson, 1978).

A major problem with these ideas is raised by the studies of wild birds carried out by Immelmann (1962a, 1965). As pointed out earlier, these showed that independence from the parents normally occurs at around 35 days of age, which is early in relation to the timing of song learning. Indeed, if conditions remain favorable for breeding, most parents will already have a fresh clutch in a different nest by this time. They also tend to become increasingly aggressive toward their fledglings at this stage, driving them away. These changes are also shown by captive birds (Eales, 1985a). After this time the father is therefore unlikely to be available for the young birds to learn from except where they are housed together experimentally. In the wild, juveniles form small flocks in the area of the colony (Immelmann, 1965), and within these groups young birds will certainly experience a variety of songs after separation from the father. Their experience during this period is likely to be the most important factor in determining the form of the song that they sing as adults. However, this is not to say that all experience before 35 days of age is irrelevant to song learning. As Böhner (1983) has shown, males removed from their parents at 40 days of age and then housed in visual and auditory contact with their father and another song tutor learn the song of the former rather than the latter. Thus experience before independence may lead to preferences in subsequent song-tutor selection, a point to which we return later.

Eales (1985b) examined whether male zebra finches might learn the songs of their fathers by removing young males from their parents at three different ages: at 35 days, the normal age of independence; at 50 days, in about the middle of the juvenile period; and at 65 days, when the birds were approaching sexual maturity. On removal from their parents, the birds were housed with their clutch mates either in both visual and acoustic isolation from adults or with a different adult pair (but separated by bars from them to avoid aggression), thus providing them with an opportunity to learn song from another male (Böhner, 1983).

Results of young moved from their father to a different song tutor suggest that the sensitive phase for song learning in zebra finches is, in the conditions of our experiments, at some stage during the period from 35 to 65 days. Males given a new tutor at 35 days learned their song from this second male. Those given a new tutor at 65 days showed no evidence of learning from him but developed songs based entirely on those of their fathers. There was a significant increase in the proportion of the song learned from the father, and decrease in that learned from the new tutor as the time spent with the father increased (Fig. 2).

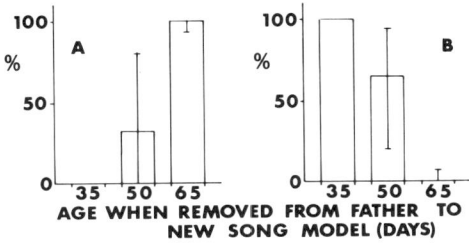
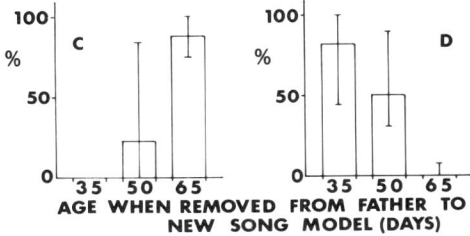

FIG. 2. Results from birds given a new song tutor when removed from their father, showing the percentage of song that was learned from the father (A) or the tutor (B), and the percentage of the father's (C) or tutor's (D) song that was learned. Median values and interquartile ranges are given. There was a significant increase in the proportion of song learned from the father among the birds given the new song tutor from Day 35, 50, or 65 (Kruskal-Wallis overall, $p < .001$; Mann-Whitney, Days 35 and 50, $p = .05$; Days 35 and 65, $p = .001$; Days 50 and 65, $p = .005$). There was a significant decrease in the proportion of song learned from the new tutor as the time spent with the father increased (overall, $p > .001$; Days 35 and 50, $p = .044$; Days 35 and 65, $p = .001$; Days 50 and 65, $p = .005$) (from Eales, 1985b).

Turning to those males that were isolated when removed from their fathers, the results again suggest that they learn their song between the ages of independence and sexual maturity, at 35–65 days (Fig. 3). The proportion of elements shared between fathers and sons increased with the time they spent together. By Day 65 each bird had learned all its father's song, although a small number of additional elements were sung by some males.

All the males moved from their parents to other adults developed normal songs regardless of when the transition was made. By contrast, seven out of nine of the birds that were isolated from adults after independence at 35 days old developed songs which were unstereotyped and lacked phrasing. While they sang frequently, with normal amplitude and posture, their songs lacked normal structure and included many repeated elements (upper trace, Fig. 4). They were also unstereotyped in that the sequence of elements in successive

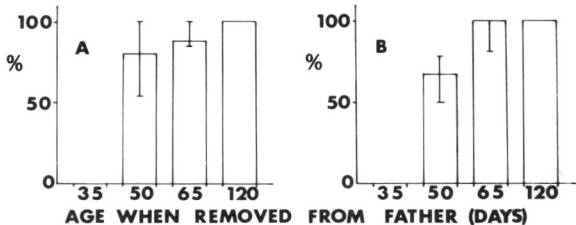

FIG. 3. Results for birds deprived of a song tutor after removal from their father, showing (A) the percentage of song learned from the father, and (B) the percentage of the father's song that was learned. Median values and interquartile ranges are given. The proportion of shared elements between fathers and sons increased with the time they spent together, both for the amount of song learned from the father (Kruskal-Wallis, $p < .001$) and for the amount of the father's song that was learned ($p < .001$). Males isolated on Days 50 or 65 learned significantly more of their song from the father than those isolated on Day 35 (Mann-Whitney, $p = .0026$ and $p = .001$ respectively). Days 50 and 65 isolates also learned significantly more of their father's song than those isolated on Day 35 ($p = .002$ and $p = .001$ respectively). For this value there was also a significant increase between Days 50 and 65 ($p = .007$) (from Eales, 1985b).

songs was often different. These birds were placed in an aviary containing normal adults at 6 months old and, interestingly, they then modified their songs to produce the species-typical pattern (Fig. 4; see also Section III,B). In no case did the final form of song match that of the father but, as the aviary contained individuals whose song had not been recorded, it is not certain whether the young birds learned new elements at this stage. Nevertheless, the result indicates that the final form of song is not achieved at a particular age but that its timing depends on experience. A last point is that there was no significant difference in the amount of the father's song that was learned between males placed in isolation and those moved to a second tutor at either 35, 50, or 65 days of age. This suggests that elements learned from the second tutor are added to those memorized from the first rather than in any way overriding them.

The lack of phrasing of birds isolated at 35 days contrasts with the results of Price (1979), who found that males visually isolated from adults at 9–12 days of age still produced species-typical patterning. A possible reason for this difference is that his birds were able to hear adults: Although our results suggest that visual isolation precludes song learning (see Section V), it may be that aspects of patterning can be acquired in this situation.

In summary, Eales (1985b) showed that male zebra finches in the standard conditions we use learn their songs mainly between 35 and 65 days of age. This is after the time when they would normally be independent from their parents. While it is possible to induce them to use song learned from their father, this occurs only in experimental situations during which the two are

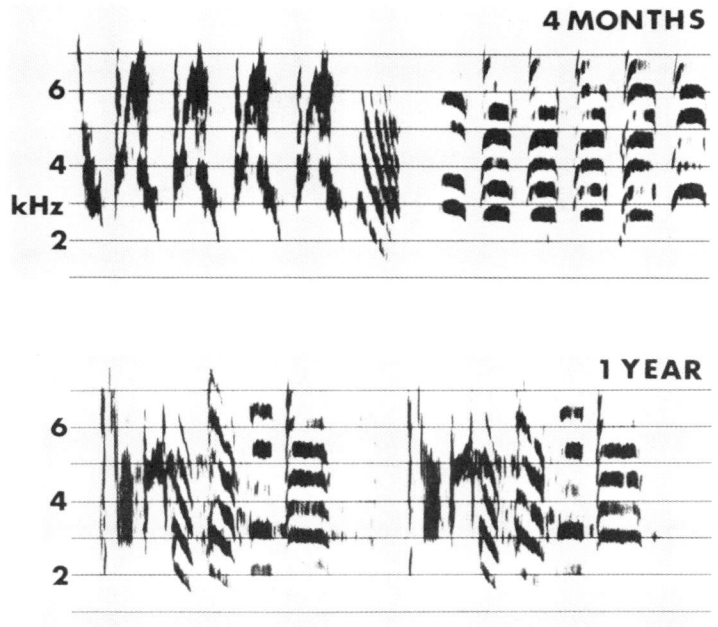

FIG. 4. Song of a male isolated from his parents at 35 days of age. His song at 4 months (top trace) was abnormal and unstructured. He was placed in an aviary containing many adult birds at 6 months, and subsequently modified his song to typical adult form (bottom trace, recorded at 1 year). This shows that the form of song can change even in a sexually mature adult if a song tutor was not available during the normal sensitive phase (from Eales, 1985b).

kept together for longer than would be normal in the wild or in situations which promote the reproduction of songs heard before 35 days (see Section IV). Birds deprived of song during this period were found to retain the capacity to modify their song into adulthood. This last finding differs from that of Böhner (1986), who has found that males removed from their parents at 35 days produce songs as similar to those of their fathers as those removed at 100 days. However, there are a number of important differences between Böhner's procedure and that which we have adopted which might account for this discrepancy. Perhaps most important of these is that he placed the young birds in individual cages in visual but not acoustic isolation from all other birds after independence (Böhner, personal communication). Thus, whereas our birds were in groups acoustically isolated from adults, his were alone but could hear adult males. As discussed in the next section, this is a situation that can lead to the production of songs heard before 35 days.

## III. Can Birds Produce Songs Heard after 65 Days?

### A. Raising by Females Alone

Male and female zebra finches normally combine to rear the young. In captivity, however, females are capable of feeding chicks successfully on their own, and this provides an easy means of studying the song of males that have not heard others singing before independence. Immelmann (1969) raised three males in this way: They could hear adult males singing and built their songs using elements of several of these neighbors instead of copying from just one. Price (1979) studied female-raised birds in acoustic isolation from all adult males: all six of these birds formed a normally structured and stereotyped song phrase using female call notes. Immelmann (1969) also found that birds cross-fostered to female Bengalese finches constructed songs using calls.

Studies of female-raised birds by Eales (1987a) add to this picture (Fig. 5). Three out of five young males reared by their mothers in soundproof boxes learned female calls and used them as song elements. Birds reared in the same way, but housed with an adult male after independence, learned the song of this adult, showing that experience of the father in the first 35 days of life is not essential for later song learning. For example, males whose father was removed before hatching but returned when they were 35 days old ($n = 4$) learned all the elements in their fathers' songs, though up to 10% of the elements they sang were additional ones that they had improvised. Female-raised males that were housed with their father from Day 50 ($n = 5$) or 65 ($n = 5$) learned 45 and 50% respectively of their fathers' elements, and these accounted for an average of 70 and 75% of their songs. The copies in these cases also appeared less precise than those of the birds housed with their fathers from Day 35. Comparing the three groups, there was no significant difference in the proportion of the birds' songs that had been learned from the father, but there was a difference among them in the proportion of the father's song that was learned (Kruskal-Wallis test, $p < .01$).

These experiments show that young male zebra finches will learn song elements from the first adult male they encounter even if this encounter does not take place until 65 days of age, when young birds that have grown up in the presence of adult males would have memorized all the elements they later use in song (Fig. 2). Although the female-raised birds have no previous experience of adult males, they must recognize some feature of them, or some quality in their song, so that they come to learn from them rather than producing a song composed of call notes as do female-raised birds denied adult male tutors altogether. This result suggests that sensitivity remains until suitable experience has been gained rather than ending at a particular age, the same conclusion as that reached from the birds isolated at independence described in the last section.

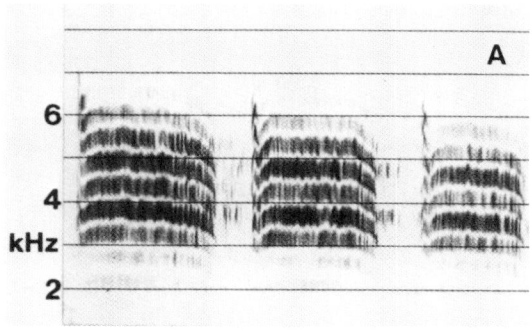
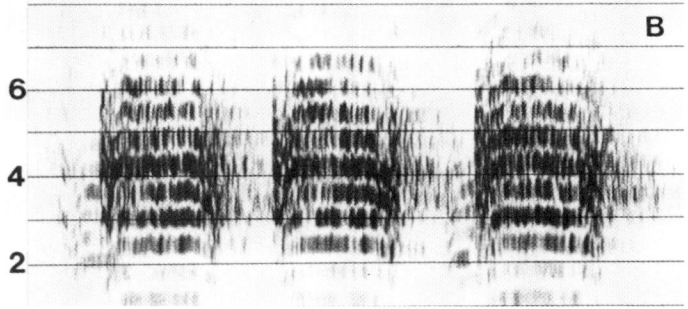
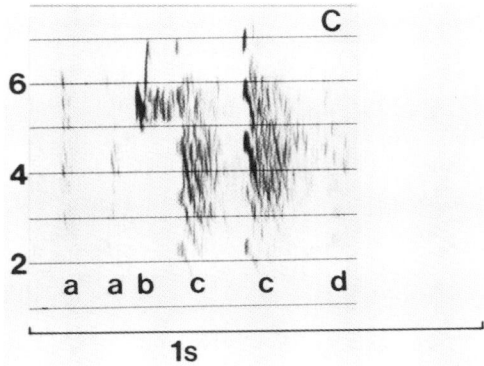

FIG. 5. A. Typical calls from a female. B. A song phrase from a male that was raised by a female and had never heard adult male song. He used female call notes as song elements. C. A song phrase of a male that was raised by its mother but housed also with its father at 35 days of age. He produced a normal song phrase learned from his father, composed of four different element types (a, b, c, and d).

While birds are capable of developing a song based on female call notes, why do they copy that of a male even if this only becomes available to them as late as age 65 days? It may be that the impoverished environment of female-raised birds leads to a delay in the memorization of the calls they will eventually use in song if no male becomes available. The copying of the male does not therefore necessarily imply a switch from a song that has already been memorized. Nevertheless, in these experiments and under normal circumstances, the young males do choose male song tutors rather than building song from other sounds that they hear, including female calls. It is perhaps most likely that features of the song phrase may label it as the best vocalization to copy: In the terms of template theory, the male song phrase may match the crude template more closely than other sounds that the young bird hears. On the other hand, as the sexes both look and behave differently, it could be that young birds are more prone to learn from males, regardless of the form of song. One such difference between the sexes is in their call-note repertoire. Zebra finches call frequently and several different calls have been described, the two most common being the contact call and the distance call (Immelmann, 1962a; Silcox, 1979; Price, 1979). The distance call differs between the sexes and is used more by males than by females. It does not develop normally in young males that are isolated from adult males during the first 40 days of life (Zann, 1984, 1985). It is the sexually dimorphic portion of this call that is absent in the deprived males. This call therefore provides another label of sex: It is possible that it allows the young female-raised male to recognize adult males of its species and so choose an appropriate song tutor.

We can only speculate on the features of male zebra finches that make them most appropriate as song tutors. However, the results we have described show that experience of the father during the nestling and fledgling period is not necessary for song learning to occur. A young male can select a suitable song tutor from his environment after independence even if no male was present before this stage. Furthermore, if a suitable tutor is not present at 35 to 65 days, when learning would normally occur under the conditions of our experiments, then learning can occur later. Thus, some aspect of the experience a bird gains during song learning is an important factor in the ending of sensitivity.

## B. Lack of Social Stimulation

Experience between independence and sexual maturity may influence song development as well as affecting which song is learned and when learning takes place. For example, particular social experiences may be necessary if a song that has been memorized is to be practiced and so develop into the adult form. Although there is clearly considerable overlap in the timing of song memorization and its motor development in the zebra finch, experience may still affect the two processes differently. The fact that males isolated at independence did not produce normal song could have resulted from influences on either or both of these processes, as the young males in these experiments were housed, after removal from their parents, in a room that contained no birds other than those in their group. In the wild, young zebra finches normally experience a stimulating social environment (Immelmann, 1962a,b, 1965); lack of this, as well as of suitable song tutors, might have been responsible for delayed song development in some of our experiments.

To investigate the effects of a stimulating environment on song development, Eales (1985a) raised males in two experimental conditions. In both of these the birds were raised by their parents until 35 days of age and then caged with only siblings from the same clutch until 65 days old, from which stage they were housed with a second adult male song tutor. In Group 1, this whole process was carried out in soundproof chambers, in visual and acoustic isolation from all other birds; in Group 2 the cages were in a large bird room containing many other zebra finches. If social stimulation were important, it was predicted that the birds in Group 2 would develop normal song phrases and not copy the second tutor, while those in Group 1 would be less stimulated and so would remain capable of learning from the second tutor.

The sample sizes of these groups were small (Group 1, $n = 4$; Group 2 $n = 5$), but they provide no support for this hypothesis; if anything, the results go in the opposite direction to that predicted. Two birds in Group 1 and all of those in Group 2 based their songs on that of the second tutor. Thus the birds in Group 2, like those studied earlier, learned after 65 days if they lacked a tutor earlier, even though they had experienced visual and vocal stimulation from birds in other cages between 35 and 65 days. Their experience at that stage was clearly not equivalent in effect to close interaction with singing adult males.

In contrast to those of our results discussed so far, both Immelmann (1969) and Böhner (1986) have reported zebra finches to reproduce elements heard before 35 days of age. In the case of zebra finches raised by their own species, this is probably because they placed the young males in visual isolation at this stage. However, Immelmann's experiments also involved the rearing of zebra finch chicks by Bengalese finch foster parents, so that the song of the male that reared them was not that typical of their species. Some of our other experiments, to be discussed in the next section, show how factors such as this can affect song development.

## IV. Can Birds Produce Songs Heard before 35 Days?

The last section showed that the timing of song learning is not fixed, but depends on experience. In particular, birds lacking experience of adult male song before 65 days of age, and therefore producing abnormal songs, are able to learn later if an appropriate tutor becomes available. In this section we show that song heard before 35 days is actually memorized and, if males are exposed after 35 days to a tutor whose song is in some way inadequate for learning although sufficient to stimulate song development, they may come to reproduce song which was heard earlier. Our studies point to three situations in which this happens:

1. Lack of visual contact with tutor. Eales (1985a) examined the influence of visual and vocal interaction on song learning in zebra finches. She found that it is not necessary for young males to have physical contact with a tutor for learning to take place (see also Böhner, 1983). She used males reared by their parents until Day 35. Some young males were then denied visual interaction but were able to interact vocally with a tutor ($n = 7$); others could hear a male singing through an audio link but could not interact with him visually or vocally ($n = 8$). Because the accuracy of copying under these circumstances was low, it was not possible to determine the proportion of song that had been learned from the tutor. However, considering the overall structure of the phrase and the configuration of elements, it was possible to classify songs as being derived in part from tutor, in part from father, or independent in origin. Three out of the seven males in visual isolation from their tutor but able to interact vocally with him developed songs based on those of their fathers; the songs of the other four were like those of their tutors. One of the eight males which could hear the tutor but could not interact with him in any way based his entire song on that of his father. All of the other seven males trained through an audio link produced quiet songs, consisting of introductory elements, distance calls, and long, indistinct improvised elements. However, in three cases these songs shared some features with those of the birds' fathers.

These results are therefore, to some extent, in agreement with those obtained by Böhner (1986) in suggesting that males isolated at 35 days can use elements learned before that stage. However, Böhner found no difference between isolation at this stage and at 100 days, and this is clearly quite different from our results. As discussed earlier, this is likely to be because Böhner's birds were in visual isolation from all other birds. However, the form of song may also differ between the two stocks that have been used. This could lead to differences in the categorization of elements and, for example, if call notes are incorporated into song more often in one stock than the other, this would lead to greater similarity among the songs of all birds regardless of when they are tutored or isolated.

As well as indicating that birds trained by tutors they cannot see can recall and use songs heard earlier, these experiments point to the importance of visual and vocal interaction in the normal song-learning process. Similar findings have been made on other species (e.g., Todt et al., 1979; Payne, 1981; see Section I), and it is a phenomenon which raises questions about the value of using tape-recorded song to determine the timing of sensitive phases. Even in the many species that have been found to learn from tape recordings, would not the period of sensitivity have been found to be longer had a live tutor been used? Just such an effect has been found by Baptista and Petrinovich (1986) in white-crowned sparrows (*Zonotrichia leucophrys*). While males of this species will not learn conspecific song from tape recordings after the age of 50 days, they will learn from live tutors with which they can interact.

2. Successive exposure to two species. Males can also be stimulated to recall song heard earlier if they are housed at independence with a tutor which belongs to a different species from their father or foster father. This has been shown by Clayton (1987a), who moved normally raised zebra finches and birds cross-fostered to Bengalese finches into cages with nonbreeding pairs of the opposite species at 35 days of age (Fig. 6, Groups C and D). Control birds were moved to pairs of the same species as that which had reared them (Groups A and B). At 70 days, all the birds were transferred to the cage of yet another pair of adults, in all cases belonging to the same species that originally reared them. Two typical Bengalese finch songs are shown in Fig. 7.

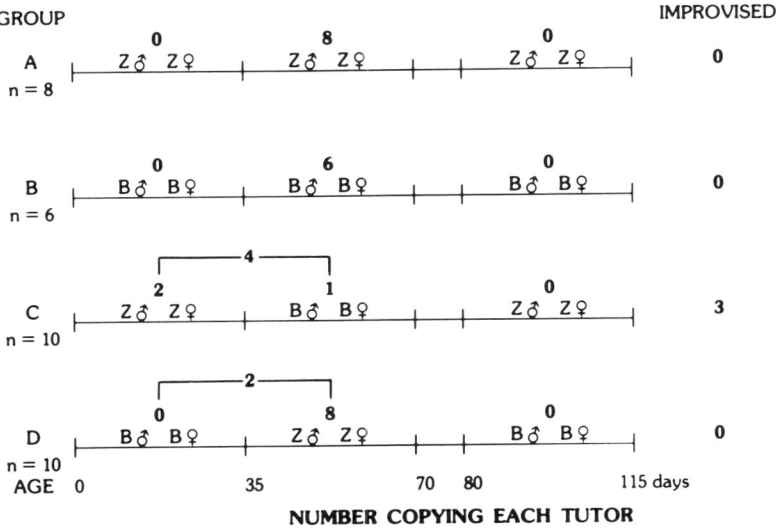

FIG. 6. Song learning in young zebra finches raised by a pair of their own species (Z) or of Bengalese finches (B) and then housed for two periods of 35 days with different adult pairs. The young birds were isolated from adults for song recording from Days 70 to 80. Figures in bold type indicate the number of young birds showing evidence of learning from each male tutor with brackets to indicate cases where young birds copied more than one tutor. Birds are labeled as having "improvised" where their song showed no evidence of learning from any of these tutors.

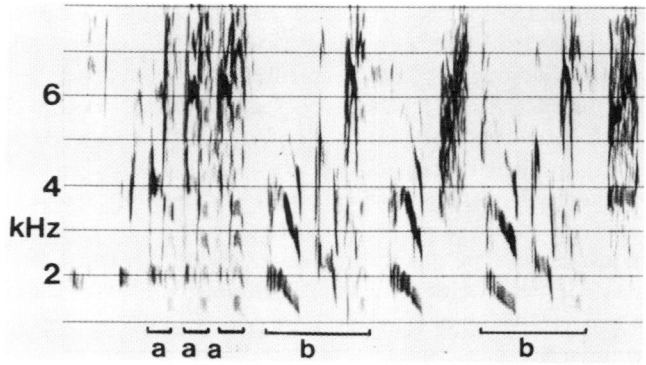

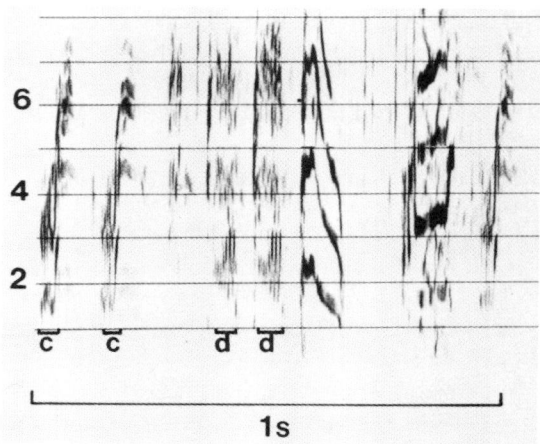

FIG. 7. Typical song phrases from two Bengalese finches. A comparison with Fig. 1 shows a number of differences between zebra finch and Bengalese finch song (see also Table II). The Bengalese finch phrase tends to be longer and contains a number of repeated elements. The first bird repeats single (a) or multiple (b) elements within a phrase; the second bird repeats two elements (c and d) twice in succession. Zebra finch phrases do not usually contain such repeats. However, for both species, the song phrase may be repeated several times during a song bout.

Males kept with the same species throughout (Groups A and B) all learned from the song tutor with which they were housed from 35 to 70 days. But if the male they were housed with at this stage was of the species that did not rear them, the tendency to learn from him was much less, and some of the young males produced songs based on those they had heard before independence. Only one male from Group C based his song solely on that of the middle tutor; the others produced at least one of their foster father's elements, except for three males in which the song consisted only of a series of call notes. None of the males in Groups A and B sang songs that contained elements both of their father and of the next tutor they heard; as would be expected from results described earlier, they all learned from the latter. However, some birds in Group C (4 out of 10) and in Group D (2 out of 10) learned from both. If Groups A and B are combined, this gives a significant difference between them and Group C (Fisher Exact test, $p < .02$), although not Group D.

Although all the birds were housed with a third tutor from Day 80 to Day 115, none was found to learn from this new tutor. Three birds in Group C and one in Group D did change their songs during this period (see Fig. 8), but there were no further differences by 6 months of age when their songs were recorded again.

3. Simultaneous exposure to two species. Clayton (1988a) found that males raised by mixed species parents (i.e., zebra finch male and Bengalese finch female or vice versa) and housed from independence with a song tutor from each species tend to learn from both tutors, but also to sing some elements heard before 35 days (Fig. 9, Groups A and B). There was no suggestion that birds tended to learn from the species to which their foster father belonged rather than that of their foster mother. However, of 18 zebra finches raised in this way, 11 sang only zebra finch elements and the other 7 all sang mixed songs. Conversely, of 17 Bengalese males raised in the same way (results not illustrated), 11 sang pure Bengalese song, 5 sang mixed songs, and one improvised. These results indicate some bias toward learning from conspecifics (see Section V). Eight of the Bengalese finches and nine of the zebra finches included elements from their foster father in their songs. This gives a significant difference from 10 controls of each species, in which none of the birds learned from their father (zebra finches, $\chi^2 = 5.25$, $df = 1$, $p < .05$; Bengalese finches, $\chi^2 = 4.62$, $df = 1$, $p < .05$. This is therefore a third situation which promotes the use of elements heard before 35 days of age.

It is interesting to compare the results obtained in these three situations with those from the birds deprived of song between 35 and 65 days, which were found to learn after 65 days (Section III,B). In all three studies just mentioned, auditory and/or visual stimulation between 35 and 65 or 70 days did not match in quality that received earlier. Such a mismatch seems to cause the bird to recall and reproduce song learned before 35 days and also to block further modification later. For young zebra finches, which are known to join mixed-species flocks (Immelmann, 1962b), this mechanism may act as a safeguard to ensure that only species-specific song is produced.

It is worth considering how these results might fit in with one or two models of learning that have been put forward. They match the idea of proactive interference quite well, songs learned earlier (before 35 days) preventing the

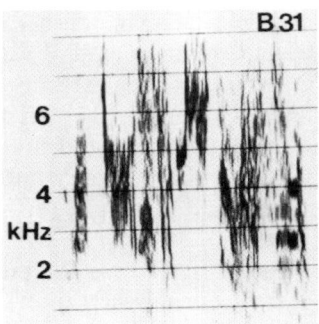
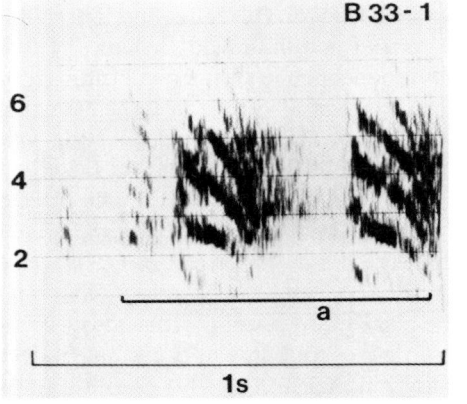
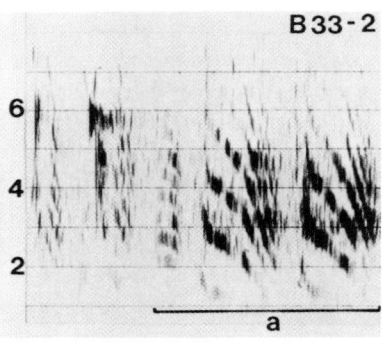

FIG. 8. Two sonagrams of B33's song (Group C), lower level. This bird did not base his song on either the father, with which he was housed until 35 days of age, or on the Bengalese finch tutor with which he was housed between 35 and 70 days of age. His song was recorded at 4 (B33-1) and 6 (B33-2) months; between these times he changed his song by incorporating new elements at the start of the phrase. These were not learned from the tutor present at this time (B31) whose song is shown above. The pacing of the song also changed during this period, the three original elements (a) being sung more rapidly.

learning of new elements at a later stage (after 70 days). This hypothesis would also suggest the converse result: Birds denied experience of song before independence should be prepared to learn later than would be normal. This is as described above for female-raised birds. McGregor and Avery (1986) suggest that the phenomenon of proactive interference is important in neighbor recognition by great tits (*Parus major*).

The results described here are also consistent with those obtained from work on sexual imprinting, for which Bateson (1987) has proposed an "updating" hypothesis. He suggests that continuing exposure to one stimulus slowly

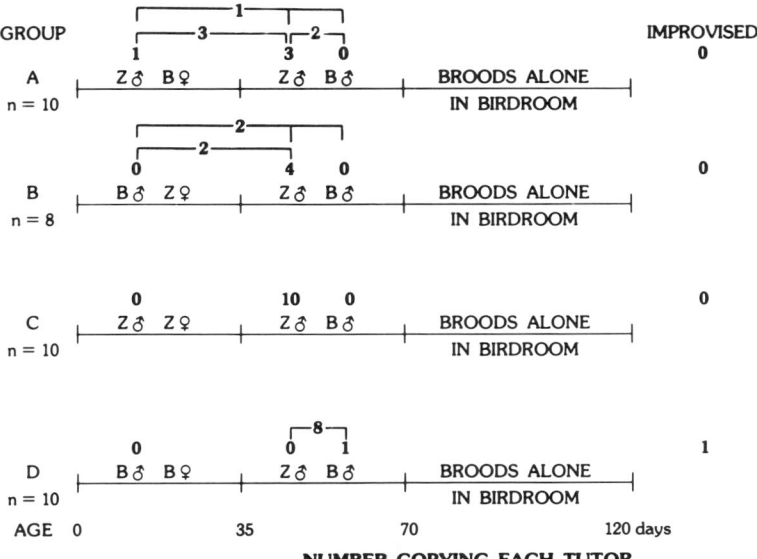

FIG. 9. The results of experiments in which young male zebra finches were given a choice of two song tutors, a zebra finch and a Bengalese finch, between 35 and 70 days of age. The birds had either been raised by mixed species pairs (Groups A and B), by their own species (Group C), or by a pair of Bengalese finches (Group D). From Days 70 to 120, each brood was housed together but in visual isolation from all other birds. Results are shown in bold type as explained in the legend to Fig. 6.

diminishes the scope for other stimuli to have an effect, with the rate at which this occurs depending on how effective the first stimulus is. If the two stimuli are quite different, two separate standards are stored. However, if they are similar and the second is a more effective one, it will modify the standard set by the first, so "updating" it. It would be a matter for empirical study to determine just how similar two stimuli must be for updating to occur.

This idea can be applied to the results of young zebra finches exposed to two species in succession (Groups C and D in Fig. 6). In the control situation (Groups A and B), the tutor heard after independence had a song similar to that of the foster father so that updating could occur with his elements. By 70 days, memorization was complete so that no elements were learned from the last tutor. The conspecific foster father used in Group C should have established a strong standard. This might have been expected to lead to no updating by the next tutor, but some from the bird of the same species heard after 70 days. However, none of the young males learned from this last individual. In Group D, the Bengalese finch foster father, being of low stimulus value, had established only a weak standard by Day 35, so that this could be updated by the conspecific tutor. All of the young birds learned form this tutor, perhaps because he provided an alternative and stronger standard. Nevertheless, two males here did copy from the foster father as well.

We can conclude that the social experiences a male zebra finch has early in life are of prime importance in governing when and how much he will learn. As far as song learning is concerned, normally raised males tend to reproduce songs heard at around 35 to 65 days of age. Birds can be deprived of appropriate experience at this time by not letting them hear adult song, by not allowing them to interact visually with a song tutor, or by giving them only a tutor belonging to a different species from the male that reared them. In these circumstances our experiments have shown that young males may produce elements from songs heard before or after this time.

## V. Is There an Own-Species Bias?

A striking feature of the results described above from cross-fostered birds and from those reared by mixed-species pairs is that in most cases the young males preferred to learn from conspecifics. This own-species bias is most obvious in birds which are reared by the other species and then exposed to song tutors of both their own species and that of their foster parents at independence (Group D, Fig. 9). Of 10 male zebra finches reared in this way, 9 learned Bengalese finch elements and 8 learned zebra finch ones (as 1 male did not show evidence of learning from either tutor, eight of the songs were hybrid). Thus their early experience did not totally override the tendency to learn from their own species. Zebra finches that have been raised by Bengalese finches and housed with this species throughout life also tend to copy their songs less accurately (Clayton, 1987a; Eales, 1987b). The Bengalese finch elements are sung in shorter phrases, like those of zebra finch song, and this is because the same element is not usually repeated in quick succession as is typical of Bengalese finch males (Clayton, 1987c).

Another line of evidence suggesting own-species bias comes from experiments in which normally raised and cross-fostered males are housed during the learning phase close to both the male that raised them and an unrelated adult male zebra finch. If both these males are zebra finches, the young male tends to learn from the father (Böhner, 1983). However, for cross-fostered birds there is less tendency to learn from the "father." Whether the young male sings his foster father's song or learns that of his own species from the other male seems to depend on how much social interaction he has with the two individuals. Eales (1987b) found that zebra finches housed with their Bengalese finch foster father until 4 to 6 months old but able to see and hear a pair of their own species through a wire lattice throughout this time still all learned Bengalese finch song ($n = 10$). Another group of 10 birds was raised in the same way but moved to the other side of the lattice at 35 days of age. Four of these incorporated zebra finch elements in their songs, despite the fact that they were still in visual and auditory contact with their foster father.

There are several possible reasons for the own-species bias. Genetic differences between the two species might be responsible, leading the crude template of the young zebra finch to match its own species song more closely than that of a Bengalese finch. Song structure certainly differs between the two species: Comparison of the songs of 20 birds of each from our stocks has revealed some marked differences (see Table I). For example, Bengalese finch phrases are considerably longer both in duration and in number of elements. It could be that this makes them more difficult for a zebra finch to memorize or reproduce. Bengalese finches also tend to repeat elements within a phrase whereas zebra finches tend not to. The structure of the elements also differs. Those of zebra finches often show eight or more stressed harmonics; harmonics are less common in Bengalese finch song and, where they do occur, there are rarely more than four. Finally, species-specific call notes, which are often incorporated into song by zebra finches, might act as a label indicating the suitability of a tutor.

Are Bengalese finch elements, even if incorporated into a zebra finch phrase, more difficult for the young male to learn? Clayton (in press b) has examined this using two zebra finch tutors, one with normal song and one that had been trained by a Bengalese finch (Fig. 10). The results suggest no tendency to select zebra finch elements. For example, in one group of 10 males raised by zebra finch females alone (Group B) before exposure to the two tutors, 2 learned from the male singing zebra finch song, 7 from that with Bengalese song, and 1 from both. However, species-specificity might still be indicated by phrase length, lack of repetition of elements, and the inclusion of zebra

TABLE I
A COMPARISON OF THE SONGS OF NORMALLY RAISED ZEBRA FINCHES AND BENGALESE FINCHES

|  | Zebra finch ($N = 20$) | | Bengalese finch ($N = 20$) | | Significance (Mann-Whitney) |
| --- | --- | --- | --- | --- | --- |
|  | Mean | SE | Mean | SE |  |
| Duration of song phrase(s) | 0.7 | 0.04 | 1.3 | 0.04 | $p < .001$ |
| Number of elements per phrase | 8.3 | 0.49 | 13.5 | 0.57 | $p < .001$ |
| Number of repeat elements in phrase[a] | 0.4 | 0.15 | 4.0 | 0.28 | $p < .001$ |
| Number of elements per second | 13.8 | 0.59 | 14.0 | 0.53 | N.S. |

[a] This measure examines the whole phrase and scores each element as being a repeat or not. Thus, the score for both the sequences aaaabcd and abccddde would be 3.

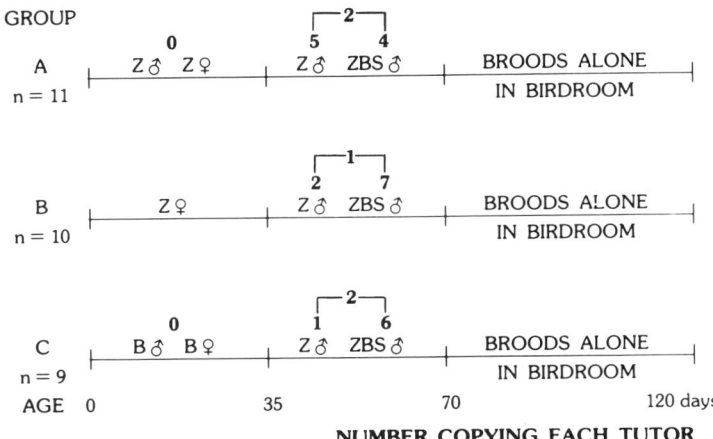

FIG. 10. Song learning in young zebra finches exposed to two tutors, a normal male zebra finch (Z) and one that had been trained by a Bengalese finch (ZBS). The young birds had either been normally reared (Group A), reared by a female of their own species (Group B), or cross-fostered to Bengalese finches (Group C). Results are shown in bold type as explained in the legend to Fig. 6.

finch call notes within the song, features which both tutors in this experiment shared.

As well as features of the song itself, we have confirmed the conclusion of Immelmann (1969) that visual interaction with a song tutor is vital if learning is to take place. Song in zebra finches is quiet, high in frequency, and rich in harmonics, qualities placing severe limits on the distance over which it will carry (Immelmann, 1968), especially as different frequencies attenuate at different rates (see, e.g., Konishi, 1970). For the young bird to be able to hear the details of such a quiet song, the adult would have to be close and therefore likely to be visible. This may be one reason why visual cues have taken on importance in this species. However, Bengalese finches and zebra finches look quite different: Could this be another reason for own-species bias? If young zebra finches are exposed to two tutors, a zebra finch singing Bengalese song and a Bengalese singing zebra finch song, they do show a tendency to learn from the former (Clayton, 1988b; Fig. 11). However, this result is not conclusive, as both the phrase length and number of repeated elements in the songs of zebra finches copied from Bengalese finches are more typical of their own species, and these could be important vocal cues.

An interesting additional factor which may bias learning stems from differences in behavior between the two species. Cross-fostered zebra finches receive less parental care from their Bengalese finch foster parents (ten Cate, 1982, 1984), and Bengalese finches are also less aggressive toward young than are zebra finches (ten Cate, 1982; Clayton, 1987c). This last difference may

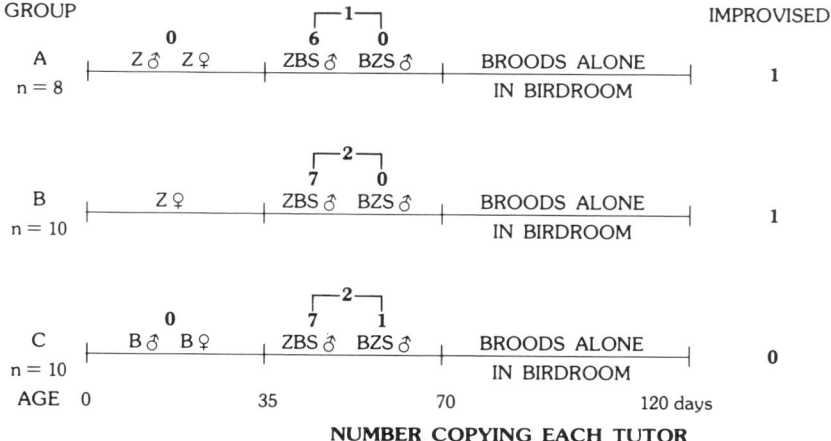

FIG. 11. Song learning in young zebra finches exposed to two tutors, a zebra finch singing Bengalese finch song (ZBS) and a Bengalese singing zebra finch song (BZS). Rearing conditions of the three groups were as for the experiments summarized in Fig. 10; results are shown in bold type as explained in the legend to Fig. 6.

be very important in song tutor choice (see Section VI). In addition to these basic differences between the species, adults may also differ in their reactions to chicks of their own species and those of the other. This is most obvious in mixed-species pairs (ten Cate, 1982) where parents tend to feed more and direct more contact behavior and aggression toward chicks of their own species (ten Cate, 1985). Young zebra finch males subsequently prefer a female of their own species in mate choice tests (ten Cate, 1982, 1984). Although it has not been tested, a preference for a conspecific song tutor could also be established through such behavioral interactions. Zebra finch chicks reared by one parent of their own species and one Bengalese finch cease to prefer a female of their own species if interactions with the conspecific parent that reared them are reduced, even though they can still see it (ten Cate, 1984). From this, ten Cate argued that behavioral interaction, rather than just visual and vocal stimulation, is the important factor leading to mate preference (see also ten Cate *et al.*, 1984). Could this be true of song tutor preference as well? The point is taken up in the next section.

## VI. How Do Zebra Finches Choose Their Song Tutors?

In the wild, zebra finches gain independence from their parents at around 35 days and thereafter join flocks consisting of other juveniles and non-breeding adults (Immelmann, 1962a). As this is also the age at which we have found song learning to begin in our standard laboratory situation, from whom is it likely that this learning takes place if birds have a choice of tutors?

Clayton (1987b) examined this question by giving young zebra finches two adult male tutors of their own species at independence. They were raised by their own parents and then housed with the two tutors, one of which had a song like that of the father (Ts: >75% of elements in common) while the other had a very different song (Td: no elements in common). The aim of using tutors with different songs was to see whether the birds were more likely to learn from Ts as a result of their earlier experience with their father. Another group of young birds was reared by their mother alone before exposure to two tutors in the same way. This group allowed examination of whether song tutor choice depended on other vocal differences between the two tutors. The tutors for this group were also chosen as belonging to different color morphs (fawn and wild-type). Using behavioral observations, this made it possible to test whether choice of song tutor was affected by visual imprinting on the mother, siblings, or the animal itself, or by differences in the interactions between the pupil and his two tutors.

Only tutors with normal song output were used in the experiments, and the song output of each male was checked for 1 hour daily throughout the experiment. Such variation as there was in output had no effect on song tutor choice (Wilcoxon test, $T = 96$, $n = 20$, n.s.), the same conclusion as reached by Böhner (1983) for those of his birds with normal output. Nor did the number of elements in the song phrase influence which tutor was chosen in either group analyzed separately or in both groups combined ($T = 43$, $n = 17$, n.s.). However, males that had been raised by both parents tended to learn from tutor Ts: 9 out of 10 chose elements common to the father and that tutor, while the tenth bird sang a song composed of elements from both tutors ($\chi^2 = 6.4$, $df = 1$, $p < .05$). Only one male sang an element peculiar to the father's song, whereas five males sang one or more elements specific to tutor TS (see Table II). This suggests that most of the elements produced that were common to the father and Ts were copied from Ts, in keeeping with the timing for song learning proposed by Eales (1985b).

Immelmann et al. (1978), using wild-type and white birds, found that males imprint on the plumage type of their parents and select a mate of the same type. It is possible that fawn and wild-type individuals would also mate assortatively in this way, although the differences between them are more subtle. There was no suggestion in the experiments of Clayton (1987b) that such imprinting, either on the mother's plumage type, on that of siblings, or on that of the bird itself, affected which male was chosen as a tutor. However, recent studies by Slater and Eales (1988), using wild-type and chestnut-flanked white males reared by both parents, do suggest that visual characteristics are important. Young birds cross-fostered to a pair of the other color and, at independence, given song tutors of each color, all learned only from the foster

TABLE II

ORIGINS OF SONGS ELEMENTS IN ZEBRA FINCHES RAISED BY
PARENTS FOR 35 DAYS, THEN HOUSED WITH TWO MALES[a]

| Clutch | Pupil | Number of elements learned from: | | | | Number of elements in pupil's songs[b] |
|---|---|---|---|---|---|---|
| | | Ts and/or F | F only | Ts only | Td only | |
| 1 | P46 | 4 | 1 | 2 | 0 | 9 |
| | P47 | 3 | 0 | 2 | 0 | 6 |
| 2 | P49 | 7 | 0 | 1 | 0 | 8 |
| 3 | P50 | 4 | 0 | 1 | 0 | 5 |
| | P52 | 6 | 0 | 0 | 0 | 6 |
| 4 | P62 | 3 | 0 | 1 | 0 | 5 |
| | P63 | 4 | 0 | 0 | 0 | 4 |
| 5 | P67 | 6 | 0 | 0 | 0 | 9 |
| | P68 | 2 | 0 | 0 | 2 | 6 |
| | P69 | 5 | 0 | 0 | 0 | 9 |

[a] F, father; Ts, male with song similar to father; Td, male with song very different from father.
[b] Includes element types not copied from any of the three males.

father and/or the tutor of the foster father's plumage type ($n = 15$). None learned from the tutor that was the same color as themselves or their siblings.

Ten Cate *et al.* (1984) suggested that aggression has an important influence on sexual imprinting: Zebra finches cross-fostered to Bengalese finches were more likely to prefer a Bengalese mate if the foster parents had been aggressive to them. A similar effect seems to occur in song learning. The 11 young zebra finches in the female-raised group were subsequently housed in the same cage as their two song tutors, and they all learned from the one that was most aggressive to them ($\chi^2 = 11.0$, $df = 1$, $p < .001$). In only 6 cases out of the 11 was this the male with the highest song output. Furthermore, it was irrespective of the overall amount of aggression displayed by the two tutors or shown to each other. The 10 males in the normally reared group were prevented from interacting physically with either tutor by a wire partition: This eliminated the effects of behavioral interactions, both of the tutors with each other and between them and their pupils, but did not stop normal song learning (Eales, 1985a).

Although this effect of aggression appears to be a strong one, with a perfect correlation between the tutor showing most aggression to a particular young male and that which he learned from, it is possible that the correlation could arise because the two variables are related to some other aspect of tutor-pupil interaction. There is no correlation between the overall level of aggression of a tutor, which includes that to the other pupils and the other tutor, and the proportion of song learned from him. Nor could a relationship be found between tutor choice and the amount of clumping or of allopreening shown between tutors and pupils. Of possible social factors, aggression specifically directed at the pupil in question appears to be the most important. A similar conclusion has been reached by Payne (1981), who found young male indigo buntings to copy the song of the male from whom they receive the greatest number of supplanting attacks.

Could learning from the individual most aggressive to the young male be an artifact of confined space in the laboratory? Levels of aggression are thought to be much lower in wild zebra finches, although parents will drive their young away once they begin a fresh clutch. But our result is unlikely to be simply explained by this, as the important factor is not the general level of aggressiveness of the tutor, but the aggression specifically directed to the pupil concerned.

Correlation need not imply causation. Pupil-directed aggression may be a consequence rather than a cause of tutor choice. Having chosen a song tutor, a young male might well interact more closely with him and thus elicit more aggression. Ten Cate (1986) has observed "listening behavior" in cross-fostered zebra finches, the young males following their tutor and turning their heads toward him when he sings. As yet, there is no evidence of this in normally reared zebra finches (ten Cate, 1986; personal observations) but, if it does occur, it could well lead to tutor aggression. It seems unlikely that this is the complete explanation, as aggression is often initiated by the tutor approaching the pupil, pecking at him, and driving him off his perch, but more detailed observations would be required to resolve this issue. It may be that the young bird is most likely to be alert and pay attention to a male that is aggressive to him and so learn his song. This could also account for the relationship between aggression and mate choice described by ten Cate *et al.* (1984, see also ten Cate, 1984). A similar phenomenon may be involved in the fact that white-crowned sparrows will learn strawberry finch (*Amandava amandava*) song, even if they can hear their own species, provided that they experience aggressive interactions with the strawberry finch tutor (Baptista and Petrinovich, 1984).

A final question to consider in this section is why young males appear to prefer to learn song from an individual that sounds like their father. This could simply ensure that species-specific song is learned by young males in mixed-species flocks. Alternatively, if closely related males have similar songs, then song could be used as a cue in mate choice to give an appropriate balance between inbreeding and outbreeding (see Bateson, 1983). Young males would be most likely to achieve this by learning songs from their father, but could also do so by choosing a tutor who shares a large proportion of his song elements with the father. If it is advantageous for a female to choose a mate who is neither too closely nor too distantly related to herself, then she might do this by selecting a male whose song differed from that of her father to a particular extent. Miller (1979) provided evidence that female zebra finches can discriminate between their fathers' songs and those of other males, and this could provide the basis of such a mechanism.

## VII. Conclusion

Studies of song learning in zebra finches have advanced considerably since the pioneering publication by Immelmann (1969), in which he drew attention to the great potential of this species for work of this sort. The influence of various rearing conditions on song learning, and especially on its timing, is now much better understood. It is clear that the sensitive phase is far from being a rigid phenomenon, but that the timing of sensitivity is affected by experience. While birds allowed to interact with one or more singing males between 35 and 65 days of age base their songs on sounds heard during this time, if their experience during this period is more restricted, they will reproduce sounds heard later (see also Kroodsma and Pickert, 1980). It is also clear that, under various conditions, song elements heard before this time may be recalled and used. While the sensitive phase in our laboratory situation starts at around the time of independence, some features of the father's song may sometimes be reproduced if subsequent experience is restricted. Even if reared by another species, young birds show some bias toward learning the song of their own and, at a more detailed level, they also prefer to learn a song similar to that of their father. They do not learn from birds with whom they cannot interact, and an important aspect of the interaction seems to be the amount of aggression the tutor shows toward them.

There are many aspects of song development in zebra finches which deserve further study. The following are a few examples:

1. How does song learning relate to sexual imprinting? From the extensive studies carried out by Immelmann (e.g., 1972), there is little doubt that sexual imprinting takes place earlier than song learning, at around 15 to 25 days of age, before the young bird leaves its parents. The finding, discussed earlier, that males prefer to learn from individuals with songs like those of their fathers, indicates that experience at this earlier stage may affect later preferences. More work is needed to discover just how these two processes relate in timing and how the effects of sexual imprinting, and of other experiences before independence, influence song learning.

2. How are performance and recognition learning related to one another? Miller (1979) has shown that female zebra finches prefer to approach the song of their father, rather than that of another male, 3 months after fledging. This implies that they learn some features of their father's song before

independence. This learning may not require memorization of details, such as those that must be copied in the learning by young males of songs that they later perform. Nevertheless, both males and females may learn features of a wide variety of songs, and this learning may help them to distinguish between individuals, between neighbors and strangers, and perhaps also between relatives. The last of these depends upon the extent to which performance learning by males involves the passage of cues that give information about kinship. The suggestion of this by Immelmann (1969) for zebra finches, and by Nicolai (1959) for bullfinches (*Pyrrhula pyrrhula*), may well be laboratory artifacts, but transmission of song from father to son does seem likely in some Darwin's finches (Grant, 1984). However, this is only one use to which learning to discriminate among songs might be put: The point we wish to stress here is that such learning may follow a very different timecourse and involve memorization of a much wider variety of songs than does the performance learning with which this article has been concerned (see McGregor and Avery, 1986; Shy *et al.*, 1986; Clayton, 1988c). More detailed work on this in zebra finches is underway.

3. How do neural and hormonal changes relate to the sensitive phase? The relationship of song learning to neural changes during development has recently been discussed in detail by Bottjer and Arnold (1986) with emphasis on zebra finches. This promises to continue to be an exciting area of research, and there is considerable scope for work on the relationship between development of the brain and that of behavior. The possibility of linking endocrine changes during development to changing sensitivity to learning is also an area where more work on zebra finches is likely to be rewarding. Hormone levels in zebra finches vary considerably and are affected by both experience and housing conditions. It has been suggested that peaks at different stages during development may be related to the timing of sexual imprinting and of song learning (Pröve 1983, 1985). If so, the role of aggression in song-tutor selection could well be mediated by endocrine changes induced by chasing (see Pröve and Sossinka, 1978, 1982). Other aspects of experience may also affect hormone levels and, through this, influence the timing of the sensitive phase. The work in this area so far provides interesting pointers but, the interactions between hormone levels and experience being complex, it is not a simple matter to determine whether hormones have a role in the timing of the sensitive phase. The fact that castrated zebra finches are still capable of song learning (Arnold, 1975) suggests that any role gonadal hormones may have in this respect is likely to be subtle.

4. How do findings in the laboratory relate to song development in the wild? In our experiments we have attempted, as far as possible, to match the experience of young birds to that they would experience in the wild. We assume that rearing by the parents until 35 days of age, followed by separating the young birds into groups, is a reasonably close fit to the situation that would

exist in the wild. However, questions about the function of song and of song learning can only be answered in relation to the environment in which that song evolved. Thus, while the controlled conditions of the laboratory are essential for carrying out experiments on development, the extent to which the results shed light on the functioning of the system in nature depends on how well the situation used mimics that in the wild. While there have been some studies of zebra finches in the wild (Immelmann, 1962a; Zann, 1984), the species is not an easy one on which to gain detailed information; more work on aspects of its biology is certainly needed. For example, information on population structure and dispersal patterns, as well as more precise details on the changing experiences of young birds as they mature, would help considerably to put the laboratory findings in a natural context. Furthermore, there is as yet no knowledge about transmission of song from one individual to another in nature. Such information is essential if the functional significance of findings on song learning in the laboratory is to be appreciated.

These are just some of the areas where further work on the song learning of zebra finches is likely to prove fruitful. Given the advantages of this species for laboratory study, it certainly has a good deal more to contribute to our understanding of the processes of song development.

### Acknowledgments

Much of the work by L. A. Eales described here was financed by a studentship from S.E.R.C., and that by N. S. Clayton was financed by a University of St. Andrews research studentship and an I.C.I. scholarship. P. J. B. Slater is grateful to S.E.R.C. and the Royal Society for funds. We are particularly grateful to Carel ten Cate, Peter Marler, and Heather Williams, as well as to the editors, for their comments on earlier drafts.

### References

Arnold, A. P. (1975). The effects of castration on song development in zebra finches. *J. Exp. Zool.* **191**, 261–278.
Baptista, L. F., and Petrinovich, L. (1984). Social interaction, sensitive phases and the song template hypothesis in the white-crowned sparrow. *Anim. Behav.* **32**, 172–181.
Baptista, L. F., and Petrinovich, L. (1986). Song development in the white-crowned sparrow: Social factors and sex differences. *Anim. Behav.* **34**, 1359–1371.
Bateson, P. P. G. (1978). Sexual imprinting and optimal outbreeding. *Nature (London)* **273**, 659–660.
Bateson, P. (1979). How do sensitive periods arise and what are they for? *Anim. Behav.* **27**, 470–486.
Bateson, P. P. G. (1983). The interpretation of sensitive periods. *In* "The behaviour of human infants" (A. Oliverio and M. Zappella, eds.), pp. 57–70. Plenum, New York.
Bateson, P. (1987). Imprinting as a process of competitive exclusion. *In* "Imprinting and Cortical

Plasticity. Comparative Aspects of Sensitive Periods" (J. P. Rauschecker and P. Marler, eds.). Wiley, New York.

Böhner, J. (1983). Song learning in the zebra finch (*Taeniopygia guttata*): Selectivity in the choice of a tutor and accuracy of song copies. *Anim. Behav.* **31**, 231-237.

Böhner, J. (1986). Der zeitliche Verlauf des Gesangerwerbs beim Zebrafinken. *Verh. Dtsch. Zool. Ges.* **79**.

Bottjer, S. W., and Arnold, A. P. (1986). The ontogeny of vocal learning in song birds. *Handb. Behav. Neurobiol.* **8**, 129-161.

Bottjer, S. W., Miesner, E. A., and Arnold, A. P. (1984). Forebrain lesions disrupt development but not maintenance of song in passerine birds. *Science* **224**, 901-903.

Brockway, B. F. (1965). Stimulation of ovarian development and egg laying by male courtship vocalization in budgerigars (*Melopsittacus undulatus*). *Anim. Behav.* **13**, 575-578.

Catchpole, C. K. (1982). The evolution of bird sounds in relation to mating and spacing behaviour. *In* "Acoustic Communication in Birds" (D. E. Kroodsma and E. H. Miller, eds.), Vol. I, pp. 297-319. Academic Press, New York.

Clayton, N. S. (1987a). Song learning in cross-fostered zebra finches: A re-examination of the sensitive phase. *Behaviour,* **102**, 67-81.

Clayton, N. S. (1987b). Song tutor choice in zebra finches. *Anim. Behav* **35**, 714-722.

Clayton, N. S. (1987c). The importance of visual, vocal and behavioural cues for song tutor choice in zebra finches. Ph.D. thesis, University of St. Andrews.

Clayton, N. S. (1988a). Song learning in Estrildids raised by two species. *Anim. Behav.*, in press.

Clayton, N. S. (1988b). Song tutor choice in zebra finches and Bengalese finches: The relative importance of visual and vocal cues. *Behaviour* in press.

Clayton, N. S. (1988c). Song discrimination learning in zebra finches. *Anim. Behav.* in press.

Dowsett-Lemaire, F. (1979). The imitative range of the song of the marsh warbler, *Acrocephalus palustris*, with special reference to imitations of African birds. *Ibis* **121**, 453-468.

Eales, L. A. (1985a). Song learning in zebra finches. Ph.D. thesis, University of Sussex.

Eales, L. A. (1985b). Song learning in zebra finches: Some effects of song model availability on what is learnt and when. *Anim. Behav.* **33**, 1293-1300.

Eales, L. A. (1987a). Song learning in female-raised zebra finches: Another look at the sensitive phase. *Anim. Behav.* **35**, 1356-1365.

Eales, L. A. (1987b). Do zebra finch males that have been raised by another species still tend to select a conspecific song tutor. *Anim. Behav.* **35**, 1347-1355.

Grant, B. R. (1984). The significance of song variation in a population of Darwin's finches. *Behaviour* **89**, 90-116.

Immelmann, K. (1962a). Beiträge zu einer vergleichenden Biologie australischer Prachtfinken (Spermestidae). *Zool. Jb. Syst. Bd.* **90**, 1-196.

Immelmann, K. (1962b). Biologische Bedeutung optischer und akustischer Merkmale bei Prachtfinken. *Verh. Dtsch. Zool. Ges.* 369-374.

Immelmann, K. (1965). "Australian Finches in Bush and Aviary." Angus & Robertson, Sydney.

Immelmann, K. (1968). Zur biologischen Bedeutung des Estildidgesanges. *J. Ornithol.* **109**, 284-299.

Immelmann, K. (1969). Song development in the zebra finch and other Estrildid finches. *In* "Bird Vocalisations" (R. A. Hinde, ed.), pp. 61-74, Cambridge Univ. Press, London.

Immelmann, K. (1972). Sexual and other long term aspects of imprinting in birds and other species. *Adv. Study Behav.* **4**, 147-174.

Immelmann, K., and Suomi, S. J. (1981). Sensitive phases in development. *In* "Behavioural Development" (K. Immelmann, G. W. Barlow, L. Petrinovich, and M. Main, eds.), pp. 395-431. Cambridge Univ. Press, London.

Immelmann, K., Kalberlah, H. H., Rausch, P., and Stahnke, A. (1978). Sexuelle Prägung als möglischer Faktor unerartliche Isolation beim Zebrafinken. *J. Ornithol.* **119**, 197-212.

Ince, S. A., and Slater, P. J. B. (1985). Versatility and continuity in the songs of thrushes *Turdus* spp. *Ibis* **127**, 355-364.

Konishi, M. (1965). The role of auditory feedback in the control of vocalisation in the white-crowned sparrow. *Z. Tierpsychol.* **22**, 770–778.
Konishi, M. (1970). Comparative neurophysiological studies of hearing and vocalizations in songbirds. *Z. Vergl. Physiol.* **66**, 257, 272.
Kroodsma, D. E. (1976). Reproductive devlopment in a female songbird: Differential stimulation by quality of male song. *Science* **192**, 574–575.
Kroodsma, D. E. (1978). Aspects of learning in the ontogeny of bird song: Where, from whom, when, how many, which and how accurately. *In* "The Development of Behavior: comparative and evolutionary aspects" (G. M. Burghardt and M. Bekoff, eds.), pp. 215–230. Garland, New York.
Kroodsma, D. E. (1984). Songs of the alder flycatcher (*Empidonax alnorium*) and willow flycatcher (*Empidonax traillii*) are innate. *Auk* **101**, 13–24.
Kroodsma, D. E., and Pickert, R. (1980). Environmentally dependent sensitive periods for avian vocal learning. *Nature (London)* **288**, 477–479.
McGregor, P. K., and Avery, M. I. (1986). The unsung songs of great tits (*Parus major*): Learning neighbours' songs for discrimination. *Behav. Ecol. Sociobiol.* **18**, 311–316.
Marler, P. (1976). Sensory templates in species-specific behavior. *In* "Simpler Networks and Behavior" (J. C. Fentress, ed.), pp. 314–329. Sinauer, Sunderland, Mass.
Marler, P., and Mundinger, P. (1971). Vocal learning in birds. *In* "Ontogeny of Vertebrate Behavior" (H. Moltz, ed.), pp. 389–449. Academic Press, New York.
Marler, P., and Peters, S. (1982a). Developmental overproduction and selective attrition: New processes in the epigenesis of bird song. *Dev. Psychobiol.* **15**, 369–378.
Marler, P., and Peters, S. (1982b). Long-term storage of learned birdsongs prior to production. *Anim. Behav.* **30**, 479–482.
Miller, D. B. (1979). Long-term recognition of father's song by female zebra finches. *Nature (London)* **280**, 389–391.
Mundinger, P. C. (1979). Call learning in the Carduelinae: Ethological and systematic considerations. *Syst. Zool.* **28**, 270–283.
Nicolai, J. (1959). Familientradition in der Gesangsentwicklung des Gimpels (*Pyrrhula pyrrhula* L.) *J. Ornithol.* **100**, 39–46.
Payne, R. B. (1981). Song learning and social interaction in indigo buntings. *Anim. Behav.* **29**, 688–697.
Price, P. H. (1979). Developmental determinants of structure in zebra finch song. *J. Comp. Physiol. Psychol.* **93**, 260–277.
Pröve, E. (1983). Hormonal correlates of behavioural development in male zebra finches. *In* "Ontogeny of Vertebrate Behaviour" (J. Balthazart, E. Pröve, and R. Gilles, eds.), pp. 368–374. Springer-Verlag, Berlin.
Pröve, E. (1985). Steroid hormones as a physiological basis for sexual imprinting in male zebra finches (*Taeniopygia guttata castanotis* Gould). *In* "The Endocrine System and the Environment" (B. K. Follett, S. Ishii, and A. Chandola, eds.), pp. 235–245. Springer-Verlag, Berlin.
Pröve, E., and Sossinka, R. (1978). Kurzberichte aus der laufenden Forschung. *J. Ornithol.* **119**, 235.
Pröve, E., and Sossinka, R. (1982). Radioimmunoassay of plasma hormones and its use in investigations of hormone and behaviour correlations in birds. *In* "Aspects of Avian Endocrinology: Practical and Theoretical Implications" (C. G. Scanes, *et al*, eds.), pp. 1–411. Texas Technical University,
Shy, E., McGregor, P. K., and Krebs, J. R. (1986). Discrimination of song types by male great tits. *Behav. Proc.* **13**, 1–12.
Silcox, A. (1979). The pair bonding in the zebra finch. Ph.D. thesis, University of Newcastle upon Tyne.
Slater, P. J. B. (1981). Chaffinch song repertoires: Observations, experiments and a discussion of their significance. *Z. Tierpsychol.* **56**, 1–24.

Slater, P. J. B. (1983). Bird song learning: Theme and variations. *In* "Perspectives in Ornithology" (G. H. Brush and G. A. Clark, eds.), Cambridge Univ. Press, New York.
Slater, P. J. B., and Clements, F. A. (1981). Incestuous mating in zebra finches. *Z. Tierpsychol.* **57**, 201-208.
Slater, P. J. B., and Eales, L. A. (1988). In preparation.
Sossinka, R., and Böhner, J. (1980). Song types in the zebra finch. *Z. Tierpsychol.* **53**, 123-132.
ten Cate, C. (1982). Behavioural differences betwen zebra finch and Bengalese finch (foster) parents raising zebra finch offspring. *Behaviour* **81**, 152-172.
ten Cate, C. (1984). The influence of social relations on the development of species recognition in zebra finch males. *Behaviour* **91**, 263-285.
ten Cate, C. (1985). Differences in the interactions between zebra finch and Bengalese finch parents with conspecific versus heterospecific young. *Z. Tierpsychol.* **67**, 58-68.
ten Cate, C. (1986). Listening behaviour and song learning in zebra finches. *Anim. Behav.*. **34**, 1267-1269.
ten Cate, C. Los, L., and Schilperoord, L. (1984). The influence of differences in social experience on the development of species recognition in zebrafinch males. *Anim. Behav.* **32**, 852-860.
Todt, D., Hultsch, H., and Heike, D. (1979). Conditions affecting song acquisition in nightingales (*Luscinia megarhynchos* L.). *Z. Tierpsychol.* **51**, 23-35.
Treisman, M. (1978). Bird song dialects, repertoire size and kin association. *Anim. Behav.* **26**, 814-817.
Zann, R. (1984). Structural variation in the zebra finch distance call. *Z. Tierpsychol.* **66**, 328-345.
Zann, R. (1985). Ontogeny of the zebra fich distance call: I. Effects of crossfostering to Bengalese finches. *Z. Tierpsychol.* **68**, 1-23.

# Behavioral Aspects of Sperm Competition in Birds

T. R. BIRKHEAD

ZOOLOGY DEPARTMENT
THE UNIVERSITY
SHEFFIELD S10 2TN, ENGLAND

## I. Introduction

Sperm competition is the competition between spermatozoa of different males to fertilize the eggs of a single female (Parker, 1970). Circumstantial evidence that sperm competition may occur in birds has been available for some time from observations of females copulating with more than one male (Selous, 1906–1907; Heinroth, 1911). The occurrence of sperm precedence, which is the outcome of sperm competition in ecological time, has also been known (at least in chickens) for some time (Aristotle, cited in Payne and Kahrs, 1961). Only since the early 1970s, however, have adaptations to sperm competition (i.e., the outcome of sperm competition in evolutionary time) been considered (Parker, 1970; Trivers, 1972). The aim of this article is to provide a review of sperm competition and behavioral adaptations to sperm competition in birds.

Among birds showing simultaneous polyandry or promiscuous mating systems (see Emlen and Oring, 1977; Faaborg and Patterson, 1981; Oring, 1982), in which females regularly copulate with more than one male prior to laying a clutch, it is obvious that sperm competition occurs. Among monogamous birds it is less obvious that it occurs, since monogamy has been defined as "the prolonged association and essentially exclusive mating relationship between one male and one female" (Wittenberger and Tilson, 1980). Nonetheless, it is known that copulations outside the pair bond (extrapair copulations, or EPCs) occur in many monogamous bird species (Birkhead, 1987a; Ford, 1983; McKinney *et al.*, 1983, 1984). Sperm competition may also occur in monogamous species when rapid mate replacement takes place (Erickson and Zenone, 1976).

Extrapair copulations have also been recorded in those polygynous species in which males form pair bonds with several females simultaneously (e.g., red-winged blackbird *Agelaius phoeniceus*; Bray *et al.*, 1975). In certain lek species, some females may copulate with more than one male in a single "copulation bout" (Lill, 1974, 1976; P. Trail, personal communication). Sperm competition may also occur between males in communally or cooperatively breeding groups, such as those of the acorn woodpecker (*Melanerpes formicivorus*) (Mumme *et al.*, 1985).

The main emphasis in the present article is on monogamy, EPCs, and associated behaviors, although sperm competition within other avian mating systems is also discussed. For monogamous birds, cuckolded males are at a selective disadvantage since they waste time and energy rearing other males' offspring at the expense of their own (Trivers, 1972). Not surprisingly, males show several behaviors which are thought to minimize their risk of being cuckolded, mainly (1) mate guarding, that is, the close following of the female by her male partner throughout the time that she can be fertilized, or (2) frequent copulations, which may devalue inseminations from EPCs (Birkhead *et al.*, 1987). Despite these paternity guards, it is now clear that some EPCs can fertilize eggs (e.g., Burns *et al.*, 1980; Gavin and Bollinger, 1985; Westneat 1987a,b). It is particularly intriguing that estimates of extrapair paternity often exceed estimates of extrapair copulation based on behavioral observations; the reason for this is as yet unknown (see Birkhead, 1987a). Indeed, the way in which copulations translate into offspring and the way sperm from different males compete to fertilize the ova within a single female are poorly known.

## II. Detecting Extrapair Paternity

The terms *mixed paternity* and *multiple paternity* are used to indicate that spermatozoa from two or more different males have each fertilized eggs within a single clutch laid by one female. However, the terms are potentially misleading since, as Westneat (1987a,b) has shown, EPCs can result in an entire brood being fathered by a male other than the female's partner. Here I use the term *extrapair paternity* to refer either to one female's brood fathered by more than one male or to a brood fathered by a male other than the one the female was paired with.

Extrapair paternity can be detected using genetic markers of two main types: those that are continuous variables (e.g., morphological characters) and those that are discontinuous variables (e.g., plumage color, enzyme polymorphisms) (see Table I).

1. Use of morphological correlates. Because this technique uses continous variables (e.g. tarsus length; Alatalo *et al.*, 1984), it provides less direct evidence for extrapair paternity than the others. It depends upon the demonstration that the characteristic in question is heritable, it requires large sample, and it cannot assign paternity to particular individuals. Nonetheless, it can be used to demonstrate that EPCs result in offspring.

TABLE I
Evidence for Sperm Competition in Birds, Using Different Methods for Paternity Determination

| Method | Extrapair paternity[a] | | Species | Breeding or mating system[b] | Reference |
|---|---|---|---|---|---|
| Morphological correlates | 618/2565 | (24%) | Pied and collared flycatcher | PP | Alatalo et al. (1984) |
|  | 83/320 | (26%) | Swallow | C-M | Moller (1987a) |
| Electrophoresis | 1/3 | (33%) | Acorn woodpecker | CB | Joste et al. (1985) |
|  | 2/186 | (2%) | Acorn woodpecker | CB | Mumme et al. (1985) |
|  | 1/20 | (5%) | Eastern bluebird | S-M | Gowaty and Karlin (1984) |
|  | 1/97 | (1%) | White-fronted bee-eater | CM CB | Wrege and Emlen (1987) |
|  | 2/12 | (17%) | Bobolink | P | Gavin and Bollinger (1985) |
|  | 15/110 | (>14%)[c] | White-crowned sparrow | M-P | Sherman and Morton (in press) |
|  | 37/257 | (>14%)[c] | Indigo bunting | M-P | Westneat (1987b) |
|  | 9/238 | (>4%)[c] | Mallard | M | Evarts and Williams (1987) |
| Plumage polymorphism | 13/156 | (8%) | Mallard[d] | M | Burns et al. (1980) |
|  | — |  | Domestic poultry | — | See Table VI |
| Vasectomy | — |  | Red-winged blackbird | P | Bray et al. (1975); Roberts and Kennelly (1980) |

[a] All values refer to numbers of young, except for bobolinks, where they refer to numbers of broods in which mixed/incorrect paternity was detected.

[b] PP, polyterritorial polygyny; C-M, colonial and monogamous; CB, communal breeder; S-M, solitary and monogamous; P, polygynous; M-P, monogamous and polygynous; M, monogamous.

[c] Electrophoresis tends to underestimate the extent of mixed paternity (see Westneat et al., 1987) in indigo buntings by up to 40%; true values lie between 27 and 42% in two years (Westneat, 1987b). For white-crowned sparrows, true values lie between 34 and 38% (Sherman and Morton, in press).

[d] Captive birds.

2. Electrophoresis. In this, the most commonly used technique for detecting extrapair paternity, enzyme polymorphisms in blood or other tissue can be detected (Hanken and Sherman, 1981; Sherman, 1981, Barrowclough, 1983). The relative paucity of paternity information for birds stems from the fact that birds generally have insufficient heterozygosity for paternity exclusion. However, considerable diversity has been found in some avian groups (Barrowclough and Corobin, 1978), and a few studies have used this technique with great success (e.g., Westnest, 1987b) (see Table I). The main disadvantage of electrophoresis is that while it allows one to estimate the proportion of young fathered by EPCs (see Westneat et al., 1987), it can only rarely be used to assign paternity to particular individuals (Chakraborty et al., 1974). In other words, paternity is assigned probabilistically rather than absolutely in most cases. Two techniques have been developed which will allow paternity to be assigned with a much higher degree of confidence: DNA fingerprinting (Jeffreys et al., 1985; Wetton et al., 1987; Burke and Bruford, 1987) and DNA restriction fragment polymorphism analysis (Quinn and White, 1988; Quinn et al., 1987).

3. Genetic plumage markers. The main restriction with this technique is that it is only rarely possible to use it on wild birds. Most sperm-competition studies of domestic poultry have assigned paternity using plumage (or some other morphological) markers. For use with wild birds, the genetic basis for the plumage polymorphism needs to be known, and paternity detection would be restricted to those cases where both pair members were of the recessive form, and where the phenotype of the offspring was apparent before fledging. At first sight, the common guillemot or murre (*Uria aalge*) would appear to be a suitable candidate for such a study, since the genetic basis of the bridling polymorphism is known, and EPCs are frequent (Jeffries and Parslow, 1976; Birkhead et al., 1985). Since the bridled form is recessive, the appearance of a normal chick reared by a bridled pair would almost certainly indicate a successful EPC. Unfortunately, bridling does not become apparent in young guillemots until long after they have left the colony (Jeffries and Parslow, 1976), so this technique is logistically difficult. In the lesser snow goose (*Anser c. caerulescens*), in which a blue and a white (recessive) form exist, gosling phenotype is obvious at hatching, and the appearance of mixed broods from two white parents could indicate a successful EPC. Unfortunately, in this species both EPC and egg-dumping (see Mineau and Cooke, 1979) are known to occur, and genetic plumage markers cannot be used to distinguish mixed paternity from mixed maternity (but see Quinn et al., 1987). The most important application of genetic plumage markers is in captive studies (e.g., Burns et al., 1980; Sims et al., 1987; T. R. Birkhead, in preparation; see below).

4. Vasectomy. This technique doe not really detect extrapair paternity but is a useful method for detecting the occurrence of EPCs, providing the following conditions are met: (1) The duration of sperm storage is known for the

species being studied and this can be excluded as a means by which females paired to vasectomized males can produce fertile eggs; (2) the ability of males to produce spermatozoa following vasectomy is checked; (3) females do not respond to vasectomized male partners by seeking EPCs, because their male's behavior has been altered in some way (e.g., reduced copulation frequency). One way round some of these problems would be to use long-lived species, perform the vasectomy one breeding season, but only use results from subsequent seasons (providing (2) is undertaken). Conclusions from vasectomy studies must be made with care: As Mock (1983) has pointed out, vasectomy can demonstrate the occurrence of EPCs, but it will undoubtedly exaggerate their success since sperm from the male performing the EPC would not face any competition from the (vasectomized) male partner. As a result, vasectomy cannot be used to detect extrapair paternity.

### III. Mechanism of Sperm Competition

At least four factors are known to influence the probability of extrapair paternity: (1) the timing and success of copulation (i.e., sperm transfer) by different males, (2) the relative numbers of copulations by different males, (3) the duration of sperm storage, and (4) sperm precedence.

#### A. Timing and Success of Copulations

For EPCs to be successful for the males performing them, they must be directed toward fertile females (see III,C). The problem with collecting information to test this idea is that the fertilization period (see below) is known for relatively few species, especially those for which other data (e.g., pair copulation and EPC frequency) are available. For some species it may be possible to estimate the female's fertilization period from the timing of pair copulations, but this is likely to be reasonable only for those species that copulate over just a few days, before and during egg laying (e.g., passerines: see Birkhead *et al.*, 1987: Fig. 2). In other species, pair members may copulate outside the female's fertilization period: This is definitely known to occur in captive ring doves (*Streptopelia risoria*) (Zenone and Sims, 1979; Lumpkin, 1983), wild mallards (*Anas platyrhynchos*) (see Elder and Weller, 1954; Weidmann, 1958), and willow ptarmigan (*Lagopus lagopus*) (Martin and Hannon, in press); it may also occur in pigeons (*Columba livia*) (see Owen, 1941; Fabricius and Jansson, 1963), and is suspected in several other species (Birkhead *et al.*, 1987).

Here I examine the relationship between EPCs, the fertilization period, and pair copulations (PC), to determine the extent to which males time their EPCs to coincide with the female's fertilization period. For no species is all the necessary information available. For the common guillemot, only data on the temporal pattern of PC and EPC are available (see below), but the data on the fertilization period are incompletely known (Birkhead et al., 1985). For none of the wild species whose fertilization period is known (e.g., mallard), are there any complete data on the temporal patterns of PC or EPC (despite several detailed behavioral studies of mallards: Titman and Lowther, 1975; Barash, 1977; Burns et al., 1980; Cheng et al., 1982, 1983). For the snow goose, the temporal pattern of EPCs is known and the fertilization period may be similar to that of domesticated geese (see Table IV), but there is little information on copulation within pairs (Mineau and Cooke, 1979). Data on the timing of EPCs relative to pair copulations are available for rather more species, but as mentioned above, these may overestimate the extent of successful EPC timing by males (Table II).

Overall, the results indicate that males time their EPCs to coincide with the female's fertilization period: Between 54 and 100% of all EPCs are directed at fertile females (excluding the snow goose, which directs only 20% of EPCs at fertile females; Table II).

In addition to the data presented in Table II, there is also circumstantial evidence, from much smaller samples on other species, that EPCs coincide with the female's fertilization period, for example, magpie (*Pica pica*, Birkhead, 1979, see below), pied flycatcher (*Ficedula hypoleuca*, Bjorklund and Westman, 1983; Alatalo et al., 1987), wheatear (*Oenanthe oenanthe*, Carlson et al., 1985), great tit (*Parus major*, Bjorklund and Westman, 1986), sand martin (*Riparia riparia*, Beecher and Beecher, 1979), and little blue heron (*Florida caerulea*, Werschkul, 1982).

TABLE II
PROPORTION OF EPCs PERFORMED WITHIN THE FERTILE (F) PERIOD OR COPULATION (C) PERIOD

| Species | % EPCs | Period[a] | Reference |
|---|---|---|---|
| Common guillemot[b] | ca 80 | F | Birkhead et al. (1985) |
| Snow goose | 20 | F | Mineau and Cooke (1979) |
| Swallow | 83 | C | Moller (1985) |
| White ibis | 54 | C | Frederick (1985, 1987b) |
| White throated bee-eater | 81 | C | Emlen and Wrege (1986) |
| Indigo bunting | ca 100 | C | Westneat (1987a) |
| Cattle egret | ca 80 | C | Fujioka and Yagamishi (1981) |
| Lesser scaup | 87 | C | Afton (1985) |
| Rook | 88 | C | Roskaft (1983) |
| Pied flycatcher | 100 | C | Alatalo et al. (1987) |

[a] Copulation period includes up to the penultimate egg laid.
[b] See also Fig. 4.

Furthermore, over and above this gross timing of EPCs, there may also be an adaptive diurnal pattern of EPCs. In mallards, egg laying occurs in the early morning, and ovulation and fertilization take place in the following hour or so. This period has been referred to as a *fertilization window*, since during this short time spermatozoa are able to move rapidly and directly to the infudibulum (the site of fertilization; see Howarth, 1974) because the oviduct does not contain a hard-shelled egg to impede the transport of sperm in the oviduct. Cheng *et al.* (1982) found that male mallards seeking EPCs attempted to waylay females as they returned to the water following egg laying. These authors were able to show by artificial insemination experiments that an insemination made during the fertilization window could fertilize the next egg (9 of 36 cases or 25%); in contrast, when females were inseminated between 1 and 4 hours after laying, only 1 of 179 (0.6%) eggs laid the next day were fertile ($p < 0.001$; Cheng *et al.*, 1983).

The fertilization window may also operate in chickens. Laying typically takes place around the middle of the day, so the fertilization window will occur during the afternoon (see Cheng and Burns, 1988). Artificial inseminations made 4 hr before laying (while there was a hard-shelled egg in the oviduct) resulted in very low fertility, whereas those made in the afternoon, after laying, resulted in the highest fertility (Bobr *et al.*, 1964; Bilgili *et al.*, 1984; Giesen and McDaniel, 1980; Bornstein *et al.*, 1960). Semen production also peaked in the afternoon (Lake and Wood-Gush 1956), as did natural copulations (Cheng and Burns, in preparation).

There is little information regarding the diurnal pattern of EPC in wild birds, even though many (particularly passerines) are thought to lay around dawn (Skutch, 1952; Schifferli, 1979; Tullet, 1985). However, in the swallow (*Hirundo rustica*), egg laying occurs early in the morning and this is followed by pair copulations and then (in some cases) by EPCs, thus providing support for the fertilization window idea among wild birds (Moller, 1987).

A sucessful EPC is defined here as one which results in cloacal contact with the female, where the duration of cloacal contact is long enough for insemination to have occurred. Table III summarizes the available information on the success of EPCs; values range from 3% in the white-throated bee-eater (*Merops bullockoides*) to 26% in the cattle egret (*Bubulcus ibis*). In general, forced extrapair copulations (FEPC) are relatively unsuccessful; the majority of successful EPCs are unforced (UEPC, see below).

Success (and our estimate of success) depends upon several factors: (1) the behavior of the female during an EPC, (2) whether the EPC is forced or unforced (i.e., the female cooperates), (3) the presence and behavior of the male partner, and (4) the relative visibility of successful and unsuccessful EPCs to the observer.

Although the data in Table III are presented as FEPC or UEPC, the distinction between these two categories may not always be clear. At one extreme,

TABLE III
APPARENT INSEMINATION SUCCESS OF EXTRAPAIR COPULATIONS

| Species | EPCs observed | | | Successful | | | | Reference |
|---|---|---|---|---|---|---|---|---|
| | N | FEPC (%) | UEPC (%) | N (%) | | FEPC | UEPC | |
| Wandering albatross | 26 | 26(100) | 0 (0) | 1 | (4.0) | 0 | 1 | S. Pickering (personal communication) |
| Northern fulmar | 44 | — | — | 9 | (15.0) | 0 | 9 | Hatch (1987) |
| Cattle egret | 147 | — | — | 38 | (25.9) | 0 | 38 | Fujioka and Yagamisha (1981) |
| White ibis | 989 | — | — | 66 | (6.7) | 0? | 66 | Frederick (1985) |
| Snow goose | 116 | 116(100) | 0 (0) | 9 | (7.7)[a] | 0 | 9 | Mineau and Cooke (1979) |
| Lesser scaup | 276 | 276(100) | 0 (0) | 54 | (19.6) | 54 | 0[b] | Afton (1985) |
| Common guillemot | 266 | 226( 85) | 40 (15) | 49 | (18.4) | 10 | 39 | Birkhead et al. (1985) |
| White-throated bee-eater | 149[c] | 149(100) | 0 (0) | 4 | (2.7) | 4 | 0 | Emlen and Wrege (1986) |
| Swallow | 387[c] | 387(100) | 0 (0) | 15 | (3.9) | 0 | 15[d] | Møller (1985) |
| Indigo bunting | 54 | — | — | 2 | (3.7) | — | — | Westneat (1987a) |
| Pied flycatcher | 20 | 17 (85) | 3 (15) | 7 | (35.0) | 4 | 3 | Alatalo et al. (1987) |

[a] Minimum value.
[b] Success determined from male postcopulatory display. This study concentrated on FEPC and may therefore have missed UEPC.
[c] Sexual chases, not mountings.
[d] See text. Most EPC attempts are forced, but females apparently 'give in' and so successful EPCs are scored here as UEPC.

some female fulmars (*Fulmarus glacialis*) appear to actively seek EPCs, and those that occur as a result are clearly UEPC (Hatch, 1987). In the common guillemot, some females may adopt copulation invitation behavior on being approached by a male, and then engage in an UEPC (personal observation). In the snow goose, most EPC attempts are forced, but some females "eventually responded...by raising [their] tail and allowing cloacal contact" (Mineau and Cooke, 1979). In the cattle egret and white ibis (*Eudocimus albus*), virtually all EPC attempts were forced but most females apparently allowed cloacal contact almost immediately. Forced EPCs occur in the common guillemot, white-throated bee-eater and lesser scaup (*Aythya affinis*) (see Table III).

Unforced EPCs are likely to be successful, but FEPC may also result in cloacal contact, either because females "give in" and allow cloacal contact (in order to get rid of the male sooner) or because males are able to pin females down and force cloacal contact. In lesser scaup, at least, FEPC can definitely result in sperm transfer despite female resistance (Afton, 1985). Almost all studies have shown that the presence of the male partner reduces the likelihood of an EPC being successful (e.g., Birkhead, 1979; Mineau and Cooke, 1979; Bjorklund and Westman, 1983; Birkhead *et al.*, 1985; Emlen and Wrege, 1986; Frederick, 1987a).

A successful EPC does not necessarily result in the fertilization of (one or more) eggs, because sperm from an EPC must compete with sperm from the male partner. Since the male partner is likely to have inseminated his female on more occasions than extrapair males, we might expect the fertilization success of EPCs to be low (see Birkhead *et al.*, 1985; Martin *et al.*, 1974). In one of the most comprehensive studies to date, the opposite result was obtained. Westneat (1987a,b) showed that EPCs were (apparently) infrequent relative to pair copulations (see below), and that EPCs had a low success rate (3.7%; Table III). Despite this, the proportion of offspring fathered by EPCs was very high, up to 42%. This result raises a number of questions regarding (1) the mechanism of sperm competition in this species, (2) the relative visibility of PCs and EPCs, and of successful and unsuccessful EPCs (see below), and (3) the proportion of copulations (pair and extrapair) that result in successful ejaculation and insemination (in domesticated Japanese quail, for example, only 50% of copulations involving cloacal contact result in sperm transfer, K. M. Cheng, personal communication.)

B. Relative Numbers of Pair Copulations and EPCs

The interspecific variation in pair-copulation frequency in birds is dramatic, ranging from a single copulation per clutch (e.g., some galliformes), to over 100 in some colonial species and raptors. Birkhead *et al.* (1987) reviewed the literature on pair-copulation behavior to examine four main hypotheses to explain the interspecific variation in (female) copulation frequency:

1. Fertilization hypothesis: The total number of copulations is positively correlated with the number of eggs in the clutch which need to be fertilized. There was no evidence for this.

2. Social bond hypothesis: The variation in copulation rate is associated with the formation and maintenance of pair bonds. This is a difficult hypothesis to test because it makes no clear predictions. However, it seems likely that in a few species copulation plays a part in pair formation, since it occurs well outside the female's fertile period (e.g., some ducks; Hohn, 1947).

3. Predation hypothesis: Species vulnerable to predation copulate less often and/or more rapidly than other species. The evidence for this hypothesis was equivocal; some predictions were supported, but others were not.

4. Sperm competition hypothesis: Copulation frequency is related to the risk of EPC; if the risk is high, pair copulations are frequent in order to devalue inseminations made by other males. Most predictions were supported by data. In particular, those species in which males are unable to guard their fertile females (because of ecological constraints), and are therefore uncertain whether their female has engaged in one or more EPCs, show a higher copulation rate than those that guard their mates. Two groups of birds were classified as nonguarders: colonial species and raptors. All others were considered to be guarders. In addition, an examination of those genera in which there were both colonial and solitary species showed that in all cases ($N = 5$) the colonial species had a high copulation rate and the solitary species a low rate (binomial test, $p = .03$). Copulation frequency also differs within species according to the social circumstances. Solitary-breeding swallows copulated significantly less often than those breeding colonially (Moller, 1985). Similarly in chickens, females kept with a single male copulated less often than those kept with two males (Cheng and Burns, in preparation).

There have been no experiments to test directly the idea that frequent copulation will increase a male's probability of paternity if his female has been subject to an EPC. Circumstantial evidence from experiments on chickens supports this idea (Martin *et al.*, 1974; see below). In fact it is unlikely that the absolute number of pair copulations will be important; rather, it is much more probable that the proportion of EPC inseminations a female receives will determine a male's probability of paternity. For example, skylarks (*Alauda arvensis*) probably copulate only once per clutch (Delius, 1963), and a single EPC would pose a much greater threat to a male's paternity than it would for a species that typically copulates many times for each clutch. Male skylarks guard their females during the fertilization period (R. Green, personal communication), but, as already pointed out, mate-guarding does not automatically prevent EPCs. It is interesting to speculate that some additional form of paternity-assurance mechanisms may exist for species like the skylark in which pair copulations occur at low frequency.

Not all individuals in a population copulate to the same extent, or perform, or are subjected to, forced EPCs at the same rate. In guillemots, for example, the mean number of copulations/female/clutch was 17.1 ± 9.1 *SD*, with a range from 3 to 45. Similarly, the mean number of FEPCs performed by males was 5.8 (range 0 to 32); for females the mean was 5.3 (range 0 to 29) (Birkhead *et al.*, 1985, and unpublished). This strongly suggests that individuals differ in their risk of EPC. Indeed, both Moller (1985) and Westneat (1987a) found that young females were particularly likely to experience EPCs, and old males particularly active in seeking EPCs.

C. SPERM-STORAGE DURATION AND THE FERTILIZATION PERIOD

Prolonged sperm storage in domesticated birds has been known for over 200 years (W. Harvey, cited in Pearl and Surface, 1909). If sperm are stored in the female reproductive tract prior to fertilization, the potential for sperm competition exists; the longer the duration of sperm storage, the greater the probability of overlapping inseminations from different males (Parker, 1970, 1984).

The duration of sperm storage (also erroneously referred to as the *period of fertility* [Howarth, 1974] and the *fertile period* [Lake, 1975]) has been determined for five avian orders: Anseriformes, Falconiformes, Galliformes, Columbiformes, and Psittaciformes (Table IV). However, it is important to note that the methods used to obtain these values, and the way in which sperm storage duration has been defined, varies among studies. For example, Elder and Weller (1954) define the duration as the interval between a female's separation from a male and the laying of the last fertile egg, whereas Howarth (1974) defines it as the period between the last mating and the production of the last fertile egg.

Several workers have used the term *fertile period* (Lake, 1975) to indicate the time period over which a female bird can be fertilized. However, this is not the sense in which Lake (1975) originally used the term, nor is it the same as the duration of sperm storage. Lake defined the fertile period, with respect to poultry breeding, as the mean period for which the maximum rate of fertilization can be maintained (following a single artificial insemination/female) once the flock is in full lay (P. E. Lake, 1975, personal communication). The period over which a female can be fertilized, that is, laying at least one fertile egg (referred to here as the *fertilization period*), differs from the duration of sperm storage. Consider the case where a female (1) can store sperm for 5 days, (2) lays a clutch of six eggs, over 6 days, starting on Day 0, and (3) each egg is fertilized shortly after ovulation, at first light in the morning, 24 hr before it is laid (Howarth, 1974). In this case, the period over which the female

TABLE IV
MEAN AND MAXIMUM SPERM STORAGE DURATION IN BIRDS

| Species | Mean duration (Days) | Maximum duration (Days) | Method[b] | Reference |
|---|---|---|---|---|
| Chinese goose | | | | |
| *Anser cygnoides* | —[a] | 10 | AI | Olver (1971) |
| Embden goose | | | | |
| *Anser anser* | — | 14 | AI | Kinney and Burger (1960) |
| Pilgrim goose | | | | |
| *Anser anser* | 9.7 | 16 | AI | Johnson (1954) |
| Moscovy duck | | | | |
| *Cairina moschata* | — | 13 | N | Tolentino (1948); Thibault and Levasseur (1973) |
| Peking duck | | | | |
| *Anas platyrhynchos* | — | 11–16 | N | Chappelier (1917); Fronda *et al.* (1940); Ash (1962); Laundau and Vancikova (1959) |
| | 8.2 | 13 | AI | Olver *et al.* (1977) |
| | 10.3 | 16 | N | Olver *et al.* (1977) |
| Mallard | | | | |
| *Anas platyrhynchos* | 9.9 | 17 | N | Elder and Weller (1954) |
| American kestrel | | | | |
| *Falco sparverius* | 8.1 | 12 | AI | Bird and Buckland (1976) |
| Turkey | | | | |
| *Meleagris gallopavo* | 43.0 | 72 | AI | Lorenz (1950) |
| | 42.6 | 62 | N | Hale (1955) |
| | 51.6 | 63 | AI | McCartney (1951) |
| Willow ptarmigan | | | | |
| *Lagopus lagopus* | 7.8 | 14 | N | Parker (1981) |
| Bobwhite quail | | | | |
| *Colinus virginianus* | 8.3 | — | AI | Kulenkamp and Coleman (1965) |
| Japanese quail | | | | |
| *Coturnix japonica* | 6.3 | 11 | N | Sittman and Abplanalp (1965) |
| Chicken | | | | |
| *Gallus domesticus* | — | 10–35 | N | 20 studies cited in Elder and Weller (1954) |
| | — | 21 | AI | Lodge *et al.* (1971) |
| | 12 | — | AI | Polge (1951) |
| Pheasant | | | | |
| *Phasianus colchicus* | 22 | 42 | N | Shick (1947) |
| | 21 | 29 | N | Twining *et al.* (1949) |
| Guinea fowl | | | | |
| *Numida meleagris* | 7 | 24 | AI | Petitjean (1966) |
| Pigeon | | | | |
| *Columbia livia* | — | 8 | AI | Owen (1941) |

TABLE IV (continued)

| Species | Mean duration (Days) | Maximum duration (Days) | Method[b] | Reference |
|---|---|---|---|---|
| Ringdove | | | | |
| Streptopelia risoria | — | 6 | N | Zenone et al. (1979); Cheng et al. (1981) |
| Hybrid dove | | | | |
| S. risoria ×, S. alba, or S. douraca | — | 8 | N | Riddle and Behre (1921) |
| Budgerigar | | | | |
| Melopsittacus undulatus | 11 | 14 | AI | J. Samour (personal communication) |
| | 11 | 20 | N | J. Samour (personal communication); T. R. Birkhead (unpublished) |
| Cockatiel | | | | |
| Nymphicus hollandicus | — | 24 | N | T. R. Birkhead (unpublished) |

[a] A dash indicates no data available.
[b] AI, artificial insemination; N, natural mating.

could be fertilized spans 10 full days, from Day $-6$ to Day $+3$. Clearly, when the clutch size is greater than one, the sperm-storage duration will always be shorter than the period over which the female can be fertilized. When the clutch is one, the two periods will be the same. Hence it is important to distinguish between sperm-storage duration and the female's fertilization period.

Many sperm-storage studies (e.g., those cited by Elder and Weller, 1954) involved a male bird being placed with several females (usually for an unspecified number of days) and then being removed. Eggs were subsequently collected and incubated to determine their fertility each day. Clearly, with this procedure the number of times particular females were mated was not recorded, nor was there any informatiton on when the male last mated with a particular female. Howarth's (1974) definition specified that the time was recorded from the last mating, but does not consider the total number of matings by each female. Lake's (1975) definition is more precise since it specifies a single natural, or artificial, insemination. However, there are limitations even with this, since for natural and artificial inseminations to be comparable, they must contain the same numbers of spermatozoa. Since it is apparently extremely difficult to determine spermatozoa numbers for natural matings (P. E. Lake, personal communication), this could be a problem.

Most studies present information for the maximum duration of sperm storage, and the values obtained vary interspecifically from 6 to 8 days in three Columbiformes to 72 days in the turkey (Table IV). The intraspecific variation in maximum sperm-storage durations is also considerable (e.g., chicken, 10–35 days; turkey 63–72 days; Table IV) and must reflect, in part at least, the different methods used to obtain the information or differences between strains used (see Taneja and Gowe, 1961). Olver et al. (1977) found significant differences in sperm-storage duration between Peking ducks, with means for individual females varying from 6.3 to 10 days.

Some studies have used natural matings (single or multiple), while others have used artificial inseminations with known volumes of semen and densities of spermatozoa (e.g., Compton et al., 1978). Olver et al. (1977) found a significant ($p < .001$) difference in mean sperm storage duration between female Peking ducks subjected to either an unspecified number of natural matings ($\overline{X} = 10.3$ days $\pm 1.8$ SD, $N = 54$) and those artificially inseminated once (8.2 days $\pm 1.5$ SD, $N = 80$). They suggest that the naturally mated females had received a greater number of spermatozoa, which resulted in a longer duration of sperm storage. Studies on turkeys (Lorenz, 1950) and chickens (Taneja and Gowe, 1961) also showed that inseminations with larger volumes of semen or numbers of spermatozoa, resulted in longer sperm storage. A similar but nonsignificant trend has also been recorded in quail (Lepore and Marks, 1966). In Taneja and Gowe's (1961) detailed study, sperm-storage duration increased with increasing numbers of spermatoza, leveling off between 60 and 120 million. The best available estimate of sperm numbers in a natural mating in chickens is about 25 million (P. E. Lake, personal communication), which means that sperm-storage duration will be maximal following three or four natural matings.

Obtaining sperm storage durations for other birds, comparable with those from domestic poultry, may be difficult. Most poultry lay (more or less) continuously, so it is relatively straightforward to obtain mean sperm-storage durations. Most other birds lay discrete clutches, and therefore the timing and number of clutches which isolated females lay will determine the nature of the data obtained. My own work with zebra finches (*Poephila guttata*) has highlighted this problem, and I suggest that the most parsimonious solution may be to pool all the data obtained to produce a fertility curve (see below) and to use the median value.

Some information on sperm storage in wild birds is available, but it is important to realize that such data have been obtained in very different ways from those for domesticated species and are not strictly comparable (cf. Phillips et al., 1985; Table 1). Moreover, it is possible that domestication may have (unintentionally) selected for prolonged sperm storage (Lake, 1975; see also Clayton, 1972) or longevity of sperm in female storage glands (K. M. Cheng, personal communication); unfortunately there are no data to test these ideas.

The information for wild birds is based on the interval between the last-observed copulation and egg laying, and is available only for seabirds. In many seabirds species, females spend relatively little time at the breeding colony (where copulation takes place) prior to egg laying, and mean intervals between the last-observed copulation and laying vary between 8.1 days in the common guillemot (personal observation), 14.6 days in the black-browed albatross (*Diomedea melanophris*, Astheimer et al., 1985), 19 days in the fulmar (*Fulmarus glacialis*, Hatch, 1983, 1988), 30 days in Buller's shearwater (*Puffinus bulleri*, Harper, 1983), to 60 days in the grey-faced petrel (*Pterodroma macoptera*, Imber, 1976). In addition to the data in Table IV and those for seabirds, there is some incomplete information (based on very small samples) which provides minimum estimates of sperm-storage duration for several other species. For three greater rheas (*Rhea americana*), the maximum interval between separation from the male and laying a fertile egg was 8 days (Bruning, 1974). The interval between artificial insemination and the last fertile egg was 4 days in the goshawk (*Accipter gentilis*, Berry, 1972), and 10 days in the peregrine (*Falco peregrinus*, Fessner, 1970). Grier (1973) considered a 10-day sperm-storage duration in his golden eagle (*Aquila chrysaetos*) excessive and suggested that manipulation during artificial insemination may have delayed ovulation. While this is a possibility, it does not alter the fact that the sperm may have remained viable for this time. Also, compared with data for other species (Table IV), a 10-day period is not excessive.

Bird and Buckland (1976) similarly questioned some of their own data from American kestrels (*Falco sparverius*); one female laid a fertile egg 15 days after artificial insemination, and 9 days after the previous egg. They did not use this 15-day value in calculating the mean maximum storage duration (in Table IV), because they assumed that the fertilized egg had been held in the oviduct for "an abnormally long period." Clearly, if females do hold fertilized eggs for long periods, this is a potential source of bias in sperm-storage studies (particularly if single maximum values are used). Indeed, in making interspecific comparisons, it is assumed that the interval between fertilization and laying is constant across species. For species that lay eggs at 24-hr intervals, this is likely to be true (Opel, 1966; Howarth, 1974). For species that lay at longer intervals, the interval between fertilization and oviposition may be longer, for example, 40 hr in doves (Riddle and Behre, 1921); ca 48 hr in budgerigars (*Melopsittacus undulatus*, J. Samour, personal communication; see also Astheimer, 1985). For species that lay only a single egg, the interval between ovulation and fertilization is unknown. As Riddle and Behre (1921) point out, the sperm-storage duration is strictly the interval between insemination and fertilization, and not oviposition.

The adaptive significance of prolonged sperm storage in birds is poorly understood, but the available information indicates that the duration of sperm storage may be linked with the ecology of particular species or groups. If we consider those groups for which we have most information (Galliformes, Columbiformes, and seabirds), we can speculate about the significance of sperm storage. However, many more data are needed for other groups (particularly passerines), and methods must be standardized, before a detailed comparative study can be undertaken. Many Galliformes produce relatively large clutches but copulate infrequently, so prolonged sperm storage would be advantageous. In their review of copulation behavior in birds, Birkhead *et al.* (1987) obtained qualitative information on the (female) copulation frequency of six Galliformes: sage grouse (*Centrocercus urophasianus*), black grouse (*Lyrurus tetrix*), capercaillie (*Tetrao urogallus*), red grouse (willow ptarmigan) (*Lagopus lagopus*), grey partridge (*Perdix perdix*), and red-legged partridge (*Alectoris rufa*). All of these have low copulation rates, probably copulating only once per clutch, and have mean clutch sizes varying from 6 to 15 eggs. Unfortunately there is only one of these species for which we have reasonably complete information: The willow ptarmigan has a low copulation rate and mean clutch of 7.5 eggs (S. Hannon, personal communication), with maximum and mean sperm-storage durations of 14 and 7.8 days respectively (Parker, 1981). It seems likely that a single insemination could fertilize the entire clutch in this species. The possible reasons why many Galliformes have very low copulation rates are discussed in Birkhead *et al.* (1987).

In seabirds (which typically produce small clutches of one or two eggs), prolonged sperm storage is advantageous because females and males may spend days or weeks apart prior to egg laying. Most species produce relatively large, yolky eggs, and females probably spend most of their time away from the colony foraging prior to laying (Birkhead *et al.*, 1985; Astheimer *et al.*, 1985, Hatch, 1987).

It is striking that the shortest sperm-storage durations recorded occur in the Columbiformes (maximum values of 6 to 8 days), in two species for which there is no obvious reason for prolonged sperm storage. Clutch size is small (two eggs, laid 2 days apart) and male and female are probably rarely apart for long prior to egg laying (see Goodwin, 1967; Kotov, 1978; Lumpkin, 1983).

Although most studies have reported maximum durations of sperm storage, the functional significance of such values is questionable for two reasons. First, they represent single maximum values from a population of females; such extreme values may represent chance events and have little relevance to paternity studies. For example, the maximum recorded duration of sperm storage in the chicken is 35 days (Table IV), but the experiments of Lodge *et al.* (1971) show that fertility is virtually zero by Day 20 and the probability of eggs being fertilized after this time is extremely low. Second, the hatching success of eggs fertilized by "old" spermatozoa is reduced: The maximum duration of sperm storage in the turkey is 72 days (Table IV), but no eggs fertilized after Day 53 have ever hatched (McCartney, 1951). Reduced hatching success of eggs fertilized by sperm that have been stored in the female reproductive tract for a long time has been recorded in four species: mallard, chicken, quail, and turkey (but not in doves, apparently; Riddle and Behre, 1921). A functional definition of sperm storage should take this into account, and in Fig. 1 data for fertilization and hatching success are combined to show functional sperm-storage curves for these four species.

Clearly, maximum sperm-storage values are of limited use, but it is difficult to decide whether any other single value is meaningful. Indeed, since the methods employed for obtaining data on sperm-storage duration have varied so much, it may be unnecessary to aim for a high level of sophistication. However, assuming that comparable techniques are used in the future, mean values are probably the most biologically meaningful, but it would perhaps be useful to also present fertility and hatching success curves so that median and maximum values for all parameters can be obtained. Table V compares sperm-storage duration for five species using different variables. In four species, the difference between maximum and minimum values are large (ratios 1.6 to 2.4), whereas in the dove the difference is relatively small; this was due in part to the lack of any decrease in hatching success with increased sperm-storage duration.

In terms of sperm competition, the decline in fertility and hatching success with increasing sperm-storage duration has different implications for males seeking EPCs and those guarding their partners. For males seeking EPCs, there would be little point obtaining EPCs at the very beginning of a female's fertilization period, since this would result in sperm being stored for close to the maximum time, and although such EPCs may result in the fertilization of eggs, it is unlikely that any young would be produced (see also Section III,D). On the other hand, a guarding male should protect a female from the onset of her fertilization period, since any egg fertilized by another male (regardless of whether it hatches or not) is one fewer for him to father.

D. Sperm Precedence

Sperm-precedence experiments have been conducted on four domestic species: chickens, turkeys, mallard ducks, and ringdoves. In all studies, paternity was determined using genetic markers, either plumage markers or some other marker such as dwarfing (e.g., Compton et al., 1978) or the number of digits (Krallinger, 1930). It has been known for a long time that sperm precedence can occur in chickens; Aristotle apparently recorded that "the bird who carries an egg conceived by a copulation, if it then has coitus with another male, will hatch all its chicks thereafter of a genus similar to the latter male" (cited in Payne and Kahrs, 1961). Subsequent studies on chickens by Crew (1926), Warren and Kilpatrick (1929), and Krallinger (1930), and the ringdove by Sims et al. (1987), confirmed that when one male was replaced by another,

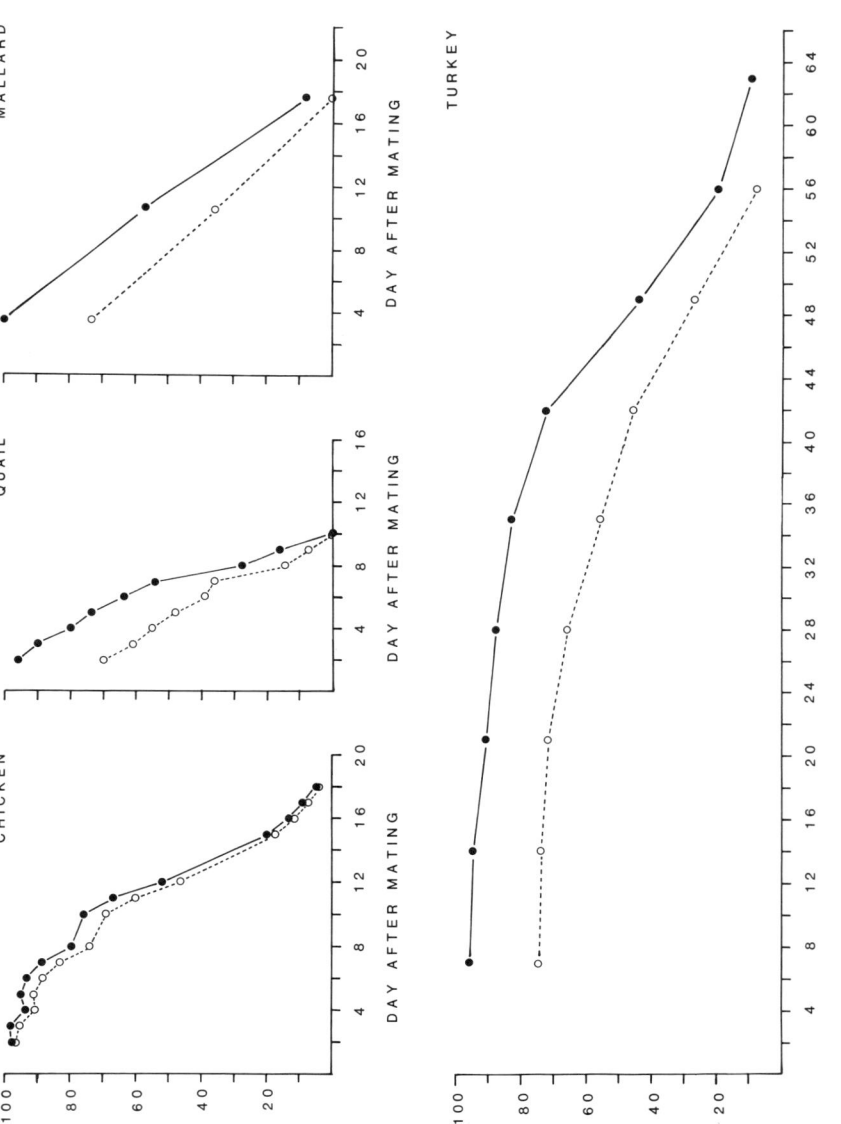

FIG. 1. Decline in fertility (—●—) following the last mating, in four species of domesticated birds. Open symbols (--○--) show the decline in the proportion of eggs which hatched. Data for chicken from Lodge et al. (1971); quail, Sittman and Abplanalp (1965); mallard, Elder and Weller (1954); and turkey, Hale (1955). (See also Table V.)

TABLE V
COMPARISON OF SPERM-STORAGE DURATIONS USING DIFFERENT MEASURES

| Species | Median value fertility × hatching success (a) | Sperm-storage duration (days) | | | | Ratio (b) : (a) | References |
|---|---|---|---|---|---|---|---|
| | | Median | Mean | SD | Maximum (b) | | |
| Mallard duck | ca 8 | 9 | 9.9 | 2.5 | 17 | 2.1 | Elder and Weller (1954) |
| Turkey | 38 | 48 | 43.0 | (?) | 62 | 1.6 | Hale (1955) |
| Quail | 4.5 | 7 | 6.3 | 2.0 | 11 | 2.4 | Sittman and Abplanalp (1965) |
| Chicken | ca 11.5 | 12 | —[a] | | 21 | 1.8 | Lodge et al. (1971) |
| Dove | ca 7 | 7 | 7.8 | 0.1 | 8 | 1.1 | Riddle and Behre (1921) |

[a] No data available.

the second male fertilized the majority of eggs, despite the fact that if the first male were removed from the females and not replaced, his spermatozoa would continue to fertilize eggs for 20 or more days in the chicken and 6 days in the ringdove (see above). The most detailed of these studies involving natural matings is that of Warren and Kilpatrick (1929); their main result is summarized in Fig. 2. Nine days after the removal of Male 1 and replacement by Male 2, over 90% of eggs were fertilized by Male 2. That this was due to sperm precedence by Male 2 can be most clearly seen by comparing their data with the decline in fertility which would have been expected had Male 2 not been introduced.

Sperm-competition studies involving natural matings neither quantified nor controlled for the number of matings, but subsequent artificial insemination studies controlled both the number of inseminations and either the volume of semen or the number of spermatozoa introduced into females. Artificial insemination studies found that, like those involving natural matings, the last insemination fertilized most eggs. When females were inseminated twice, at intervals of 4 hr, 24 hr, or several days, with spermatozoa from two different males, the second insemination fertilized 70 to 90% of the eggs; with shorter intervals both males fathered approximately equal numbers of offspring (Table VI).

Neither of these two types of experiment, however, accurately mimics the situations where a female bird is subject to an EPC. First, in the natural mating

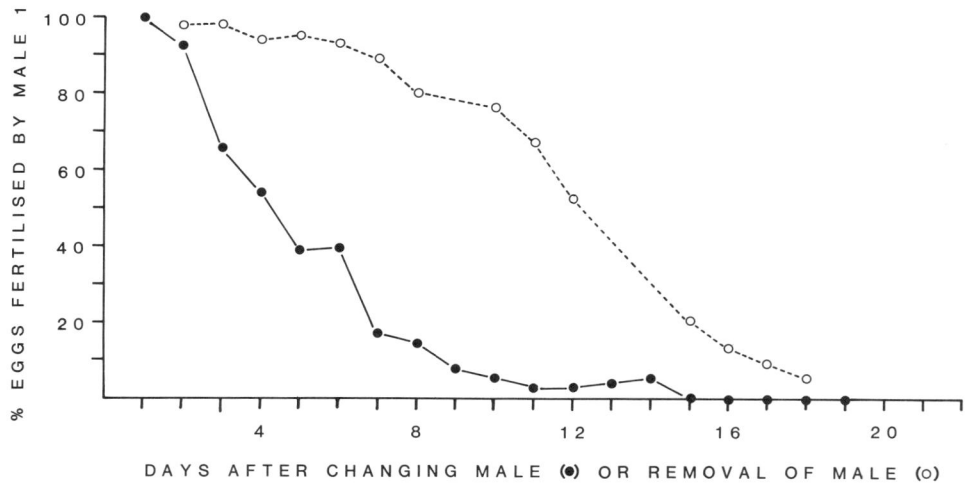

FIG. 2. Decline in proportion of eggs fertilized by the first male (●) following a change in males (data from Warren and Kilpatrick, 1929), compared with the decline in fertility (--○--) following the removal of a male from the females (data from Lodge et al., 1971). The difference between the two curves is the result of sperm precedence by the second male.

TABLE VI
ARTIFICIAL INSEMINATION STUDIES OF SPERM COMPETITION IN BIRDS

| Species insemination pattern[a] | Insemination interval | N[b] | $P_2$[c] | Reference |
|---|---|---|---|---|
| Chicken single | 0 days[d] | 173 | .53 NS | |
|  | 2–4 days | 329 | .81** | Warren and Gish (1943) |
|  | 7 days | 604 | .93** | |
| Chicken single | 4 hr | 246 | .77** | Compton et al. (1978) |
| Chicken single (?) | 1 day? | ? | high | DeMerritt (1979) |
| Chicken multiple | ca 1 day | 47 | .87** | Bonnier and Trulson (1939) |
| Turkey single | 10 days | 484 | .71** | Payne and Kahrs (1961) |
| Mallard single | 1 hr | 69 | .48 NS | |
|  | 3 hr | 77 | .58 NS | Cheng et al. (1983) |
|  | 6 hr | 79 | .79* | |

[a] Single, one insemination from each male at the interval specified, with a total of two; multiple insemination, one insemination from each male alternating between days, total inseminations > 2.

[b] Number of offspring for which paternity was determined.

[c] Proportion of offspring attributable to the second male. Deviations from 50 : 50 ratio: $\chi^2$ tests; **, $p < .001$; *, $p < .01$; NS, not significantly different from 50 : 50. Note that $P_2$ values given here are as in the original sources. However, it is not always clear whether the values have been calculated from the number of days in which the first and second males' inseminations could *both* potentially fertilize eggs.

[d] Warren and Gish (1943) state: "Females which had been given freedom of a pen with males of one breed were caught, inseminated immediately with semen from males of another breed and isolated." The actual interval between the first (natural) inseminaton and the second (artificial) insemination is not stated.

experiments one male was simply replaced by another, and second, in most of the artificial insemination studies, sperm competition occurred between equal numbers of spermatozoa from the two males. While the latter may occur in some Galliformes and a few other bird species which copulate infrequently, it is unlikely to be the case in the majority of species (see above, and Birkhead et al., 1987). The study by Bonnier and Trulson (1939) more closely resembles what might occur with an EPC; females were inseminated on several occasions, with spermatozoa from two males being introduced on alternate days. As in the other experiments, however, the last insemination before laying (excluding eggs laid within 24 hr following artificial insemination) fertilized most eggs (see Table VI).

The second (or last) male advantage is thought to occur because sperm from different matings are layered in the sperm storage glands, with those from the last mating lying on top of those from previous inseminations, and because spermatozoa leave the glands in the reverse order from which they were introduced (Compton *et al.*, 1978). In other words, as in many insects, a "last-in first-out" system appears to operate (see Gwynne, 1984; Thornhill and Alcock, 1983). Although Compton *et al.* (1978) did not point it out, the data they present show good quantitative agreement with this idea. They artificially inseminated hens twice, 4 hr apart. Sperm from each of the two inseminations were genetically labeled so that the success of each insemination could be determined. Van Krey *et al.* (1971) had previously shown that a single insemination resulted in about 50% of sperm storage glands receiving sperm. In Compton *et al.*'s (1978) experiment, then, the first insemination would have resulted in half the glands receiving sperm, as would the second, but assuming the glands received sperm at random, on average 50% of the sperm from the second insemination would have gone into empty glands and 50% into glands already containing sperm from the first insemination. In other words, 75% of the sperm storage glands will have had either (1) sperm only from the second insemination (25%), or (2) sperm from the second insemination overlying that of the first. The remaining 25% of glands would have contained sperm from the first insemination only. If sperm leak out of the sperm storage glands at random, as Compton *et al.* (1978) suggest, then one would predict that the second insemination should fertilize 75% of eggs, and the first, 25%: Compton *et al.*'s (1978) figures of 77% and 23%, respectively, are remarkably close to these values.

At first sight, the experiments cited appear to provide abundant evidence for a relatively simple form of sperm precedence with the last male to mate having a .7 to .9 probability of fertilizing the next egg to be ovulated. However, two experiments suggest that sperm competition is unlikely to be this simple in the wild. First, as stated above, Warren and Kilpatrick (1929), working with chickens, showed that if Male 1 was replaced by Male 2, Male 2 fertilized most eggs within a few days (Fig. 2). If however, Male 2 was not allowed to remain with the hens, but was removed after 2 days, he fertilized only 50% of the subsequent eggs (Fig. 3), indicating that in Warren and Kilpatrick's initial experiment the second-male advantage may have occurred as a result of repeated copulations. Unfortunately, no information on the numbers of copulations was recorded in these experiments. Second, Martin *et al.* (1974) showed by means of artificial insemination that if females were inseminated with a mixture of spermatozoa from two males mixed in different proportions, the probability of fertilization was directly proportional to the number of spermatozoa from each male.

Both these studies suggest that if the copulations are close together in time the relative number of spermatozoa from two different males will influence the probability of paternity, but if the copulations are far apart in time then sperm precedence would favor the second male. However, it is important to

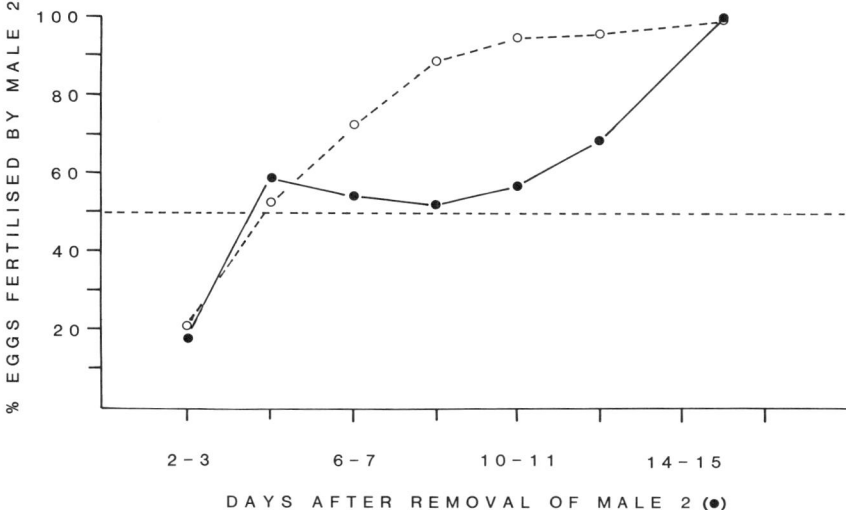

FIG. 3. Proportion of eggs fertilized by the second male (— ● —) after he was removed from females after 3 days, compared with another experiment (--○--) in which the second male was allowed to remain with the females (data from Warren and Kilpatrick, 1929). From Days 4-5 onwards the data (— ● —) do not differ significantly from 50:50 ratio (horizontal dotted line) until after Days 14-15. In contrast, all points (--○--) after Days 4-5 differ significantly from 50:50 ratio ($\chi^2$ tests), and between Days 8-9 to 12-13 inclusive the difference between the two curves is significant.

note that neither experiment shows exactly how sperm competition following an EPC would work in the wild, for different reasons. First, in Warren and Kilpatrick's experiments it is difficult to draw any conclusions other than that there is a difference in paternity in the two experiments (Figs. 2 and 3), because no information on the number of copulations made by each male is presented. Second, in Martin *et al.*'s study, spermatozoa from the two males were mixed and introduced simultaneously, not sequentially as would most likely occur in an EPC (see also Table VI, for paternity; following inseminations <4 hr apart).

Overall, sperm competition experiments on domesticated birds suggest three things. (1) For birds that copulate once or very infrequently, such as Galliformes and a few other species, the last male to mate may fertilize a disproportionate number of eggs. (2) Assuming a similar pattern of sperm competition in species that copulate frequently, a successful EPC has the greatest chance of fertilizing an egg if it is the last one prior to ovulation. Even if the EPC is the last one, its probability of fertilizing an egg may depend upon the the number of inseminations it has to compete with. (3) If a female changes her male partner, the second male will fertilize most eggs, providing he inseminates her prior to ovulation and the ejaculates from the two males are of similar quality.

The results of artificial insemination sperm-precedence studies for three species in two orders (Galliformes and Anseriformes; Table VI) and for the ringdove are remarkably similar. Nonetheless, the possibility that sperm competition may operate in different ways in other avian orders should not be ignored. The pattern of sperm precedence in rodents, for example, varies markedly from species to species (Dewsbury, 1984; Huck et al., 1985). All sperm competition studies have been conducted on domesticated species. This may give us a distorted view, since it has been suggested that sperm competition may be particularly well developed in such birds (as an indirect result of artificial selection; Clayton, 1972; Cheng and Burns, in preparation). Clearly, there is a need to undertake sperm competition studies with nondomesticated species; we also need quantitative and qualitative comparisons of sperm storage glands, semen physiology, and ejaculate parameters (e.g., volume, sperm density, sperm motility) in wild and domesticated forms of the same species.

## IV. Case Studies

### A. Magpie (Pica pica): Solitary, Territorial, Monogamous Guarder

The male magpie plays an important part in breeding, feeding the incubating female, and helping to feed the young. The average clutch consists of six eggs (range 2–9), and only a single brood is reared each year. Mate-guarding and extrapair copulation have been examined by Birkhead (1979, 1982) and Buitron (1983). The main features relevant to sperm competition are that (1) extrapair courtship and extrapair copulation attempts occur; (2) pair copulations are extremely infrequent; and (3) males guard their females during their fertile period, from about 3 days before the first egg until the third egg is laid. Differences in mate-guarding between Buitron's and my study may have been related to differences in the social organization of the two populations: In my study area, the magpie breeding density was 10 times higher than in Buitron's (see Birkhead et al., 1986).

The most complete EPC attempt observed consisted of mounting but without cloacal contact. However, the male partner may not have been able to tell whether the EPC was successful or not (Birkhead, 1979). Probably as a result, the male initiated a new breeding attempt with the same female within 24 hr of the EPC, by building a new nest (see Birkhead and Biggins, 1987).

If sperm competition in magpies follows a pattern similar to that of domestic species (above), with the last male having the greatest chance of fertilizing subsequent eggs, we can speculate about the possible outcome of EPCs in magpies. The EPC occurred at 3:30 P.M. on Day +3; if it had resulted in insemination, it is unlikely that it would have fertilized the next (fourth) egg, which was laid the next morning, because it is almost certain that the EPC occurred outside any fertilizaton window. However, the fifth and sixth eggs to be laid could have been fertilized by the EPC, providing the male partner did not copulate with the female again. Since magpies probably copulate only about three times for each clutch the likelihood of this occurring is low. Although the sample size is small, pair copulations ($N = 9$) have been recorded only between Days $-4$ and $+1$. Interestingly, the majority of extrapair courtship visits recorded by Buitron fell during the second half of the laying period of particular females (i.e., Days 0 to +5). This may have occurred because (1) the intensity of male guarding declines through egg laying, and so access to females was easier than it would have been earlier, and (2) males seeking EPCs attempt to minimize the risk of their inseminations having to compete with subsequent inseminations from the male partner.

### B. Common Guillemot (*Uria aalge*): Colonial, Monogamous Nonguarder

This seabird breeds in large, very dense colonies. Guillemots are long-lived and pair bonds may persist for several years. The clutch size is one and parental duties are shared almost equally between the sexes. EPCs are frequent, with both forced and unforced EPCs resulting in cloacal contact. EPCs occur mainly during the 12 days before a female lays and sperm storage may exceed 16 days. Pair copulations are frequent and take place only at the colony (as do EPCs). In boreal regions where guillemots visit their breeding site throughout the winter, pair copulations may occur 6 months prior to egg laying; their function at this time is unknown. During the 3 weeks prior to laying, females copulate with their partners about 17 times (Norrevang, 1958; Birkhead, 1979; Birkhead *et al.*, 1985). Males do not guard their partners by following them; instead they remain at the colony for most of the time, and by doing so are able to protect their female from EPCs (to some extent), as well as attempt to obtain EPCs themselves. Females spend relatively little time at the colony in the 14 days before laying, and are virtually never at the colony in the 4 days preceding egg laying (Birkhead *et al.*, 1985; Birkhead and Biggins, 1987; Birkhead and del Nevo, 1987; Wanless and Harris, 1986). Both the pair copulation rate and the rate at which females are subjected to EPCs increase toward the female's laying date (Fig. 4): If sperm precedence occurs as it does in other species, males may be competing for the last copulation prior to laying for particular females.

Earlier it was speculated that since EPCs had only a 5% chance of insemination and that each EPC had to compete with about 8 pair copulations during

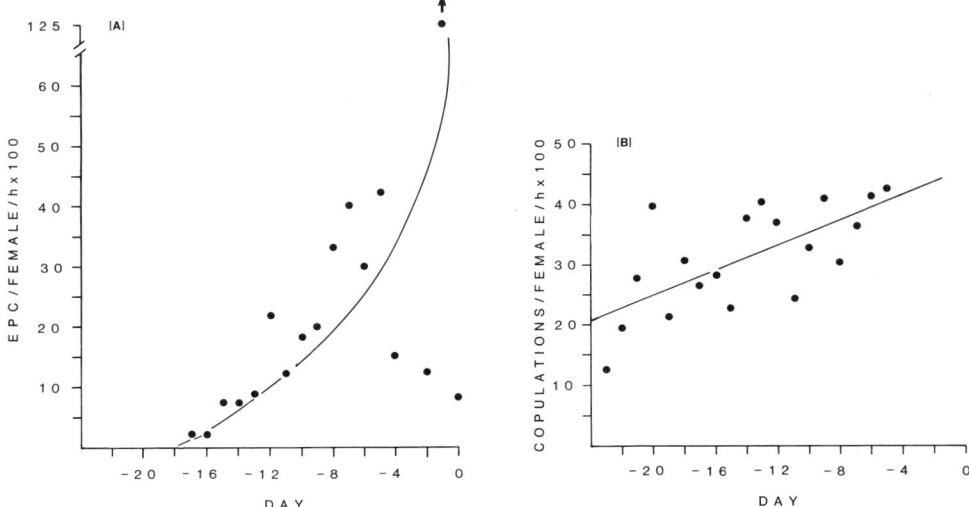

FIG. 4. (A) Rate at which female common guillemots were subjected to extrapair copulation attempts relative to their day of egg laying (the relationship, using log (1 + $n$) EPC rate, is significant, $r = .787$, 16 $df$, $P < .001$). (B) Pair copulation rate on the same time scale ($r = .627$, 17 $df$, $P < .01$); linear regression line is plotted (from Birkhead et al., 1985).

the 12 days before laying, only 1 in 200 EPCs would result in fertilization (Birkhead et al., 1985). However, if the last male to mate has a .7 to .9 probability of fertilizing the egg, as in domesticated species, the overall success rate of EPCs could be much higher than this. Moreover, such a system would give females a certain amount of control over which male fertilized her egg, since females effectively control copulations through the timing of their visits to the colony. For a female to be fertilized by her partner, she could leave the colony after a successful pair copulation (during her fertilization period) and not return until after the egg was fertilized. Indeed some females may have done this, since some of them did not visit the colony between Day −16 and egg laying (Birkhead et al., 1985; personal observation). A detailed study of common guillemots at another location, Skomer Island, Wales, by Hatchwell (in press) gave similar results to those above with 4.5% (9 out of 200) EPCs resulting in cloacal contact. In addition, Hatchwell found that all of these successful EPCs were followed by one or more pair copulations prior to egg laying.

C. SWALLOW (*HIRUNDO RUSTICA*): SEMICOLONIAL, MONOGAMOUS GUARDER

This species breeds both solitarily and colonially. The mean clutch size is five eggs, only the female incubates, and the male's role in chick-rearing is variable. Extrapair copulations and mate guarding have been investigated by

Moller (1985, 1987a–c): Extrapair chases are directed mainly at fertile females, and successful EPCs occur only on unguarded females and are not forced. Solitarily breeding female swallows were never seen to experience EPCs. Males that had had their tails artificially lengthened were particularly successful in EPC (Moller, 1988a). Pair copulations are frequent (about 40 per clutch) and may commence up to 25 days before the first egg. Copulation rates in solitary swallows are significantly lower than among colonial ones. During the laying period, copulations tend to occur within 1 hr after oviposition, presumably within the fertilization window. Males guard their females by close following, starting around Day $-25$ in colonial breeders, but later in solitary breeders. (The onset of the fertilization period is unknown.) Mate-guarding intensity is reduced when the operational sex ratio is female-biased. Most EPCs occur during the egg-laying period and may be better timed in this respect than pair copulations, but most EPCs tend to occur later in the day than pair copulations (probably outside the fertilization window). However, an EPC in the late morning of Day $+2$ (after the third egg had been laid) could fertilize the fifth egg, if no further pair copulations occurred. Parent–offspring regression for tarsus length indicates that among colonial (but not solitary) swallows some EPCs result in fertilization (Table I). Males apparently assess the likelihood of their partner being involved in an EPC by the number of times she is chased by other males. Males increase their pair copulation rate and feed "their" chicks less if their partner has been involved in many chases. Males also increase the amount of chick-feeding with the number of copulations. In other words, the amount of paternal care is positively correlated with the degree of paternity assurance.

### D. Ringdove (Barbary Dove, *Streptopelia "Risoria"*): Monogamous Guarder

This "species" (the long-domesticated form of the African collared dove, *S. rosegrisa*) has been studied mainly in captivity (Erickson and Zenone, 1976; Zenone and Sims, 1979; Cheng *et al.*, 1981; Lumpkin *et al.*, 1982; Lumpkin, 1983). As a result, data exist on several aspects of sperm competition which are not available for any wild bird. Pairs copulate at least 12 times per clutch. EPCs occur: Females will solicit copulation from other males if their partner is temporarily removed. EPCs and EPC attempts have also been reported for wild Columbiformes (Heinroth and Heinroth, 1958; Goodwin, 1967; Irby, 1964; McKinney *et al.*, 1983). The maximum duration of sperm storage is 6 days. Ovulation and fertilization occur 40 hr before egg laying, and the two eggs which comprise the clutch are laid 40 hr apart (Riddle and Behre, 1921). The fertilization period therefore extends from Day $-8$ to Day 0. Males guard their females prior to egg laying, and guarding ceases abruptly after the first egg is laid (Lumpkin *et al.*, 1982). Females may solicit copulation as early as Day $-10$, that is, outside their fertilization period, and males may commence guarding after the first female solicitation. Lumpkin (1983) has suggested that females manipulate males by soliciting copulation at this early stage in order to be guarded for longer. She suggests that the benefits that females may obtain from prolonged guarding include reduced predation risk, female evaluation of male quality, and prevention of male desertion. An alternative explanation for the early start to guarding is that the female cannot predict precisely when she will lay her first egg.

Sperm-competition studies with natural matings show that, as in other species, if one male is replaced by another, the last male to mate has the greatest probability of fertilizing the egg. Which male fertilizes the egg(s) depends upon the timing of copulation relative to fertilization. Females which laid 4 or more days after males had been exchanged all produced offspring fathered by the second male. When females laid within 2 days of exchange, eggs were fertilized only by the first male (because the time available for fertilization by male 2 was very short). For eggs laid 3 days after exchange, some were fathered by Male 1, others by Male 2, and in two cases the two eggs of the clutch were fertilized by different males (Sims *et al.*, 1987). These results are similar to those for domestic poultry in which the same experimental protocol was followed. The results from the ringdove study provide useful information on sperm competition following mate replacement, but further experiments are needed to enable us to predict the likelihood of a single EPC fertilizing eggs.

E. INDIGO BUNTING (*PASSERINA CYANEA*): SOLITARY, TERRITORIAL, MONOGAMOUS–POLYGYNOUS

This species has been the subject of detailed field study and electrophoretic analysis of paternity by Westneat (1987a,b). EPCs were frequent, with male territorial intrusions and EPC attempts peaking on Day $-3$. Both forced and unforced EPCs occurred. Pair copulations were extremely frequent, averaging 70 per clutch (D. Westneat, personal communication), starting around Day $-12$ and peaking on Day $-3$. Clutch size was three or four eggs. Mate guarding was not well developed; between Days $-12$ and $-1$, males spent only 40 to 50% of their time within 30 m of their female. On Days 0 and $+1$ this declined to about 20%. However, males tended to follow their females rather than vice versa. Only 2 (3.3%) out of 61 EPC attempts observed were successful. However, using electrophoresis, Westneat estimated that 27 to 42% (data for 2 years) of all young resulted from EPCs. There are several explanations for this discrepancy. First, EPCs may be inconspicuous; Westneat found no evidence for this. Second, EPCs may be more "potent" than pair copulations. This could arise (1) if males performing EPC produced larger or more ejaculates than in pair copulations (Hatch, 1987, found that multiple inseminations were more frequent among EPCs in fulmars than they were among pair copulations); (2) by chance; the explanation offered by Westneat (1987b); (3) if EPCs were better timed than pair copulations; or (4) if there is some error in the estimate derived from the electrophoresis.

The intensity with which male indigo buntings guard their mates clearly does little to protect their genetic paternity. However, as in nonguarders, male indigo buntings copulate with their partners very frequently, presumably in an attempt to devalue EPCs (see Birkhead *et al.*, 1987). Despite this, a substantial proportion of offspring are fathered by EPCs. The low degree of paternity assurance may explain the small (and variable) amount of paternal care (Westneat, 1987a).

## V. Conclusions and Directions for Future Research

Sperm competition undoubtedly occurs in birds, but the information currently available is not sufficient to draw many firm conclusions. All sperm competition studies have either (1) examined sperm precedence where equal volumes or numbers of spermatozoa from different males are employed, or (2) simply replaced one male with another. Since type (1) is likely to be uncommon in wild birds, the relevance of such experiments is limited. This type may occur only in those species in which females generally copulate only once per clutch but occasionally copulate with a second male. Under these circumstances the second male is likely to fertilize the majority of eggs. Situation (2) (rapid replacement of male mates, both of which inseminate the female) is known to occur in some species (e.g., Moller, 1985). The lack of information on the mode of sperm competition following an EPC has arisen because most experiments were not designed to answer the type of question which is now being asked, that is, "what factors determine the way in which copulations translate into offspring?"

Most of the available material is extremely fragmented, with small amounts of data from a range of species. Piecing this material together to make generalizations is potentially dangerous and misleading at this relatively early stage. We need studies which simultaneously examine as many aspects of sperm competition as possible within a single species. Ideally these studies should comprise field and laboratory (aviary) observations and experiments. To date studies have been either entirely field based or conducted only on captive birds. Some of the most comprehensive field studies are those on swallows by Moller (1985, 1986, 1987a–c) and indigo buntings by Westneat (1987a,b). Of species studied in captivity, ringdoves (Erickson and Zenone, 1976; Zenone and Sims, 1979; Lumpkin *et al.*, 1982; Lumpkin, 1983; Cheng *et al.*, 1981, 1987; Sims *et al.*, 1987) and mallards (Burns *et al.*, 1980; Cheng *et al.*, 1982, 1983) are the best known. However, gaps still exist; the field studies suffer from a lack of information on sperm-storage duration and the mechanism of sperm competition, while studies of captive birds tend to be deficient in information on pair copulations and EPCs.

## 1. Sperm Storage

Detailed information is limited to just five orders of birds (mainly domesticated), with incomplete information for some seabirds. There are a number of other "domesticated" species (see Sossinka, 1982; Wood-Gush, 1985) for which sperm-storage durations could readily be obtained, for example, Passerines, including several estrildine finches such as the Bengalese finch, *Lonchura straita*; Java sparrow, *L. oryzivora*; zebra finch, *Poephila guttata*; long-tailed grassfinch, *P. acuticauda*; and gouldian finch, *Chloebia gouldiae*. Other taxa are the canary (*Serinus canaria*); Psittaciformes, for example, several parakeets; Struthioniformes, specifically the ostrich (*Struthio camelus*), which is farmed in South Africa; and Pelecaniformes, specifically the cormorant (*Phalacrocorax carbo*), bred commercially in China. In addition, several species of diurnal and nocturnal raptors are regularly bred in captivity (see Newton, 1979) and would repay a study of sperm storage. Indeed, the reproductive physiology of raptors may deserve special attention given their extraordinarily high copulation rates (see Birkhead *et al.*, 1987; Birkhead and Lessells, in press; Moller, 1987d). We also need to know if sperm are stored in the same way in different species, since this could have important implications for sperm precedence.

It is important to determine whether "domestication" has resulted in any change in sperm-storage duration; Lake (1975) suggested it may be longer in domesticated birds than in their wild ancestors, and differences are known to exist between different breeds of chickens (Taneja and Gowe, 1961). In addition, domestication is known to have influenced sexual behavior in some species (Clayton, 1972; Sossinka, 1982). There are several species in which comparisons between wild and domesticated forms could be made (using identical techniques), for example, mallard, canary, Bengalese finch and its wild ancestor the white-backed munia (*L. striata*), Gouldian finch, and zebra finch (Birkhead, in preparation).

Remarkably little is known about the glands in which spermatozoa are stored in the female reproductive tract in any species other than the chicken. They have been looked for and found only in the following wild (w) and domesticated (d) species: fulmar (w), Leach's petrel (*Oceanodroma leucorhoa*) (w) (Hatch, 1983), duck (*Anas* sp.) (d) (Pal, 1977), American kestrel (w) (Bakst and Bird, 1987), turkey (d) (Ogasawara and Fuqua, 1972), quail (d) (Friess *et al.*, 1978), chicken (d) (Burke *et al.*, 1972), pheasant (*Phasianus colchicus*) (d) (Makos, in Smyth, 1968), American woodcock (*Philohela minor*) (w) (Walker and Causey, 1982), horned puffin (*Fratercula corniculata*) (w) (Hatch, 1983), pigeon (Berens v. Rautenfeld *et al.*, 1979), swallow (w) (T. R. Birkhead, unpublished), magpie (T. R. Birkhead, unpublished), willow warbler (*Phylloscopus trochilis*) (w) (T.R. Birkhead, unpublished), canary (d) (Thiede *et al.*, 1981), red-winged blackbird (*Agelaius phoeniceus*) (w) (Bray *et al.*, 1975), and zebra finch (d) (Birkhead, 1987b).

Because of the relationship of the timing of ovulation, fertilization, and copulation in birds (see Howarth, 1974), sperm-storage glands may well prove to be ubiquitous in birds. However, data from many more species, from as many different taxonomic groups and ecological types as possible, are needed. Comparisons of the size, density, and total numbers of sperm-storage glands should be made between domesticated and wild forms of the same species and species which differ in ecology or copulation patterns.

Details of ejaculate size or sperm density are known for few birds (see Bird and Lague, 1977; Moller, 1988b). Spermatozoa morphology is remarkably diverse (Romanoff, 1960; McFarlane, 1963), but it is not known whether this is related in any way to sperm storage or sperm competition.

## 2. Copulation

Considering the importance of mating and insemination, there is remarkably little information on any aspect of copulation behavior in birds. There have been few attempts to record all copulations of particular females per clutch; the available information suggests a remarkable interspecific range, from one to several hundred, and that this is related to sperm competition (Birkhead *et al.*, 1987). In this respect it is particularly important that the proportion of apparently successful copulations that result in ejaculation be determined in a range of species (see Penquite *et al.*, 1930; Parker *et al.*, 1942). More quantitative studies of copulation frequently relative to the female's laying date are needed for a range of species, particularly those that copulate infrequently (e.g., many territorial solitary passerines).

## 3. Sperm Precedence

If we are to produce quantitative models of how copulations translate into offspring, we need to conduct sperm competition studies which mimic naturally occurring situations (this in turn depends upon good field studies on which to base such experiments). As the diversity of sperm competition mechanisms in groups other than birds is large (see Dewsbury, 1984), it is essential that data are obtained from a wide range of bird species.

### Acknowledgments

I am grateful to the following for their helpful comments on the manuscript: Drs. C. Beer, M-F. Cheng, P. E. Lake, C. M. Lessells, A. P. Moller, and P. J. B. Slater, but in particular K. M. Cheng, whose comments were especially useful. I also thank those individuals who kindly allowed me to cite their unpublished results: G. F. Ball, M-F. Cheng, K. M. Cheng, S. Hatch, A. P. Moller, S. Pickering, J. Samour, and M. E. Sims. I also thank Jayne Pellatt for drawing the figures and for help with the references.

## References

Afton, A. D. (1985). Forced copulation as a reproductive strategy of male lesser scaup: A field test of some predictions. *Behaviour* **92**, 146–167.

Alatalo, R. V., Carlson, A., Lundberg, A., and Ulfstrand, S. (1981). The conflict between male polygamy and female monogamy: The case of the Pied Flycatcher *Ficedula hypoleuca*. *Am. Nat.* **117**, 738–753.

Alatalo, R. V., Gustafsson, L., and Lundberg, A. (1984). High frequency of cuckoldry in Pied and Collared Flycatchers. *Oikos* **42**, 41–47.

Alatalo, R. V., Gottlander, K., and Lundberg, A. (1987). Extra-pair copulations and mate-guarding in the polyterritorial pied flycatcher *Ficedula hypoleuca*. *Behaviour* **101**, 139–154.

Ash, W. J. (1962). Studies of reproduction in ducks. I. The duration of fertility and hatchability in White Peking Duck eggs. *Poult. Sci.* **41**, 1123–1126.

Astheimer, L. B., (1985). Long laying intervals: A possible mechanism and its implications. *Auk* **102**, 401–409.

Astheimer, L. B., Prince, P. A., and Grau, C. R. (1985). Egg formation and the pre-laying period of Black-browed and Grey-headed Albatrosses *Diomedea melanophris* and *D. chrysostoma* at Bird Island, South Georgia. *Ibis* **127**, 523–529.

Bakst, M. R., and Bird, D. M. (1987). Localization of oviductal sperm-storage tubules in the American kestrel *Falco sparverius*. Auk **104**, 321–324.

Barash, D. P. (1977). Sociobiology of rape in Mallards *Anas platyrhynchos*: Responses of the mated male. *Science* **197**, 788–789.

Barrowclough, G. F. (1983). Biochemical studies of microevolutionary processes. *In* "Perspectives in Ornithology" (A. H. Brush and G. A. Clark, eds.), pp. 223–261, Cambridge Univ. Press, London.

Barrowclough, G. F., and Corobin, K. W. (1978). Genetic variation and differentiation in the parulidae. *Auk* **95**, 691–702.

Beecher, M. D., and Beecher, I. M. (1979). Sociobiology of Bank Swallows: Reproductive strategy of the male. *Science* **205**, 1282–1285.

Berens v. Rautenfeld, D., Bley, G., and Hickel, E.-M. (1979). Technik der künstlichen Besamung und Sterilisation bei der (*Colomba livia*). *Prakt. Tierarzt* **12**, 1103–1105.

Berry, R. B. (1972). Reproduction by artifical insemination in captive American goshawks. *J. Wildl. Manage.* **36**, 1283–1288.

Bilgili, S. F., Renden, J. A., and McDaniel, G. R. (1984). Relationship of fertility to day of insemination during the laying sequence. *Poult. Sci.* **63**, 813–815.

Bird, D. M., and Buckland, R. (1976). The onset and duration of fertility in the American Kestrel. *Can. J. Zool.* **54**, 1595–1597.

Bird, D. M., and Lague, P. C. (1977). Semen production in the American kestrel. *Can. J. Zool.* **55**, 1351–1358.

Birkhead, T. R. (1979). Mate guarding in the Magpie *Pica pica*. *Anim. Behav.* **27**, 866–874.

Birkhead, T. R. (1982). Timing and duration of mate-guarding in magpies. *Pica pica. Anim. Behav.* **30**, 277–283.

Birkhead, T. R. (1987a). Sperm competition in birds. *Trends in Ecol. Evol.* **2**, 268–272.

Birkhead, T. R., (1987b). Sperm storage glands in a passerine: The zebra finch *Poephila guttata* (Estrildidae). *J. Zool. London* **212**, 103–108.

Birkhead, T. R., and Biggins, J. D. (1987). Reproductive synchrony and extra-pair copulation in birds. *Ethology* **74**, 320–334.

Birkhead, T. R., and del Nevo, A. (1987). Egg formation and the prelaying period of the Common Guillemot *Uria aalge*. *J. Zool. London* **211**, 83–88.

Birkhead, T. R., Johnson, S. D., and Nettleship, D. N. (1985). Extra-pair matings and mate guarding in the Common Murre *Uria aalge*. *Anim Behav.* **33**, 608–619.

Birkhead, T. R., and Lessells, C. M. (1988). Copulation behaviour in Ospreys *Pandion haliaetus*. *Anim. Behav.*, in press.

Birkhead, T. R., Eden, S. F., Clarkson, K., Goodburn, S. F., and Pellatt, J. (1986). Social organization of a population of magpies. *Ardea* **74**, 59-68.

Birkhead, T. R., Atkin, L., and Moller, A. P. (1987). Copulation behaviour in birds. *Behaviour* **101**, 101-138.

Bjorklund, M., and Westman, B. (1983). Extra-pair copulations in the Pied Flycatcher *Ficedula hypoleuca*. *Behav. Ecol. Sociobiol.* **13**, 271-275.

Bjorklund, M., and Westman, B. (1986). Mate-guarding in the Great Tit: Tactics of a territorial forest-living species. *Ornis Scand.* **17**, 99-105.

Bobr, L. W., Ogasawara, F. X., and Lorenz, F. W. (1964). Distribution of spermatozoa in the oviduct and fertility in domestic birds. II. Transport of spermatozoa in the fowl oviduct. *J. Reprod. Fertil.* **8**, 49-58.

Bonnier, G., and Trulsson, S. (1939). Selective fertilization in poultry. *Hereditas* **25**, 65-76.

Bornstein, S., Schindler, H., Gabriel, I., and Moses, E. (1960). Fertilization rate of chickens inseminated in the morning or in the afternoon. *Isr. J. Agric. Res.* **10**, 183-191.

Bray, O., Kennelly, J. J., and Guarino, J. L. (1975). Fertility of eggs produced on territories of vasectomized Red-Winged Blackbirds. *Wilson Bull.* **87**, 187-195.

Bruning, D. F. (1974). Social structure and reproductive behaviour in the Greater Rhea. *Living Bird* **13**, 251-294.

Buitron, D. (1983). Extra-pair courtship in Black-billed Magpies. *Anim. Behav.* **31**, 211-220.

Burke, T., and Bruford, M. W. (1987). DNA fingerprinting in birds. *Nature (London)* **327**, 149-152.

Burke, W. H., Ogasawara, F. X., and Fuqua, C. L. (1972). A study of the ultrastructure of the uterovaginal sperm-storage glands of the hen, *Gallus domesticus*, in relation to a mechanism for the release of spermotozoa. *J. Reprod. Fertil.* **29**, 29-36.

Burns, J. T., Cheng, K. M., and McKinney, F. (1980). Forced copulation in captive mallards. 1. Fertilization of eggs. *Auk* **97**, 875-879.

Carlson, A., Hillstrom, L., and Moreno, J. (1985). Mate guarding in the Wheatear *Oenanthe oenanthe*. *Ornis Scand.* **16**, 113-120.

Chakraborty, R., Shaw, M., and Schull, W. J. (1974). Exclusion of paternity: The current state of the art. *Am. J. Hum. Genet.* **26**, 477-488.

Chappellier, A. (1917). A propos de la durée du pouvoir fécundateur des spermatoyoides chez les oiseaux. *Bull. Soc. Nat. Acclim. Fr.* **4**, 21-29.

Cheng, K. M., and Burns, J. T. (in preparation). Dominance relationship and mating strategies of domestic cocks.

Cheng, K. M., Burns, J. T., and McKinney, F. (1982). Forced copulation in captive Mallards *Anas platyrhynchos*, II. Temporal Factors. *Anim. Behav.* **30**, 695-699.

Cheng, K. M., Burns, J. T., and McKinney, F. (1983). Forced copulation in captive Mallards. III. Sperm competition. *Auk* **100**, 302-310.

Cheng, M. F., Porter, M., and Ball, G. (1981). Do Ring Doves copulate more than necessary for fertilization? *Physiol. Behav.* **277**, 659-662.

Clayton, G. A. (1972). Effects of selection on reproduction in avian species. *J. Reprod. Fertil. Suppl.* **15**, 1-21.

Compton, M. M., van Krey, H. P., and Siegel, P. B. (1978). The filling and emptying of the uterovaginal sperm-host glands in the domestic hen. *Poult. Sci.* **57**, 1696-1700.

Cramp, S., and Simmons, K. E. L. (1980). "Handbook of the Birds of Europe, the Middle East and North Africa. The Birds of the Western Palearctic," Vol. II. Oxford Univ. Press, London.

Crew, F. A. E. (1926). On fertility in the domestic fowl. *Proc. R. Soc. Edinburgh* **46**, 230-238.

Delius, J. D. (1963). Das Verhalten der Feldlerche. *Z. Tierpsychol.* **20**, 297-348.

De Merritt, R. J. (1979). The role of the uterovaginal junction in sperm cell storage and release in the domestic fowl. *Poult. Sci.* **58**, 1049.

Dewsbury, D. A. (1984). Sperm competition in Muroid rodents. *In* "Sperm Competition"

(R. L. Smith, ed.), pp. 547–571. Academic Press, Orlando, Fla.

Elder, W. H., and Weller, M. W. (1954). Duration of fertility in the domestic Mallard hen after isolation from the drake. *J. Wildl. Manage.* **18**, 495–502.

Emlen, S. T., and Oring, L. W. (1977). Ecology, sexual selection, and the evolution of mating systems. *Science* **197**, 215–223.

Emlen, S. T., and Wrege, P. H. (1986). Forced copulations and intra-specific parasitism: Two costs of social living in the White-fronted Bee-eater. *Z. Tierpsychol.* **71**, 2–29.

Erickson, C. J., and Zenone, P. G. (1976). Courtship differences in male Ring Doves: Avoidance of cuckoldry? *Science* **192**, 1353–1354.

Evarts, S., and Williams, C. J., (1987). Multiple paternity in a wild population of mallards. *Auk* **104**, 597–602.

Faaborg, J., and Patterson, C. B. (1981). The characteristics and occurrence of co-operative polyandry. *Ibis* **123**, 477–484.

Fabricus, E., and Jansson, A. M. (1963). Laboratory observations on the reproductive behaviour of the Pigeon *Columba livia* during the pre-incubation phase of the breeding cycle. *Anim. Behav.* **11**, 534–547.

Fessner, W. (1970). Success breeding peregrine falcons. *Captive Breed. Diurnal Birds Prey* **1**, 22.

Ford, N. L. (1983). Variation in mate fidelity in monogamous birds. *Curr. Ornithol.* **1**, 329–356.

Frederick, P. C. (1985). Mating strategies in White Ibis. *Eudocimus albus*. Unpubl. Ph.D. thesis, University of North Carolina.

Frederick, P. C. (1987a). Responses of male white ibises to their mate's extra-pair copulations. *Behav. Ecol. Sociobiol.* **21**, 223–228.

Frederick, P. C. (1987b). Extra-pair copulations in the mating system of white ibis (*Endocimus albus*). *Behaviour* **100**, 170–201.

Friess, A. E., Sinowatz, F., Wrobel, K.-H., and Scklek-Winnisch, R. (1978). The uterovaginal sperm host glands of the quail (*Corturnix coturnix japonica*). *Cell. Tissue Res.* **191**, 101–114.

Fronda, F. M., Zialcita, L. P., and Dalisay, A. M. (1940). The fertility of the duck egg. *Philipp. Agric.* **29**, 111–123.

Fujioka, M., and Yamagishi, S. (1981). Extra marital and pair copulations in the Cattle Egret. *Auk* **98**, 134–144.

Giesen, A. F., and McDaniel, G. R. (1980). Effects of time of day of artificial insemination and oviposition and oviposition-insemination interval on the fertility of broiler breeder hens. *Poult. Sci.* **59**, 2544–2549.

Goodwin, D. (1967). "Pigeons and Doves of the World." British Museum, London.

Gowaty, P. A., and Karlin, A. A. (1984). Multiple maternity and paternity in single broods of apparently monogamous eastern Bluebirds *Sialia sialis*. *Behav. Ecol. Sociobiol.* **15**, 91–95.

Grier, J. W. (1973). Techniques and results of artificial insemination with Golden Eagles. *Raptor Res.* **7**, 1–12.

Gwynne, D. T. (1984). Male mating effort, confidence of paternity, and insect sperm competition. *In* "Sperm Competition and the Evolution of Animal Mating Systems" (R. L. Smith, ed.), pp. 117–119. Academic Press, Orlando, Fla.

Hale, E. B. (1955). Duration of fertility and hatchability following natural matings in turkeys. *Poult. Sci.* **34**, 228–223.

Hanken, J., and Sherman, P. W. (1981). Multiple paternity in Belding's Ground Squirrel litters. *Science* **212**, 351–353.

Harper, P. C. (1983). Biology of the Bullers Shearwater *Puffinus bulleri* at the Poor Knights Islands, New Zealand. *Notornis* **30**, 299–318.

Hatch, S. A. (1983). Mechanism and ecological significance of sperm storage in the Northern Fulmar with reference to its occurrence in other birds. *Auk* **100**, 593–600.

Hatch, S. A. (1987). Copulation and mate-guarding in the Northern Fulmar. *Auk* **104**, 450–461.

Hatchwell, B. (1988). Intraspecific variation in extra-pair copulation and mate defence in Common Guillemots *Uria aalge*. *Behaviour*, in press.

Heinroth, O. (1911). Beiträge zur Biologie, namentlich Ethologie and Psychologie der Anatiden. *Verh. Int. Ornithol. Kanyr.,* **5th,** 589-702.
Heinroth, O., and Heinroth, K. (1958). "The Birds." Univ. of Michigan Press, Ann Arbor.
Hohn, E. O. (1947). Sexual behaviour and seasonal changes in the gonads and adrenals of the Mallard. *Proc. Zool. Soc. London* **117,** 281-304.
Howarth, B. (1974). Sperm storage as a function of the female reproductive tract. In "The Oviduct and its Functions" (A. D. Johnson and C. E. Foley, eds.), pp. 237-270. Academic Press, New York.
Huck, U. W., Quinn, R. P., and Lisk, R. D. (1985). Determinants of mating success in the golden hamster (*Mesocricetus auratus*), IV. Sperm competition. *Behav. Ecol. Sociobiol.* **17,** 239-252.
Imber, M. J. (1976). Breeding biology of the Grey-Faced Petrel *Pterodroma macroptera gouldi*. *Ibis* **118,** 51-64.
Irby, M. D. (1964). The relationship of calling behaviour to mourning dove populations and production in southern Arizona. Ph.D. thesis, Univ. of Arizona, Tucson.
Jeffries, D. J., and Parslow, J. L. F. (1976). The genetics of bridling in Guillemots from a study of hand-reared birds. *J. Zool. London* **179,** 411-420.
Jeffreys, A. J., Wilson, V., and Thein, S. L. (1985). Hypervariable 'minisatellite' regions in human DNA. *Nature (London)* **314,** 67-70.
Johnson, A. S. (1954). Artificial insemination and the duration of fertility in geese. *Poult. Sci.* **33,** 638-640.
Joste, N., Ligon, J. D., and Stacey, P. B. (1985). Shared paternity in the Acorn Woodpecker *Melanerpes formicivorus*. *Behav. Ecol. Sociobiol.* **17,** 39-41.
Kinney, T., and Burger, R. E. (1960). A technique for the insemination of geese. *Poult. Sci.* **39,** 230-232.
Kotov, A. A. (1978). On the ecology and development of *Columba livia* in the southern Urals and western Siberia. *Byull. Mosk. Obshch. Isp. Priv. Otd. Biol.* **83,** 71-80.
Kulenkamp, A. W., and Coleman, T. H. (1965). Artificial insemination of bobwhite quail. *Poult. Sci.* **44,** 1392.
Krallinger, M. F. (1930). Beobachtungen über die Befruchtung beim Huhn. *Arch. Gefluegelkd.* **5,** 47-50.
Lake, P. E. (1975). Gamete production and the fertile period with particular reference to domesticated birds. *Symp Zool. Soc. London* **35,** 225-244.
Lake, P. E., and Wood-Gush, D. G. M. (1956). Diurnal rhythms in semen yields and mating behaviour in the domestic cock. Nature (*London*) **178,** 853.
Landau, L., and Vancikova, R. J. (1959). Fertility of eggs produced by ducks after the removal of drakes. *Pol'nohospondarstuo* **6,** 755-764.
Lepore, P. D., and Marks, H. L. (1966). Intravaginal insemination of Japanese quail: Factors influencing the basic technique. *Poult. Sci.* **45,** 888-891.
Lill, A. (1974). Sexual behaviour of the lek-forming white-bearded manakin *Manacus manacus*. *Z. Tierpsychol.* **36,** 1-36.
Lill, A. (1976). Lek behaviour in the golden-headed manakin, *Pipra erythrocephala* in Trinidad (West Indies). *Z. Tierpsychol. Suppl.* **18,** 1-83.
Lodge, J. R., Fechheimer, N. S., and Jaap, R. G. (1971). The relationship of *in vivo* sperm storage interval to fertility and embryonic survival in the chicken. *Biol. Reprod.* **5,** 252-257.
Lorenz, F. W. (1950). Onset and duration of fertility in turkeys. *Poult. Sci.* **29,** 20-26.
Lumpkin, S. (1983). Female manipulation of male avoidance of cuckoldry behaviour in the Ring Dove. *In* "Social Behaviour of Female Vertebrates" (S. K. Wasser, ed.). Academic Press, London.
Lumpkin, S., Kessel, K., Zenone, P. G., and Erickson, C. J. (1982). Proximity between the sexes in ring doves; social bonds or surveillance? *Anim. Behav.* **30,** 506-513.
McCartney, M. G. (1951). The physiology of reproduction in turkeys: 2. Degree and duration of fertility and hatchability in broody and non-broody pullets. *Poult. Sci.* **30,** 663-667.

McFarlane, R. W. (1963). The taxonomic significance of avian sperm. *Proc. Int. Ornithol. Congr.* **13th**, 91-102.

McKinney, F., Derrickson, S. R., and Mineau, P. (1983). Forced copulation in Waterfowl. *Behaviour* **86**, 250-294.

McKinney, F., Cheng, K. M., and Bruggers, D. (1984). Sperm competition in apparently monogamous birds. *In* "Sperm Competition and the Evolution of Animal Mating Ssytems" (R. L. Smith, ed.). Academic Press, New York.

Marsden, S. J., and Martin, J. H. (1949). "Turkey Management," (5th Ed.). Interstate, Danville, Ill.

Martin, K., and Hannon, S. (1988). Early pair and extra-pair copulations in willow ptarmigan. *Condor*, in press.

Martin, P. A., Reimers, T. J., Lodge, J. R., and Dzuik, P. K. (1974). The effect of ratios and numbers of spermatozoa mixed from two males on the proportion of offspring. *J. Reprod. Fertil.* **39**, 251-258.

Mineau, P., and Cooke, F. (1979). Rape in the lesser Snow Goose. *Behaviour* **70**, 280-291.

Mock, D. W. (1983). On the study of avian mating systems. *In* "Perspectives in Ornithology" (A. M. Brush and G. A. Clark, eds.). Cambridge Univ. Press, London.

Moller, A. P. (1985). Mixed reproductive strategy and mate guarding in a semi-colonial passerine. The Swallow *Hirundo rustica*. *Behav. Ecol. Sociobiol.* **17**, 401-408.

Moller, A. P. (1987a). Behavioural aspects of sperm competition in Swallows *Hirundo rustica*. *Behaviour* **100**, 92-104.

Moller, A. P. (1987b). An experimental study of mate-guarding in the swallow *Hirundo rustica*. *Behav. Ecol. Sociobiol.* **21**, 119-123.

Moller, A. P. (1987c). Extent and duration of mate-guarding in swallows *Hirundo rustica*. *Ornis Scand.* **18**, 95-100.

Moller, A. P. (1987d). Copulation behaviour in the Goshawk *Accipiter gentilis*. *Anim. Behav.* **35**, 755-763.

Moller, A. P. (1988a). Female choice selects for male sexual tail ornaments in the monogamous swallow. *Nature (London)* **332**, 640-642.

Moller, A. P. (1988b). Testes size, ejaculate quality and sperm competition in birds. *Biol. J. Linn. Soc.* **33**, 273-283.

Mumme, R. L., Koenig, W. D., Zinc, R. M., and Marten, J. A. (1985). Genetic variation and parentage in a California population of Acorn Woodpeckers. *Auk* **102**, 305-312.

Newton, I. (1979). "Population Ecology of Raptors," Poyser, Berkhampsted.

Norrevang, A. (1958). On the breeding biology of the guillemot. *Dansk Orn. Foren. Tidsskr.* **52**, 48-74.

Ogasawara, F. X., and Fuqua, C. L. (1972). The vital importance of the utero-vaginal spermhost glands for the turkey hen. *Poult. Sci.* **51**, 1035-1039.

Olver, M. D. (1971). Artificial insemination and duration of fertility in Chinese Geese. *Agroanimalia* **3**, 79-86.

Olver, M. D., Kuyper, M. A., and Mould, D. J. (1977). Artificial insemination and duration of fertility in Pekin Ducks. *Agroanimalia* **9**, 27-30.

Opel, H. (1966). The timing of oviposition and ovulation in the quail (*Cortunix coturnix japonica*). *Brt. J. Poult. Sci.* **7**, 29-38.

Oring, L. W. (1982). Avian mating systems. *Avian Biol.* **6**, 1-92.

Owen, R. D. (1941). Artificial insemination of pigeons and doves. *Poult. Sci.* **20**, 428-431.

Pal, D. (1977). Histochemistry of the utero-vaginal junction with special reference to the sperm-host glands in the oviduct of the domestick duck. *Folia Histochem. Cytochem.* **15**, 235-242.

Parker, G. A. (1970). Sperm competition and its evolutionary consequence in the insects. *Biol. Rev.* **45**, 525-567.

Parker, G. A. (1984). Sperm competition and the evolution of animal mating strategies. *In* "Sperm Competition and the Evolution of Animal Mating Systems" (R. L. Smith, ed.), pp. 1-60. Academic Press, Orlando, Fla.

Parker, H. (1981). Duration of fertility in Willow Ptarmigan hens after separation from the cock. *Ornis Scand.* **12**, 186-187.
Parker, J.E., McKenzie, F. F., and Kempster, H. L. (1942). Fertility in the male domestic fowl. *Univ. Missouri Agric. Exp. Sta. Res. Bull.* 1-50.
Payne, L. F., and Kahrs, A. J. (1961). Competitive efficiency of turkey sperm *Poult. Sci* **40**, 1598-1604.
Pearl, R., and Surface, F. M. (1909). The fertility and hatching of eggs. *Maine Agric. Exp. Stn. Bull.*, **168**.
Penquite, R., Croft, W. A., and Thompson, R. B. (1930). *Poult. Sci.* **9**, 247-256.
Petitgean, M. J. (1966). De quelques applications pratiques de l'insémination artificielle en aviculture. *Rev Elev.* **21**, 109-117.
Phillips, J. G., Butler, P. J., and Sharp, P. J. (1985). "Physiological Strategies in Avian Biology." Blackie, Glasgow.
Polge, C. (1951). Artificial insemination in fowl. *Proc. Soc. Study Fertil.* **2**, 16-22.
Quinn, T. W., and White, B. N. (1988). Identification of restriction fragment length polymorphism in genomic DNA of the lesser snow goose (*Anser c. caerulescenus*). *Mol. Biol. Evol.*, in press.
Quinn, T. W., Quinn, J. S., Cooke, F., and White, B. N. (1987). DNA marker analysis detects multiple maternity and paternity in single broods of the Lesser Snow Goose. *Nature (London)* **326**, 392-394.
Riddle, O., and Behre, E. M. (1921). Studies on the physiology of reproduction in birds. IX. On the relation of stale sperm to a fertility and sex in ring-doves. *Am. J. Physiol.* **57**, 228-249.
Roberts, T. A., and Kennelly, J. J. (1980). Variation in promiscuity among Red-winged Blackbirds. *Wilson Bull.* **92**, 110-112.
Romanoff, A. L. (1960). "The Avian Embryo." Macmillan, New York.
Roskaft, E. (1983). Male promiscuity and female adultery by the Rook *Corvus frugilegus*. *Ornis Scand.* **14**, 175-179.
Schick, C. (1947). Sex ratio-egg fertility relationships in the ring-necked pheasant. *J. Wildl. Manage.* **11**, 302-306.
Schifferli, L. (1979). Warum legen Sinvogel (Passeres) ihre Eier am frühen Morgen? (Why do passerines lay their eggs early in the morning?) *Ornithol. Beobachter* **76**, 33-36.
Selous, E. (1906-1907). Observation tending to throw light on the queston on sexual selection in birds, including a day-to-day diary on the breeding habits of the Ruff *Machetes pugnax*. *Zoologist* **10**, 201-219, 285-294, 419-428; **11**, 60-65, 161-182, 367-381.
Sherman, P. W. (1981). Electrophoresis and avian genealogical analyses. *Auk* **98**, 419-421.
Sherman, P. W., and Morton, M. L. (1988). Extra-pair fertilizations in Mountain White-crowned sparrows. *Behav. Ecol. Sociobiol.*, in press.
Sims, M. E., Gall, G. F., and Cheng, M. F. (1987). Sperm competition after sequential mating in the ringdove. *Condor* **89**, 112-116.
Sittman, K., and Abplanalp, H. (1965). Duration and recovery fertility in Japanese quail *Coturnix coturnix japonica*. *Brt. Poult. Sci.* **6**, 245-250.
Skutch, A. F. (1952). On the hour of laying and hatching of birds eggs. *Ibis* **94**, 49-61.
Smyth, R. J. (1968). Poultry. *In* "The Artificial Insemination of Farm Animals" (E. J. Perry, ed.), 4th Edi., pp. 258-300. Rutgers Univ. Press, New Brunswick, New Jersey.
Sossinka, R. (1982). Domestication in birds. *In* "Avian Biology" (D. S. Farner, J. R. King, and K. C. Parkes, eds.), Ch7, pp. 373-403. Academic Press, New York.
Taneja, G. C., and Gowe, R. S. (1961). Effect of varying doses of undiluted semen on fertility in the domestic fowl. *Nature (London)* **191**, 828-829.
Thibault, C., and Levasseur, M.-C. (1973). Conservation et survie prolongée des spermatozoides dans les voies génitales femelles des vertèlres. *Ann. Biol. Anim. Biochem. Biophys.* **13**, 767-784.
Thiede, H., Gerrits, D., and Berens v. Rautenfeld, D. (1981). The problems and techniques of artificial insemination in small birds. *Prakt. Tierarzt* **62**, 879-882.
Thornhill, R., and Alcock, J. (1983). "The Evolution of Insect Mating Systems." Harvard Univ.

Press, Cambridge, Mass.

Titman, R. D., and Lowther, J. K. (1975). The breeding behaviour of a crowded population of mallards. *Can. J. Zool.* **53**, 1270–1283.

Tolentino, L. J. (1948). The fertility of Muscovy duck eggs. *Philipp. Agric.* **31**, 212–215.

Trivers, R. L. (1972). Parental investment and sexual selection. "Sexual Selection and the Descent of Man" (B. Campbell, ed.). Aldine, Chicago.

Tullett, S. G. (1985). Laying. *In* "A Dictionary of Birds" (B. Campbell and E. Lack, eds.). Poyser, Calton.

Twining, H., Hjersman, H. A., and MacGregor, W. (1948). Fertility of eggs of the ring-necked pheasant. *Calif. Fish Game* **34**, 209–216.

Van Krey, H. P., Siegel, P. B., and Leighton, A. T. (1971). Repeatability estimates and quantification of uterovaginal sperm-host gland numbers and population patterns. *Biol. Reprod.* **4**, 31–34.

Walker, W. A., and Causey, M. R. (1982). Breeding activity of American woodcock in Alabama. *J. Wildl. Manage.* **46**, 1054–1057.

Wanless, S., and Harris, M. P. (1986). Time spent at the colony by male and female guillemots, *Uria aalge* and razorbills *Alca torda*. *Bird Study* **33**, 168–176.

Warren, D. C., and Gish, C. L. (1943). Value of artificial insemination in poultry breeding work. *Poult. Sci.* **22**, 108–117.

Warren, D. C., and Kilpatrick, L. (1929). Fertilization in the domestic fowl. *Poult. Sci.* **8**, 237–256.

Weidmann, U. (1958). Verhaltensstudien an der Stockente *Anas platyrhychos* L. I. Das Aktionssystem. *Z. Tierpsychol.* **13**, 108–271.

Werschkul, D. F. (1982). Nesting ecology of the little blue heron: Promiscuous behaviour. *Condor* **84**, 381–384.

Westneat, D. F. (1987a). Extra-pair copulations in a predominately monogamous bird: Observations of behaviour. *Anim. Behav.* **35**, 865–876.

Westneat, D. F. (1987b). Extra-pair fertilizations in a predominantly monogamous bird: Genetic evidence. *Anim. Behav.* **35**, 876–886.

Westneat, D. F., Frederick, P. C., and Wiley, H. R. (1987). The use of genetic markers to estimate the frequency of successful alternative reproductive tactics. *Behav. Ecol. Sociobiol.* **21**, 35–45.

Wetton, J. H., Carter, R. E., Parkin, D. T., and Walters, D. (1987). Demographic study of a wild house sparrow population by DNA "fingerprinting." *Nature (London)*, **327**, 147–149.

Wittenberger, J. F., and Tilson, R. L. (1980). The evolution of monogamy: Hypotheses and evidence. *Annu. Rev. Ecol. Syst.* **11**, 197–232.

Wood-Gush, D. G. M. (1985). Domestication. *In* "A Dictionary of Birds" (B. Campbell and E. Lack, eds.). Poyser, Calton.

Wrege, P. H., and Emlen, S. T. (1987). Biochemical determination of parental uncertainty in white-fronted bee-eaters. *Behav. Ecol. Sociobiol.* **20**, 153–160.

Zenone, P. G., Sims, M. E., and Erickson, C. J. (1979). Male ring dove behavior and the defence of genetic paternity. *Am. Nat.* **114**, 615–626.

# Neural Mechanisms of Perception and Motor Control in a Weakly Electric Fish

WALTER HEILIGENBERG

NEUROBIOLOGY UNIT
SCRIPPS INSTITUTION OF OCEANOGRAPHY
UNIVERSITY OF CALIFORNIA AT SAN DIEGO
LA JOLLA, CALIFORNIA 92093

## I. Introduction

An early goal of ethology was to explain behavioral phenomena at the level of the nervous system (Lorenz, 1937; Tinbergen, 1951). These efforts, however, were hampered by technical difficulties, leaving this field open to speculations and the construction of models founded on intuition and arguments by analogy. Only with the advent of powerful techniques of electrophysiological recording and anatomical tracing, particularly the ability to label physiologically identified neurons, has the pursuit of this goal become realistic. "Neuroethologists" have learned how receptors and higher-order neurons detect and encode biologically relevant stimulus patterns and how neurons can orchestrate coordinated motor responses (see reviews by Camhi, 1984; Ewert, 1980). The understanding of neurons at the interface of sensory perception and motor control would seem more difficult, however, since high-order neurons appear to participate in the control of various forms of behavior and to change their response properties under the influence of more global conditions of the system. This complexity makes simple descriptions and classifications of such neurons impossible, and it raises the question whether more central functions of the nervous system can at all be explained at the single-neuron level.

Neuronal systems are most complex processors of information, and any study of their organization is likely to be trapped into the analysis of epiphenomena unless it is guided by knowledge of the functional significance of its components. In the exploration of neuronal mechanisms of sensory information processing, scientists have been most successful and their results most exciting in those cases where detailed studies of the animal's natural behavior and ecology have identified natural forms of stimulus patterns so that corresponding specializations for their analysis could be sought in the nervous system. The full complexity of cortical auditory neurons in bats (Suga, 1982, 1984), for example, would never have been discovered without prior knowledge about echolocation behavior.

It is thus an important role of behavioral studies to identify relevant stimulus patterns and to propose possible mechanisms for their perception and evaluation. Following the strategy of early ethology, one can systematically modify artificial stimulus patterns in order to determine their necessary components and the computational rules for their recognition as part of the pattern. To the extent that modified versions of stimulus patterns then cause predictable behavioral consequences, we will gain confidence in our theories of perception. Following this behavioral phase of research, neurophysiological and neuroanatomical studies then serve to identify specific implementations of abstract perceptional mechanisms that were postulated on the basis of behavioral tests.

This strategy has guided explorations of electroreception in weakly electric fishes and has led to a rather detailed analysis of neuronal mechanisms underlying the perception of biologically relevant stimulus patterns and the control of adaptive behavioral responses. This presentation raises questions as to how far one can understand complex behavioral phenomena at the cellular level. It also demonstrates that a physiological study of neuronal systems necessarily raises speculations about their evolution and ontogeny.

## II. The Mechanism of Electrolocation: "Seeing" Objects as Perturbations of Electric Fields

Weakly electric fishes repetitively discharge an electric organ located in the tail section of their body, and they monitor the electric current penetrating their body surface by means of electroreceptors embedded in their skin. Each discharge of the electric organ is triggered by a command pulse which originates in the pacemaker nucleus of the hindbrain, and the firing rate of this pacemaker can be modulated through inputs from the midbrain (see reviews by Bennett, 1971; Dye and Meyer, 1986).

Objects that differ electrically from the surrounding water distort the animal's current field and thus offer cues about their size, distance, velocity, and material quality (Lissmann and Machin, 1958; see reviews by Heiligenberg, 1977; Bastian, 1986). Fish of the genus *Eigenmannia* produce a nearly sinusoidal electric organ discharge (EOD) with a highly stable, though individually distinct, fundamental frequency in the range of 250 to 600 Hz. Electroreceptors on the animal's body surface code the local amplitude of this signal as well as the timing of its zero-crossings, also referred to as *phase*. Both amplitude and phase may change in the presence of objects moving through the animal's electric field (Fig. 1), and separate sets of receptors and

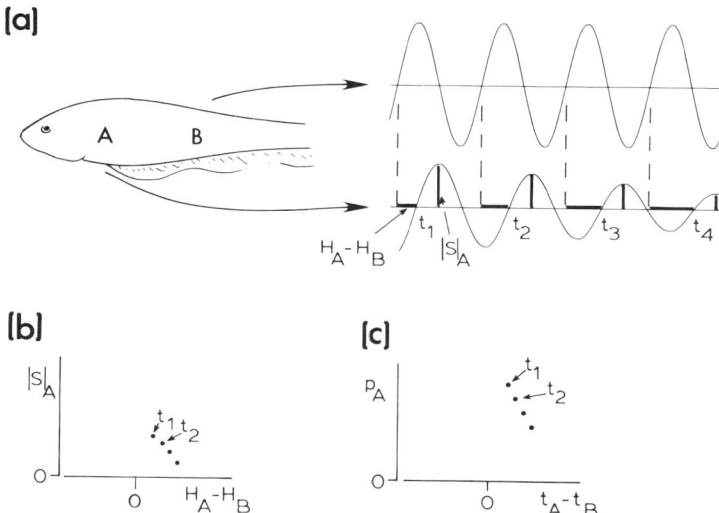

FIG. 1. (a) Schematic representation of sinusoidal EOD cycles, measured at two points, A and B, on the body surface. The two EOD traces represent local voltages (ordinate) recorded over time (abscissa). The moments of the positive zero-crossings of the signal in A are labeled $t_1, t_2, \ldots$, and successive differences in the timing of the zero-crossings of the two signals are marked by thick bars. An object is assumed to move in the vicinity of A, causing a gradual change in the local amplitude $|S|_A$ of the signal as well as a gradually changing difference, $H_A - H_B$, in the timing of the zero-crossings, or phase, of the signal with reference to that in B. The size of the amplitude and phase modulations has been exaggerated for demonstration purposes. In the absence of the object, the differential phase, $H_A - H_B$, would be zero. (b) Plotting successive amplitude and differential phase values, sampled at the moments $t_1, t_2, \ldots$, in a two-dimensinal state plane yields a succession of points which form the contour of a graph. (c) Contours in the amplitude-phase plane are coded in the joint activity of two types of electroreceptors. P-type receptors fire intermittently and raise their probability of firing with increasing stimulus amplitude. T-type receptors fire on each EOD cycle, phase locking their spike to the positive zero-crossing, or steepest positive slope, of the signal. The probability $p_A$ of firing of P-receptors in A reflects the local amplitude $|S|_A$, while the difference in the timing $t_A - t_B$, of firing of T-receptors in A and B reflects the differential phase $H_A - H_B$.

higher-order neurons allow for an independent analysis of amplitude and phase information.

As an object passes through the animal's electric field, amplitude and phase of the EOD current are modulated in a specific way at any given point on the animal's body surface. By recording the amplitude and phase of successive EOD cycles in a two-dimensional plane having amplitude and phase as its axes, one can plot this joint modulation progressively in the manner of a Lissajous figure. Modulations are strongest for points in the vicinity of the object, and the shape of the contours drawn in the amplitude-phase plane over time depends upon various characteristics of the object, such as its size, velocity, distance, as well as the ohmic and capacitive properties of its material. Fig. 2

gives examples for artificial and natural objects. The values of the amplitude and of the phase were recorded near and perpendicular to the animal's cheek. The current measured perpendicularly to the body surface is proportional to the current component acting upon local electroreceptors.

Since moving objects generate specific trajectories in the amplitude-phase plane, the analysis of local changes of phase and amplitude values of the EOD signal provides information about the nature of such objects. In addition, these animals show patterns of behavior that serve to enhance these stimulus

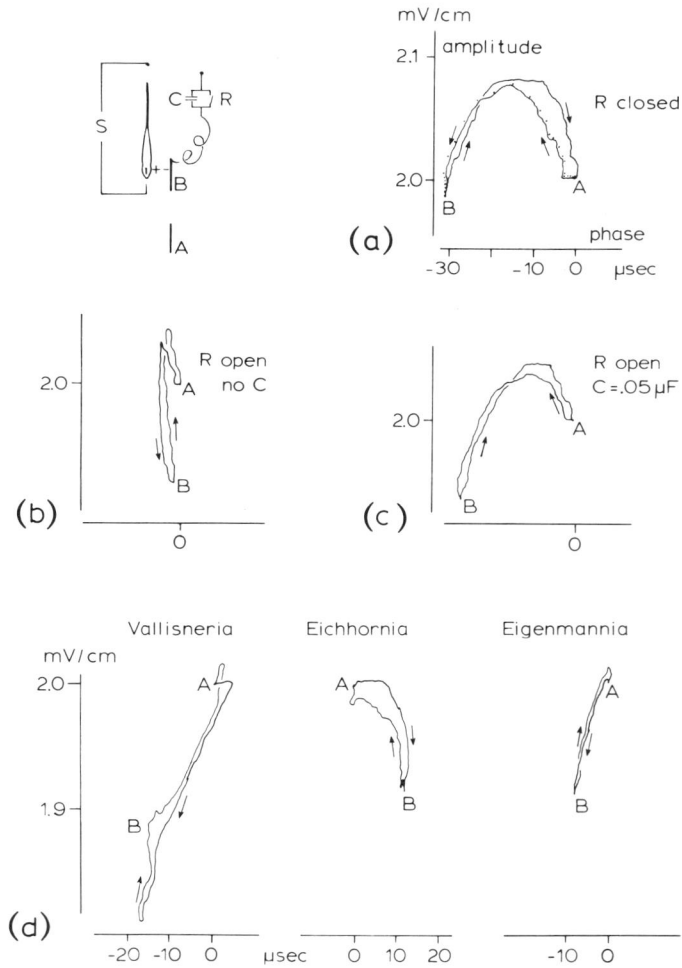

features. The fish explores novel objects by passing them repeatedly with elegant parallel seesaw motions of its body, scanning their electric image on the body surface. Moreover, by bending its tail section around an object of interest and thereby distorting its electric field intentionally, the animal can enhance the spatial contrast of electric images on its body surface (Heiligenberg, 1977).

The graphs in Fig. 2 reflect the modulation of the EOD signal at a single point on the body surface. Since electroreceptors are scattered over the entire surface of the body, though most densely in the region of the head, electric images of objects can be analyzed by spatial comparison of inputs from different sites on the body surface. Different, somatotopically ordered strata of higher-order neurons, that is, layers of neurons that maintain the spatial relations of their receptor inputs, serve this function. Of particular interest in this regard is the analysis of phase information. For sinusoidal electric signals, phase is defined as the timing of the zero-crossing of this signal with reference to a fixed point in time. The animal's own pacemaker signal which triggers each EOD signal would be a natural reference point for the phase of EOD signals in different locations of the body surface. This reference signal, however, is not used in gymnotiform fish which, instead, assess modulations in the phase of their EOD by comparing the timing of zero-crossings in different parts of their body surface. These fish, therefore, only evaluate differential phase on the basis of reafferent information and have no entirely internal efference copy of their pacemaker activity.

FIG. 2. Object-induced modulations of amplitude and phase of the animal's electric signal. The experimental design is shown in the insert, top left. Since the animal is immobilized by curarization, which also silences the electric organ, a sinusoidal EOD substitute, S, is provided through electrodes placed inside its mouth and at the tip of its tail. The signal is monitored by a pair of electrodes placed near and perpendicular to the animal's cheek, close to the path of an object which moves sinusoidally between two points, A and B. The modulation in peak-to-peak amplitude of the signal is plotted on the ordinate, while the modulation of the timing of the zero-crossings, or phase, is plotted on the abscissa. An amplitude of 2.0 mV/cm and a phase defined as zero are measured as the object is in position B, approximately 5 cm away from the animal. The phase values plotted on the abscissas would thus correspond to the differential phase between a point on the animal's cheek, near the object, and a reference point on the body surface far away from the object. In (a) to (c), the object is a thin, 1.8 cm wide, vertically suspended strip of metal foil, insulated on the side facing away from the animal. The foil is connected via a capacitor, C, or an electrical short (R closed) to a distant point in the water. In diagram (a), dots mark every tenth cycle of the EOD-like signal, S, as the object travels from A to B. Since the period of the cycle of S is 2 ms, the separation of successive points is 20 ms. Arrows indicate the direction of motion in the amplitude-phase plane. Although the motion from A to B is, theoretically, symmetrical to the motion from B to A, small mechanical asymmetries cause differences in the shape of the corresponding trajectories in the amplitude-phase plane. In (d), different natural objects were chosen: a leaf of the water plant *Vallisneria*, approximately 1.5 cm wide; a bulbous leaf stem of the water hyacinth, *Eichhornia*, approximately 2 cm in diameter and a conspecific fish, with its EOD silenced by MS222 anesthesia to avoid electrical interference. (From Rose and Heiligenberg, 1986a.)

## III. THE JAMMING AVOIDANCE RESPONSE

The interference of EODs of similar frequencies causes modulations in the amplitude and phase of the electric signal perceived by the animal that are similar to the modulations caused by moving objects. As a consequence, the animal's ability to detect objects may suffer in the presence of a neighbor with a similar EOD frequency. *Eigenmannia*, however, is able to minimize the detrimental effects of signal interference by shifting its EOD frequency away from that of its neighbor. This *jamming avoidance response* (JAR, Bullock *et al.*, 1972; see review by Heiligenberg, 1986) is so robust and predictable that it has become a favorite model system for the analysis of neuronal circuits underlying the perception and evaluation of biologically relevant stimulus patterns. Since behavioral and neurophysiological aspects of the JAR have been reviewed in great detail, only a short summary is given here before more general issues of neuronal organization are addressed. Some general concepts that have emerged from studies of the JAR are the following. First, the actual neuronal solutions to problems of signal processing can be very different from those a human engineer might propose. Second, the perception of stimulus patterns and the control of adaptive behavioral responses are executed in a parliamentary fashion by large populations of neurons in which individual elements are of little significance. Monitoring of single neurons may tell us very little about the outside world. Third, nervous systems are full of improvizations and patchwork, burdened with traces of their evolutionary history.

Electroreceptors are driven predominantly by the animal's own EOD, while the interfering EOD of a neighbor is perceived as a relatively small perturbation of the animal's own signal. If the two interfering EODs are of similar frequencies, amplitude and phase of the signal at the animal's body surface are modulated at a rate which is equal to the difference $Df$ of the two frequencies, and the depth of these modulations increases with the relative strength of the interfering EOD. Much as demonstrated in Fig. 1, one can record the instantaneous amplitude $|S|_A$ at a given point on the body surface, A, and the instantaneous differential phase, $H_A - H_B$, of this signal, measured with reference to the signal in some area B which is uncontaminated by the interfering EOD. If these two quantities are then plotted in a two-dimensional state plane, a circular graph is obtained. The modulation in phase and amplitude is described by a rotation about this circle in the counterclockwise sense for positive $Df$s, that is, when the neighbor's EOD is of higher frequency, and in the clockwise sense for negative $Df$s. If phase is measured in radians and amplitude is measured relative to the amplitude of the animal's uncontaminated signal, the radius of the circle approximates the local intensity ratio of the interfering signal to the animal's own signal (Fig. 3).

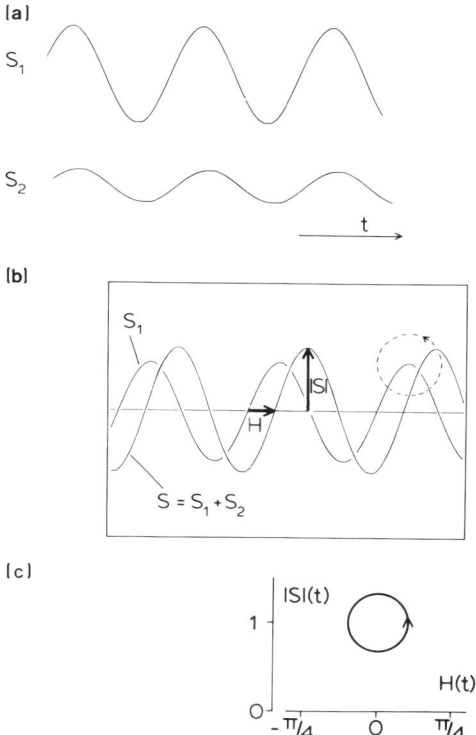

FIG. 3. The addition of two sine waves simulating the EODs of two fish with slightly different frequencies. (a), Two sine waves, $S_1$ and $S_2$, plotted as functions of time, $t$. The stronger signal, $S_1$, represents the animal's own EOD. $S_2$ is the EOD of a neighbor. (b), Oscilloscope display, triggered by $S_1$ so that $S_1$ appears stationary. Simultaneous display of the added signals $S_1 + S_2$ yields a nearly sinusoidal signal whose instantaneous amplitude $|S|$ and phase angle $H$ are modulated at the difference frequency $Df = f_2 - f_1$. The animal would perceive the signal $S = S_1 + S_2$ in an area of its body surface where both EODs interfere, while it would perceive a pure form of its own signal $S_1$ in areas that are not exposed to the neighbor's EOD current field. As a consequence of the joint modulation of $|S|$ and $H$, the peak of $S_1 + S_2$ is seen to rotate around the stationary peak of $S_1$ as indicated by the dashed circle. (c), Lissajous figure display of $|S|$ versus $H$ in a two-dimensional state plane. The nearly circular graph rotates in the counterclockwise sense for positive $Df$s. The mean amplitude of $|S|$ is the amplitude of the dominant signal $S_1$, which is considered unity. The mean value of $H$ is zero, which corresponds to the timing of the positive zero-crossing of $S_1$. The radius of the graph is equal to the amplitude ratio $|S_2| / |S_1|$. A positive $H$ implies that the zero-crossing of $S_1 + S_2$ lags with respect to that of $S_1$. $2\pi$ corresponds to the period of the $S_1$ cycle, which is 2 msec if $f_1$ is 500 Hz. (From Heiligenberg, 1980.)

As mentioned earlier, *Eigenmannia* has no internal access to the timing of its pacemaker and, therefore, cannot measure the local phase $H_A$ of the contaminated signal on its body surface directly. Nevertheless, by comparing the timing of the zero-crossing of the signal in Area A with that in a different area, B, the animal can monitor the differenial phase $H_A - H_B$. The value of this differential phase is proportional to the difference in the degree of contamination of the animal's signal in A and B by that of its neighbor, and, as a consequence, the animal can obtain differential phase information by comparison of differentially contaminated areas of its body surface. A certain dilemma now arises as the fish symmetrically compares electrosensory inputs from two areas, A and B, of which A is assumed to be more heavily contaminated by the neighbor's EOD than B. A plot of the local amplitude $|S|_A$ in A versus the differential phase, $H_A - H_B$, yields a graph with a counterclockwise sense of rotation for positive *Df*s, while a plot of the local amplitude $|S|_B$ in B versus the corresponding differential phase, $H_B - H_A$, yields a graph with the opposite sense of rotation (Fig. 4). This is a consequence of the fact that the two ordinates, $|S|_A$ and $|S|_B$, are of the same sign and, therefore, travel in the same direction, up or down, as time progresses, while the two abscissas are opposites of each other. In accordance with the opposite sense of rotation of their respective graphs, Area A and Area B provide opposite inputs to the pacemaker in this interaction. Area A, however, due to its larger amplitude modulation, outweighs the contribution of Area B and predominates (Heiligenberg and Bastian, 1980).

The presentation in Fig. 4 assumes that the local vectors of the interfering current in A and B both form either acute or obtuse angles with the animal's own current vector. As a consequence, both areas experience net currents that reach maximal or minimal amplitudes in synchrony. The fish, however, can also compare areas in which the vector angles between the two currents are opposite. This holds for the right and the left side of the body under exposure to a transverse jamming field. In this case, the modulations experienced by the two sides are half a cycle out of phase so that one side of the body, A, will experience a net current maximum while the opposite side, A', will experience a minimum. Both areas see rotations of the same sign, and since, for similar degrees of contamination, $H_A$ is approximately the negative of $H_{A'}$, the differential phase, $H_A - H_{A'}$, is approximately $2 \times H_A$. The comparison of such "antipodal" areas thus doubles the depth of the phase modulations and yields differential phase information, even if the two sides experience the same degree of contamination (for more details see Heiligenberg and Rose, 1986a, Fig.10).

One can demonstrate that pairwise comparisons of inputs from areas of the body surface provide a distributed and parliamentary control of the JAR. Input from any area can be compared with input from any other area. Amplitude inputs from the head, however, carry more weight than those from

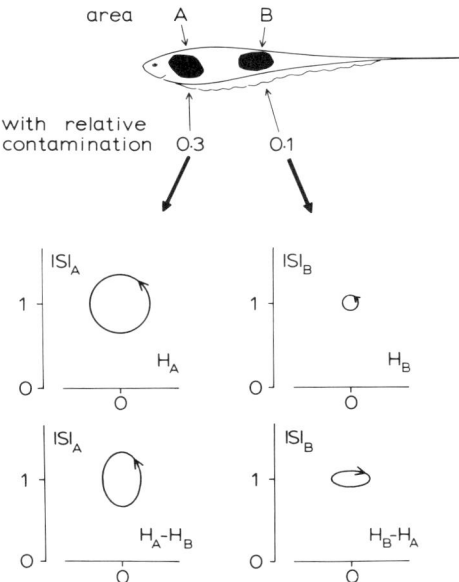

FIG. 4. Information about phase can be obtained by comparing areas of body surface with different amplitude ratios between the interfering signals $S_1$ and $S_2$. Let the animal's EOD or its substitute, $S_1$, be contaminated by the foreign signal $S_2$ by 30% and 10% of the amplitude of $S_1$ in Areas A and B respectively. The stimulus modulation graphs, $|S|_A$ versus $H_A$ and $|S|_B$ versus $H_B$, have radii equal to the local amplitude ratios between $S_2$ and $S_1$ and rotate synchronously and in the counterclockwise direction for positive $Df$s. By replacing the local phase modulations $H_A$ and $H_B$ by the differential phase modulations, $H_A - H_B$, and $H_B - H_A$, elliptical graphs with opposite rotations are obtained. Whereas the counterclockwise rotation of the graph in Area A lowers the pacemaker frequency, the clockwise rotation in Area B raises the pacemaker frequency. As can be shown experimentally, Area A wins in this competition due to its larger amplitude modulation. Note that the animal has no direct access to either $H_A$ or $H_B$, but that it can evaluate their difference by comparing the timings of spike arrivals from T-type receptors from these two parts of the body surface. (From Heiligenberg, 1980.)

more caudal regions, and the contribution from two areas is less strong the farther they are separated from each other (Heiligenberg and Bastian, 1980).

The graphs of amplitude and phase modulations generated by the interference of EODs (Fig. 4) resemble those that are associated with the motion of certain objects (Fig. 2), and very general neuronal networks could serve for the analysis of these patterns in the context of electrolocation as well as jamming avoidance.

At this point, it should be mentioned that *Eigenmannia* could have opted for other solutions to control the JAR. As was said earlier, the fish does not use its pacemaker signal as a phase reference, a design principle that a human engineer certainly would have preferred. Also, a very different strategy for computing the sign of a frequency difference would have been the simultaneous evaluation of modulations in amplitude and instantaneous frequency. The latter, defined as the inverse of the interval between successive EOD cycles, could have been chosen instead of differential phase, but behavioral experiments show that this form of information is not exploited for the control of the JAR (Heiligenberg *et al.*, 1978). This, however, does not rule out the evaluation of frequency modulations in other behavioral contexts, such as social communication (Hopkins, 1974; Hagedorn and Heiligenberg, 1985), and the existence of higher-order neurons that are extremely sensitive to frequency modulations (Bastian and Heiligenberg, 1980b) supports this assumption.

## IV. The Neuronal Substrate for the Analysis of Phase and Amplitude Information

When a neuron is seen to respond to a given stimulus pattern that is known to elicit a certain behavioral response, it is difficult to determine whether this neuron is indeed involved in the control of the behavior or whether it might only respond incidentally and not be significant for this particular behavior. Only rarely, as in the case of the Mauthner cell system (see review by Eaton and Hackett, 1984), are we able to demonstrate the significance of a given neuron in a vertebrate system directly by intracellular stimulation and observation of immediate behavioral effects. Since behavioral responses in vertebrates are normally controlled by large populations of neurons, the significance of any single neuron can never be proven in this manner. Therefore, we have to use indirect evidence to interpret the behavioral significance of a given class of neurons. If, for example, these neurons are part of a structure or pathway the removal of which eliminates a specific behavioral response, or if these neurons share certain dynamic properties, such as a stimulus-filter characteristic or a time constant that is characteristic for this behavior, then we might gain confidence in our interpretation of their role. This becomes very apparent in the study of the neuronal substrate of the JAR where practically all known behavioral phenomena can be related to specific neuronal mechanisms.

The physiology and anatomy of electroreceptors and higher-order electrosensory neurons have been reviewed in great detail (Carr and Maler, 1986; Bell, 1986; Bell and Szabo, 1986). Therefore, a brief summary of the system should suffice here. The following description portrays the situation in the genus *Eigenmannia*, a gymnotiform electric fish, or South American knifefish, with continual, nearly sinusoidal EODs.

Two types of so-called tuberous electroreceptors, T-units and P-units, are distributed over the body surface (Scheich et al., 1973). T-units fire one action potential, or *spike*, on each EOD cycle and at a fixed phase within this cycle. The timing of T-unit spikes, therefore, reflects the timing of the zero-crossings of the electric signal at the site of the receptor, and a comparison of the timing of T-unit spikes generated in two different locations, A and B, on the body surface thus reflects the difference in phase between A and B. P-units, on the other hand, fire intermittently, and their probability of firing a spike within an EOD cycle increases with the amplitude of the signal. The animal can thus monitor a change in signal amplitude in any part of its body surface on the basis of local P-unit activity, while a change in signal phase is reflected in a change of the differential timing of T-unit spikes received from different sites of the body surface.

Primary afferents relay receptor inputs to the electrosensory lateral line lobe (ELL) of the hindbrain which contains three topographic representations of the body surface (Fig. 5). These representations receive identical afferent information as each primary afferent sends collaterals to all three maps (Heiligenberg and Dye, 1982). The cytoarchitecture of these maps is similar, and so far no functional differences have been detected. Phase and amplitude information are processed in separate circuits of the ELL (Maler et al., 1981). Inputs from several neighboring T-receptors converge via electrotonic synapses onto "spherical cells" which fire one action potential in response to the near synchronous arrival of several T-unit spikes. The timing of firing of spherical cells thus reflects the timing of the zero-crossing of the signal in their receptive fields on the body surface, and the spikes of spherical cells lock to the zero-crossing with even less jitter in the timing of their action potentials than do individual T-receptor afferents. Spherical cells project their axons to Lamina 6 of the torus semicircularis of the midbrain where a special, somatotopically ordered network computes differences in the arrival time of spikes of different spherical cells. Lamina 6 thus computes differential phase (Carr et al., 1986a,b; for more details see Fig. 10).

Two types of pyramidal cells in the ELL, basilar and nonbasilar, receive direct or, via inhibitory interneurons, indirect input from P-units. Basilar pyramidal cells, or *E-units*, are excited by a rise in stimulus amplitude within their receptive field, while nonbasilar pyramidal cells, or *I-units*, are excited by a fall in stimulus amplitude (Maler et al., 1981; Bastian and Heiligenberg, 1980a; Saunders and Bastian, 1984). These two types of neurons thus code for temporal changes in local stimulus amplitude. Their axons project to various lamina of the torus semicircularis, with the exception of Lamina 6, and also send collaterals to the nucleus praeeminentialis of the midbrain (Maler et al., 1982).

In accordance with the higher density of electroreceptors on the surface

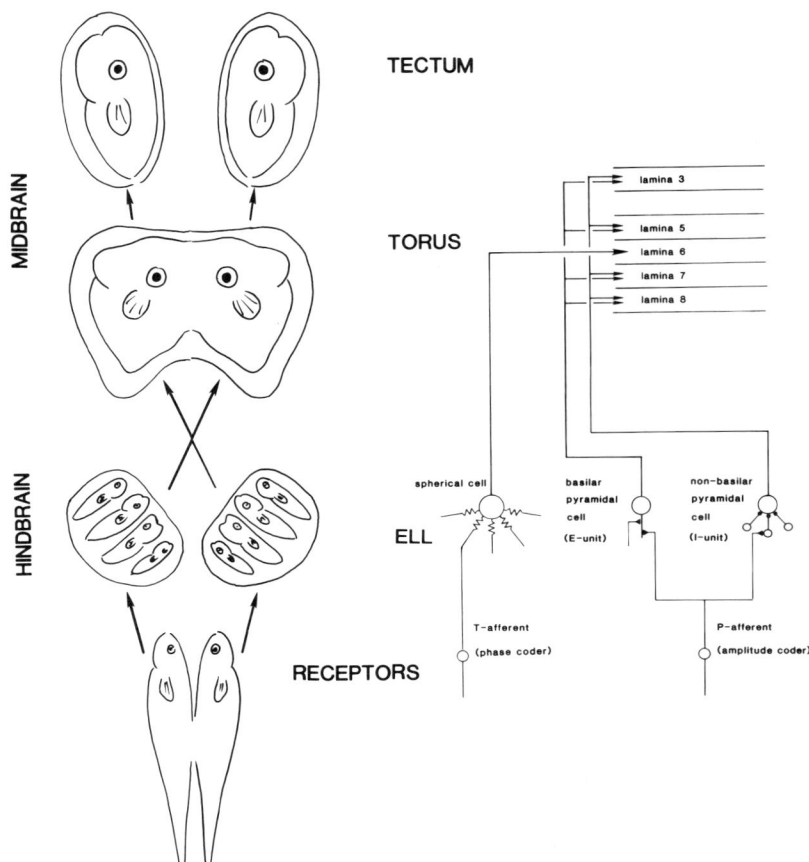

FIG. 5. Left: The spatial order of electrosensory information is preserved in somatotopically structured layers of higher-order neurons in the hindbrain and midbrain. Primary afferent neurons relay the responses of electroreceptors on the body surface to the ELL of the hindbrain. The three lateral representations of the body surface in the ELL receive identical input from P- and T-type receptors, while the most medial map only receives input from ampullary receptors (which only respond to low-frequency electrical signals and are not considered further in this presentation). The electrosensory maps of the ELL project predominantly to the contralateral torus semicircularis of the midbrain and merge into a single body map, represented in several stacked laminae which are vertically in topographic register with each other. The torus projects topographically to the optic tectum, where visual and electrosensory information are represented in spatial register. Right: A simplified neuronal flow diagram, demonstrating the separation of phase and amplitude channels in the ELL and torus. Spherical cells relay local phase information to Lamina 6 of the torus semicircularis of the midbrain. Basilar pyramidal cells, or E-neurons, are excited by a rise in local stimulus amplitude, while nonbasilar pyramidal cells, or I-neurons, are excited by a fall in amplitude. Both types of pyramidal cells project to various laminae of the torus, above and below Lamina 6.

of the head, this area is overrepresented in the body maps of the ELL and, even more so, in their projection to the torus semicircularis. This provides a physiological correlate for the behavioral observation that the JAR is driven most strongly by stimulus regimens applied to the region of the head.

Although the electrosensory body surface is represented in triplicate in the ELL, only a single body map is found in its projection to the dorsal torus semicircularis, a vertical stack of 12 laminae that are in topographic register (Carr *et al.*, 1981). While Lamina 6 is solely devoted to the computation of differential phase, other laminae receive amplitude information. Vertical connections between different laminae allow for a joint computation of amplitude information from a specific point on the body surface and its concurrent differential phase in reference to some other point on the body surface. These phase reference points, apparently, are chosen randomly in the process of cytological organization, since closely spaced toral neurons may have very different phase reference points. This implies that a vertical column of the torus, corresponding to a location A on the body surface, contains neurons in specific laminae that report amplitude modulations in A. These amplitude-sensitive neurons are vertically in register with neurons that are driven by the differential phase between Area A and individually different reference areas, B, C, D, and so on.

This spatial organization provides a neuronal substrate for the joint evaluation of amplitude information from a specific area A and differential-phase information between A and a score of different reference areas. This structure offers the following functional advantage: The degree of the modulation of the differential phase between two points on the body surface depends upon the orientation of the interfering field of the neighbor. As the current lines of the neighbor's EOD field enter the fish's body surface in one region, they exit again on the opposite side, and strongest modulations of differential phase are caused between these two antipodal regions (Heiligenberg and Rose, 1985a). The location of these antipodal regions, of course, varies with the relative orientation of the two animals so that, at any moment, the differential phase between some areas is modulated strongly, while that between other areas is hardly modulated at all. Depending upon the choice of the particular reference area, some differential phase coders at the site of the toral representation of a given area, A, of the body surface will then be driven very strongly while others will be idle. As a consequence, at least some differential-phase coders should be recruited sufficiently at any moment to contribute to the control of the JAR, regardless of the relative orientation of the interfering EOD fields.

The torus semicircularis projects topographically to the optic tectum such that visual information is in spatial register with electrosensory information derived from the dorsal torus and mechanosensory–auditory information derived from the ventral torus. In accordance with this convergence of different sensory modalities, individual multimodal tectal neurons respond to the different sensory modalities of moving objects (Bastian, 1982).

A variety of types of electrosensory neurons of the dorsal torus project to the tectum (Heiligenberg and Rose, 1985a). These include neurons that respond only to modulations in amplitude, neurons that respond only to the modulation of the differential phase between specific sites on the body surface, and neurons that respond to both aspects of a signal, amplitude and phase. Since the projection of these neurons maintains the somatotopic order of the torus, further spatial computations of phase and amplitude modulations can be executed in the tectum. More commonly than at the level of the torus, neurons in the tectum perform certain logical operations by integrating phase and amplitude information that render them particularly sensitive to certain patterns of "motion" in the phase-amplitude plane (Rose and Heiligenberg, 1985a, 1986a; Heiligenberg and Rose, 1986). For example, a neuron may be excited by a fall in amplitude in a certain area A on the body surface but may also be facilitated by a phase lead of this area with reference to a certain area B. This neuron is then recruited preferentially by graphs in the phase-amplitude plane, with the local amplitude $|S|_A$ and the differential phase $H_A - H_B$ as coordinates, that combine a fall in amplitude with a phase lead (Fig. 6, right). A jamming regimen resulting in a circular graph with a counterclockwise rotation (Fig. 4, lower left) would fulfill this condition as would the particular motion of an object that causes a similar section of a trajectory in the phase-amplitude plane (Fig. 2a, second section of travel from point A to point B). Since such neurons respond differentially to the sense of rotation in the amplitude-phase plane, which, in a jamming regimen, is determined by the sign of the *Df*, they are called *sign selective*.

The response properties of sign-selective neurons could readily account for certain behavioral phenomena of the JAR, particularly for the fact that the JAR is reversed, that is, that the pacemaker frequency is shifted in the wrong direction, when the phase center of a stimulus graph in the amplitude-phase plane is sufficiently offset from zero (Heiligenberg and Bastian, 1980). This phenomenon can be explained in the following way: A sign-selective cell may be excited by a rise in the local stimulus amplitude $|S|_A$ and may also respond to a phase advance of the signal in this area, A, with reference to that in a certain area, B (Fig. 7). Similar to neurons that only encode differential phase between given points on the body surface (Rose and Heiligenberg, 1986b), sign-selective cells respond only to a small range of phase values that is centered on either side of zero (Fig. 7a). This same range also facilitates the response to amplitude modulations (Fig. 7b). As a consequence, a neuron being excited by a phase advance and a rise in amplitude "prefers" a clockwise sense of rotation, provided that this circle has a phase center near zero (Fig. 7c). If, however, the phase center is shifted to the new position, −T, a counterclockwise

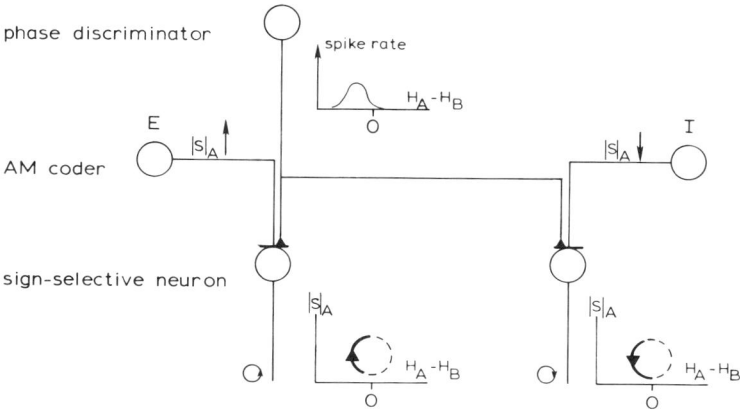

FIG. 6. The logical computation of differential-phase information and amplitude information within the central nervous representation of a particular site, A, on the body surface. A phase discriminator codes the difference $H_A - H_B$ in timing of zero-crossings in Area A with reference to zero-crossings in some other area B by firing maximally for a short phase lead of A. The phase discriminator is assumed to facilitate the input of amplitude ($|S|_A$) modulation coders (an E-unit on the left and an I-unit on the right) to sign-selective cells. Clockwise and counterclockwise motion in the state plane implies, respectively, coincidence of a rise and fall in stimulus amplitude with the activity of the phase lead-selective cell illustrated. As a consequence, sign-selective cells follow the input of amplitude-modulation coders preferentially during the active phase of the phase discriminator and thus respond best for one particular sense of rotation in the amplitude-phase plane. The sign-selective neuron on the left thus prefers clockwise rotations, while the neuron on the right prefers counterclockwise rotations. Within the same representation of site A, other phase discriminators could have any other phase reference points on the body surface, and these units could facilitate other sign-selective cells in the same manner. As a consequence, part of this network would always be recruited, regardless of the orientation of the interfering fields and the ensuing degree of differential-phase modulations between specific points on the body surface.

rotation will combine optimal phase and amplitude conditions, and the neuron will prefer the opposite sense of rotation.

Under the assumption that sign-selective neurons preferring a clockwise rotation, with a center phase near zero, accelerate the pacemaker, while neurons preferring a counterclockwise rotation decelerate the pacemaker, the following behavioral consequences should ensue. As long as a clockwise rotation is centered at phase zero, accelerating neurons will be recruited preferentially and the pacemaker frequency will rise. With the same rotation offset from phase zero, these neurons will be recruited to a lesser extent, as they now prefer the opposite sense of rotation (see Fig. 7c). Decelerating neurons, however, will now be recruited more strongly, and the pacemaker frequency will shift in the opposite direction, as is indeed observed. Finally, if rotations

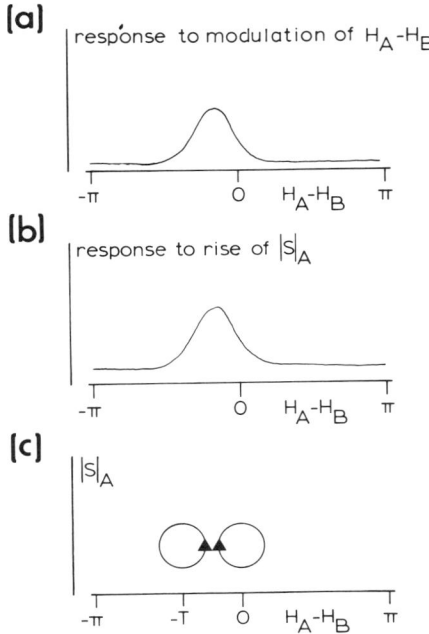

FIG. 7. The response of a sign-selective neuron to combined modulations of amplitude and differential phase can be explained on the basis of its responses when either form of stimulation, amplitude or phase, is presented alone. (a) When differential phase between two areas, A and B, which could be head and trunk, is modulated over the range from $-\pi$ to $+\pi$, the unit responds within a small phase range to the left of zero, that is, a moderate phase advance of A with respect to B. (Note that, in a natural situation, phase modulations are limited to a small range around zero and that values as large as $\pi$ are never reached.) (b) When amplitude in A is modulated while an unmodulated phase reference signal is presented in B, the neuron responds to a rise in stimulus amplitude. This response, however, is strongest for the same range of phase differences, $H_A - H_B$, that is also excitatory for pure phase modulations (a). (c) As a consequence, the neuron "prefers" a clockwise rotation with a phase center at zero, while it prefers a counterclockwise rotation with a phase center at $-T$, since both stimuli combine a rise in amplitude with the preferred phase range.

are offset from phase zero still further, so that the sensitive phase range is no longer covered, rotations are poorly discriminated, which is also observed at the behavioral level (Heiligenberg and Bastian, 1980).

The pathway from the tectum to the control of motor patterns has not yet been explored at the single-cell level. Large neurons in the deep tectum respond to the motion of objects and often discriminate the sense of rotations of graphs in the amplitude-phase plane, and these neurons project to various targets in the diencephalon, midbrain, and hindbrain (Rose and Heiligenberg, 1986a).

Some of these targets appear to be premotor nuclei which project to the spinal cord. Some of the tectal neurons that discriminate the sense of rotation in the amplitude-phase plane have been found to send collaterals toward the nucleus electrosensorius in the region of the pretectum. Neurons with similar properties have been recorded in this pretectal nucleus (Bastian and Yuthas, 1984), and a projection from this region to the prepacemaker nucleus of the midbrain, the only known source of input to the pacemaker in the hindbrain (Heiligenberg *et al.*, 1981), strongly suggests that these elements participate in the control of the JAR. This assumption is further supported by the observation that these sign-selective neurons prefer the same magnitude of difference frequencies that are also optimal for the JAR, namely, 4 to 6 Hz. Moreover, electrical stimulation of the region of the nucleus electrosensorius produces pacemaker responses with time constants typical for the JAR (Bastian and Yuthas, 1984).

The separate neuronal representation of phase and amplitude information in the electrosensory system finds a parallel in a similar separation of phase and amplitude information in the auditory system of owls (Sullivan and Konishi, 1984, 1986; Takahashi *et al.*, 1984; see reviews by Konishi, 1986; Heiligenberg, 1986, 1987). Much as in the case of electric fish, a separation of phase and amplitude information was first observed at the behavioral level, and it appears likely that in many more cases where behavioral studies have demonstrated an independent evaluation of certain aspects of stimulus patterns a corresponding separation of their neuronal substrates will also be found.

## V. The Ambiguity of Messages Encoded by Individual Neurons

The motion of objects and the interference of the animal's EOD with that of a neighbor elicit very different behavioral responses, bodily maneuvers in the first case and the JAR in the latter. Since these two forms of behavior employ nonoverlapping motor components, muscles or the electric organ, they can be executed simultaneously and without mutual interference. Both patterns are elicited by modulations of phase and amplitude in the animal's EOD that can be characterized as trajectories in the amplitude-phase plane. Neurons in the torus and in the tectum that are recruited by specific aspects of such trajectories, such as a combination of a rise in amplitude with a lead in phase at a specific site on the body surface, are recruited by the appearance of such trajectories regardless of whether they are part of a graph elicited by the motion of an object or a graph associated with EOD interference.

This means that monitoring an individual neuron, even at a level as high as the midbrain and only a few synapses away from the motor output, tells us little about the stimulus situation outside. We can certainly learn more by monitoring such a neuron over a longer period of time, but since the fish responds to a given stimulus regimen appropriately within a fraction of a second, it must interpret the nature of a stimulus pattern by parallel evaluation of responses of many such neurons. In the particular example given here, patterns caused by moving objects are characterized by a progression of phase and amplitude events along a circumscribed pathway on the body surface, while a jamming regimen generates such events synchronously over larger areas. A spatial analysis of the activation of higher-order neurons within a somatotopically ordered stratum, therefore, should allow for the discrimination between object motion and jamming. Since higher-order neurons of the torus and tectum individually project to various targets, different forms of analysis of their messages could be performed simultaneously at different loci in the brain. A certain stimulus pattern could then have the necessary global features for activating a particular behavioral response in one higher-order nucleus, whereas it would be inappropriate for other nuclei and could not initiate their respective behavioral performances.

The principle of behavioral control by a large population of neurons with rather general response properties is very prominent in the case of the JAR. The sign-selective neurons in the torus and in the tectum of *Eigenmannia* fire much more frequently for one sign of the frequency difference, Df, between a neighbor's EOD and the animal's own EOD than for the opposite sign. These neurons, therefore, were also called *Df-decoders*. (Scheich, 1974, 1977). A closer analysis of the physiology of such cells shows, however, that they only encode the sense of rotation of graphs in the amplitude-phase plane in a manner which does not unambiguously reflect the sign of Df. As was shown in the comparison of two areas of body surface contaminated differentially by the interfering EOD, the same sign of Df can lead to graphs with opposite rotations in the two areas (Fig. 4, bottom). In accordance with this rule, a midbrain neuron preferring a positive Df in one stimulus regimen may switch to prefer the opposite sign of Df if the geometry of the interfering stimulus field and, therefore, the pattern of contamination over the animal's body surface is altered appropriately (Rose and Heiligenberg, 1986a; Heiligenberg and Rose, 1986). This means that monitoring a single cell of this type will not reveal the sign of the Df unless we know the distribution of the intensity of the interfering EOD field over the receptive fields of this neuron. How then is the animal able to generate a correct JAR on the basis of the information provided by such neurons?

A possible mechanism is presented in Fig. 8. Consider two areas, A and B, on the body surface (as shown in Fig. 4). One set of neurons, represented on the left, receives amplitude information, $|S|_A$, from Field A, while the other set, represented on the right, receives amplitude information $|S|_B$ from Field B. Each set of neurons evaluates the respective differential phase, $H_A - H_B$ or by $H_B - H_A$, by comparing the timing of the zero-crossings of the signals in the two fields. Neurons marked *CW* are more strongly excited

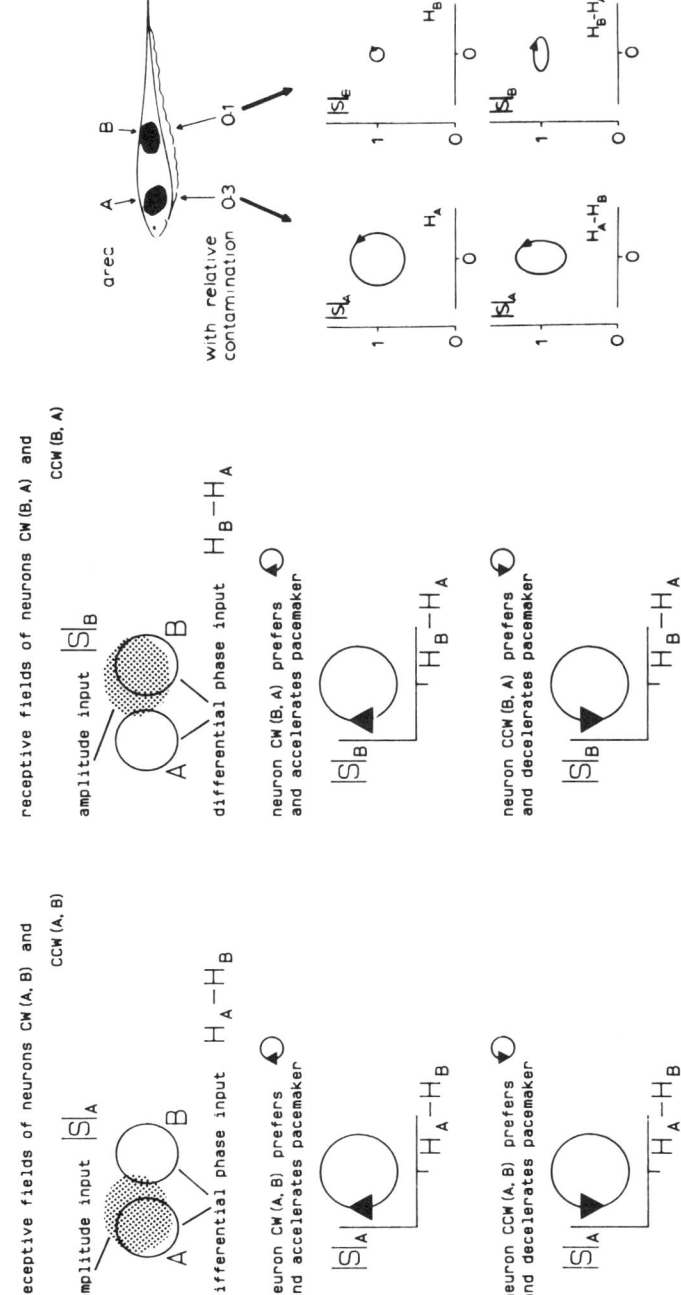

FIG. 8. A set of four types of neurons with receptive fields A and B. The two neurons of the left receive amplitude input $|S|_A$ (shaded area) from Field A and use the phase input from B as a reference for the computation of the differential phase $H_A - H_B$. The two neurons on the right execute the reciprocal operations. Neurons marked *CW* prefer clockwise rotations in their respective amplitude-phase planes and accelerate the pacemaker according to the level of their recruitment. Neurons marked *CCW* prefer counterclockwise rotations and decelerate the pacemaker. The insert on the right is a copy of Fig. 4. (From Heiligenberg and Rose, 1986.)

by clockwise than by counterclockwise rotations of graphs in their amplitude-phase plane (with a center phase near zero), while neurons marked *CCW* prefer counterclockwise rotations. Note that the modulations in the two fields will be identical if both fields are contaminated to the same degree and $H_A = H_B$. Since $H_A - H_B$ is zero in this case, all graphs will collapse into vertical streaks reflecting the modulation in amplitude only. With different degrees of contamination, however, $H_A - H_B$ will be nonzero, and, since $H_A - H_B$ is the negative of $H_B - H_A$, the graphs in A and B must have opposite rotations as long as changes in $|S|_A$ and $|S|_B$ are of the same sign. The latter condition holds if the vectors of the interfering currents form either acute or obtuse angles in both areas, A and B (see discussion in connection with Fig. 4).

Assume now that Field A is more heavily contaminated than Field B and that Df is positive (this situation is shown in Fig. 4). Field A will see a counterclockwise rotation, while Field B will see a clockwise rotation, and, due to the stronger contamination of the signal in A, the amplitude modulation in A will exceed that in B. This situation will cause the following pattern of neuronal recruitments: A neuron, CCW(A,B), with amplitude input from A and a preference for counterclockwise rotations will be more active than a neuron, CW(A,B), which prefers a clockwise rotation, while the opposite will hold for the neurons with amplitude input from Field B, CW(B,A) and CCW(B,A). Under the same assumption that was made in connection with Fig. 7, namely, that neurons preferring a clockwise rotation, centered at phase zero, accelerate the pacemaker in proportion to their level of recruitment, while neurons preferring counterclockwise rotations decelerate the pacemaker, the net contribution of neurons with amplitude input from Field A should decelerate the pacemaker, while the net contribution of neurons with amplitude input from Field B should accelerate the pacemaker. Since the neurons of Field A, however, are more strongly recruited than those of Field B, the decelerating effect of the former should outweigh the accelerating effect of the latter, that is, CCW(A,B) will predominate over CW(B,A).

Following the same logic, one can show that the set of neurons symbolized in Fig. 8 will lead to a net acceleration of the pacemaker for negative Dfs, that is, CW(A,B) will win over CCW(B,A). With Field B being more heavily contaminated than Field A, the roles of A and B would change, and, again, the net contribution from this pair of receptive fields would yield the correct shift of the pacemaker frequency. Simultaneously, other neurons with amplitude input from Field A could have other phase reference fields, C,D, and so on, and all of these pairwise interactions should contribute correct shifts of the pacemaker frequency. Large populations of neurons with reciprocal interactions would thus yield a correct and parliamentary control of the JAR, regardless of the momentary orientation of the animals and the ensuing patterns of signal contamination along their body surfaces, while the messages of single neurons at this level of the brain would not necessarily reflect the true sign of $Df$. All of this is not to imply that these particular cells directly and individually act upon the pacemaker, but rather that such a convergence and comparison of competing influences must occur at some point of pacemaker control, such as, perhaps, the nucleus electrosensorius of the diencephalon or the prepacemaker nucleus of the midbrain.

### VI. The Improvisational Character of Neuronal Systems and Traces of Their Evolution

The study of the neuronal substrate of the JAR suggests its evolutionary derivation from networks that evolved for the detection of moving objects. As was pointed out initially, the fish detects phase shifts of its EOD signal by comparing the timing of zero-crossings in different regions of its body surface, and a joint evaluation of differential-phase and local amplitude information provides cues about the nature and motion of objects. By pooling the outputs from higher-order neurons that are recruited by particular trajectories in the amplitude-phase plane, the animal could generate new networks that discriminate the sense of rotations of circular graphs in the amplitude-phase plane and thus serve in the control of the JAR. It is of particular interest in this context that the related genus *Sternopygus*, which does not show a JAR and is believed to reflect the ancestral state of gymnotiform fish with wave-type EODs, nevertheless has midbrain neurons that discriminate rotations in the amplitude-phase plane (Rose *et al.*, 1987).

This possible evolutionary scenario may explain why the neuronal substrate of the JAR is not simple and straightforward and would appear unnecessarily complex. A JAR mechanism could have been built with fewer levels of neuronal integration. Note, for example, that all necessary information about amplitude and phase is available in the torus, but relatively few cells in the torus are capable of discriminating the sense of rotation in the amplitude-phase plane. Instead, these computations are mainly executed at the next level, the optic tectum, which is specialized for the analysis of spatial patterns of information and the control of spatially oriented behaviors. As far as the JAR is concerned, the way through the tectum would seem to be an unnecessary detour.

Threshold measurements of the JAR have shown that *Eigenmannia* is able to discriminate phase modulations with temporal disparities as small as a few hundred nanoseconds (Carr *et al.*, 1986a; Rose and Heiligenberg, 1985b). This value appears very small if one considers that the animal compares the timing of zero-crossings partly between very distant areas of its body surface and that nerve conduction time over these distances is not negligible. *Eigenmannia* has coped with this problem at different levels. First, axons of primary afferents of T-type receptors show higher conduction speeds with increasing distance of the receptor pore from the brain (Heiligenberg and Dye, 1982).

This compensation, however, is not perfect, and spikes from T-receptors in very caudal regions of the body still arrive with a delay of up to 1 ms in the brain (Carr et al., 1986a). This imperfection in timing does have behavioral consequences. If the animal is experimentally limited to compare phase only between the head and a distant region of the trunk it produces JARs of the wrong sign, that is, it misinterprets the sense of rotations in the amplitude-phase plane and shifts its pacemaker frequency in the wrong direction (Heiligenberg and Bastian, 1980). Since the animal recognizes the sense of rotation on the basis of a pairing between amplitude events and concurrent phase values, and since the delay of a reference signal will make a physical phase delay of the signal at the head appear as a phase advance, this confusion is to be expected (see Fig. 9). Fortunately, *Eigenmannia* normally evaluates phase differences predominantly between closely spaced areas on the body surface, where conduction delays are less critical, and the correct contributions for the JAR derived from the phase comparison between nearby areas outweigh those erroneous contributions drawn from the comparison of very distant areas. The animal thus can afford a certain amount of imperfection in the temporal tuning of its afferent system.

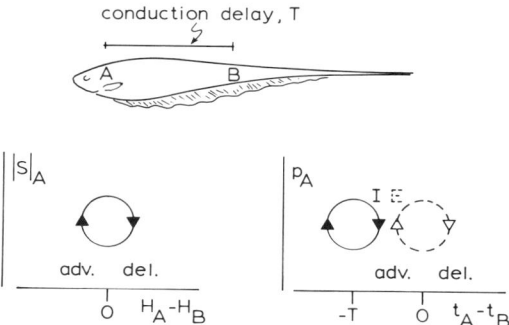

FIG. 9. Phase comparisons between distance areas of the body surface may provide erroneous information due to considerable differences in conduction delays of afferent channels. A plot of the amplitude $|S|_A$ in Area A versus the differential phase $H_A - H_B$ may yield a clockwise rotation, which is centered at zero (lower left). Due to a difference $T$ in the conduction time of afferent pathways originating at A and B, spikes that are fired at Location B will arrive $T$ units of time later in the brain than spikes that are synchronously fired at Site A. As a consequence, the neuronal representation of the differential phase $H_A - H_B$, which is expressed in the difference of the arrival times of spikes from A and B, $t_A - t_B$, is offset from zero by the value $T$ (lower right). The modulation of stimulus amplitude $|S|_A$ is expressed in the rate $p_A$ of firing of P-type receptors, and while a rise in $p_A$ activates E-type neurons, a fall in $p_A$ activates I-type neurons. Without the offset $T$, the nervous system would "see" the graph centered at zero (dashed line), and the pairing of E activity and a small phase advance would have recruited neurons that accelerate the pacemaker (see Fig. 7). With the graph being offset by $T$, however, a small phase advance is paired with I activity instead, and this combination will recruit neurons that decelerate the pacemaker. As a consequence, the animal shifts its frequency in the wrong direction.

Finally, there is an additional remedy for coping with the imperfect timing of signals. Neurons that evaluate modulations in differential phase have been found to be particularly sensitive to the temporal change of phase differences and to respond to such changes in the same manner even if they are not centered exactly at zero (Rose and Heiligenberg, 1986b). A limited offset of the mean difference phase from zero, due to imperfect compensation in nerve conduction time, can, therefore, be tolerated at the level of the central nervous system.

It thus seems that *Eigenmannia* has updated and improved the neuronal machinery of the JAR by a patchwork of modifications at various levels, giving the whole system a haphazard appearance. The exceptional precision of performance at the behavioral level, therefore, makes this system all the more remarkable.

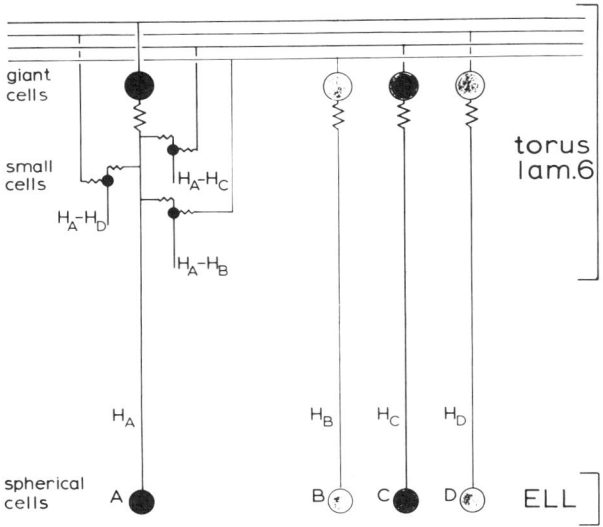

FIG. 10. The neuronal substrate for the computation of differential phase. Spherical cells in the ELL receive somatotopically ordered information about the timing of zero-crossings of stimuli on the body surface. The somatotopic arrangement of this information, $H_A$, $H_B$, ..., is preserved in the projections of spherical cells onto the somata of giant cells and nearby dendrites of small cells of Lamina 6 of the torus. The somata of small cells, in turn, receive input from a giant cell axon whose timing of spikes reflects phase in that part of the body surface which projects to the soma of this particular giant cell. The firing rate of a small cell is thus controlled by the difference in timing between spike arrivals on their dendrites and spike arrivals on their soma, that is, by the difference between local phase and a reference phase from some other part of the body surface. Small cells within a given column of Lamina 6 all receive dendritic phase input from the same region of the body surface, while the source of phase input to their soma appears to be chosen randomly from passing axon collaterals of giant cells. (Redrawn after Carr *et al.*, 1986b.)

## VII. Developmental Considerations

In studying the functional and anatomical organization of a neuronal system, one cannot avoid asking questions about the rules that might govern its development. Since animals certainly do not have sufficient genetic information for the formation of individual synapses, one expects to find more general rules by which a complex network can be organized. Simple sets of instructions that can be iterated in space and time are particularly appealing, and neuronal models for complex computational functions will appear more realistic the more readily they can be implemented by simple and robust rules of developmental self organization. The study of differential-phase computations in Lamina 6 of the torus in *Eigenmannia* provides an illuminating example. This network can develop on the basis of a few and very general statistical instructions that lead to a pattern of connections iterated for every patch in the representation of the body surface (Fig. 10; Carr *et al.*, 1986a,b; Heiligenberg and Rose, 1985b). Phase comparisons between any two points of the body surface can be executed in this network, a computational property that was postulated on the basis of behavioral evidence. And a preponderance of connections between the representations of proximal areas of body surface (Carr *et al.*, 1986b) is in accord with the behavioral observation that the JAR is driven most strongly by interactions of stimulus inputs to pairs of closely spaced areas of body surface (Heiligenberg and Bastian, 1980).

**Acknowledgments**

I thank John Dye, Gary Rose, Masashi Kawasaki, and Catherine Carr for their kind criticism of this manuscript. This research was supported by grants from NIMH, NINCDS, and NSF.

**References**

Bastian, J. (1982). Vision and electroreception: Integration of sensory information in the tectum of the weakly electric fish *Apteronotus allbifrons*. *J. Comp. Physiol. A* **147**, 287–297.

Bastian, J. (1986). Electrolocation: Behavior, anatomy and physiology. *In* "Electroreception." (T. H. Bullock and W. Heiligenberg, eds.), pp. 577–612. Wiley, New York.

Bastian, J., and Heiligenberg, W. (1980a). Neural correlates of the jamming avoidance response in *Eigenmannia*. *J. Comp. Physiol.* **136**, 135–152.

Bastian, J., and Heiligenberg, W. (1980b). Phase sensitive midbrain neurons in *Eigenmannia*: Neural correlates of the jamming avoidance response. *Science* **209**, 828–831.

Bastian, J., and Yuthas, J. (1984). The jamming avoidance response of *Eigenmannia*: Properties of a diencephalic link between sensory processing and motor output. *J. Comp. Physiol. A* **154**, 895–908.

Bell, C. C. (1986). Electroreception in mormyrid fish. Central physiology. *In* "Electroreception." (T. H. Bullock and W. Heiligenberg, eds.), pp. 375–421. Wiley, New York.

Bennett, M. V. L. (1971). Electric organs. *Fish Physiol.* **5**, 347–491.

Bullock, T. H., and Hamstra, R. H., and Scheich, H. (1972). The jamming avoidance response

of high-frequency electric fish. *J. Comp. Physiol.* **77,** 1-48.
Bullock, T. H., Behrend, K., and Heiligenberg, W. (1975). Comparison of the jamming avoidance responses in Gymnotoid and Gymnarchid fish: A case of convergent evolution of behavior and its sensory basis. *J. Comp. Physiol.* **103,** 97-121.
Camhi, J. M. (1984). "Neuroethology." Sinauer, Sunderland, MA.
Carr, C. E., and Maler, L. (1986). Electroreception in gymnotiform fish. Central anatomy and physiology. *In* "Electroreception." (T. H. Bullock and W. Heiligenberg, eds.), pp. 319-373. Wiley, New York.
Carr, C. E., Maler, L., Heiligenberg, W., and and Sas, E. (1981). Laminar organization of the afferent and efferent systems of the torus semicircularis of gymnotiform fish: Morphological substrates for parallel processing in the electrosensory system. *J. Comp. Neurol.* **203,** 649-670.
Carr, C. E., Heiligenberg, W., and Rose, G. J. (1986a). A time-comparison circuit in the electric fish midbrain. I. Behavior and physiology. *J. Neurosci.* **6,** 107-119.
Carr, C. E., Maler, L., and Taylor, B. (1986b). A time-comparison circuit in theo electric fish midbrain. II. Functional morphology. *J. Neurosci.* **6,** 1372-1383
Dye, J. C., and Meyer, J. H. (1986). Central control of electric organ discharges in weakly electric fish. *In* "Electroreception" (T. H. Bullock and W. Heiligenberg, eds.), pp. 71-102. Wiley, New York.
Eaton, R. C., and Hackett, J. (1984). The role of the Mauthner cell in fast starts involving escape in teleost fishes. *In* "Neural Mechanisms of Startle Behavior" (R. C. Eaton, ed.), pp. 213-266. Plenum, New York.
Ewert, J. P. (1980). "Neuroethology." Springer Verlag, Berlin.
Hagedorn, M., and Heiligenberg, W. (1985). Court and spark: Electric signals in the courtship and mating of gymnotoid fish. *Anim. Behav.* **33,** 254-265.
Heiligenberg, W. (1977). Principles of electrolocation and jamming avoidance. *In* "Studies of Brain Function," Vol. 1, pp. 1-85. Springer-Verlag, Berlin.
Heiligenberg, W. (1980). The jamming avoidance response in the weakly electric fish *Eigenmannia. Naturwissenschaften* **67,** 499-507.
Heiligenberg, W. (1986). Jamming avoidance responses: Model systems for neuroethology. *In* "Electroreception" (T. H. Bullock and W. Heiligenberg, eds.), pp. 613-649. Wiley, New York.
Heiligenberg, W. (1987). The control of behavioral performance in networks processing temporal and spatial patterns of sensory information. *In* "Aims and Methods in Neuroethology" (D. M. Guthrie, ed.), pp. 207-230. Univ. of Manchester Press.
Heiligenberg, W., and Bastian, J. (1980). The control of *Eigenmannia*'s pacemaker by distributed evaluation of electroreceptive afferences. *J. Comp. Physiol.* **136,** 113-133.
Heiligenberg, W., and Dye, J. (1982). Labelling of electroreceptive afferents in a gymnotoid fish by intracellular injection of HRP: The mystery of multiple maps. *J. Comp. Physiol. A* **148,** 287-296.
Heiligenberg, W., and Rose, G. (1985a). Phase and amplitude computations in the midbrain of an electric fish: Intracellular studies of neurons participating in the Jamming Avoidance Response (JAR) of *Eigenmannia. J. Neurosci.* **5,** 515-531.
Heiligenberg, W., and Rose, G. (1985b). Neural correlates of the jamming avoidance response (JAR) in the weakly electric fish *Eigenmannia. TINS* **8,** 442-449.
Heiligenberg, W., and Rose, G. (1986). Gating of sensory information: Joint computations of phase and amplitude data in the midbrain of the electric fish *Eigenmannia. J. Comp. Physiol. A* **159,** 311-324.
Heiligenberg, W., Baker, C., and Matsubara, J. (1978). The jamming avoidance response in *Eigenmannia* revisited: The structure of a neuronal democracy. *J. Comp. Physiol.* **127,** 267-286.
Heiligenberg, W., Finger, T., Matsubara, J., and Carr, C. E. (1981). Input to the medullary pacemaker nucleus in the weakly electric fish, *Eigenmannia* (Sternopygidae, Gymnotiformes). *Brain Res.* **211,** 418-423.
Hopkins, C. D. (1974). Electric communication: Functions in the social behavior of *Eigenmannia virescens. Behaviour* **50,** 270-305.

Konishi, M. (1986). Centrally synthesized maps of sensory space. *TINS* **9**, 163-168.

Lissmann, H. W., and Machin, K. E. (1958). The mechanism of object location in *Gymnarchus niloticus* and similar fish. *J. Exp. Biol.* **35**, 451-486.

Lorenz, K. (1937). Über die Bildung des Instinktbegriffs. *Naturwissenschaften* **25**, 289-300, 307-318, 324-331.

Maler, L., Sas, E., and Rogers, J. (1981). The cytology of the posterior lateral line lobe of high-frequency weakly electric fish (*Gymnotoidei*): Dendritic differentiation and synaptic specificity in a simple cortex. *J. Comp. Neurol.* **195**, 87-140.

Maler, L., Sas, E., Carr, C. E., and Matsubara, J. (1982). Efferent projections of the posterior lateral line lobe in gymnotiform fish. *J. Comp. Neurol.* **211**, 154-164.

Rose, G., and Heiligenberg, W. (1985a). Structure and function of electrosensory neurons in the torus semicircularis of *Eigenmannia*: Morphological correlates of phase and amplitude sensitivity. *J. Neurosci.* **5**, 2269-2280.

Rose, R., and Heiligenberg, W. (1985b). Temporal hyperacuity in the electric sense of fish. *Nature (London)* **213**, 178-180.

Rose, G., and Heiligenberg, W. (1986a). Neural coding of difference frequencies in the midbrain of the electric fish *Eigenmannia*: Reading the sense of rotation in an amplitude-phase plane. *J. Comp. Physiol. A* **158**, 613-624.

Rose, G., and Heiligenberg, W. (1986b). Limits of phase and amplitude sensitivity in the torus semicircularis of *Eigenmannia*. *J. Comp. Physiol. A* **159**, 813-822.

Rose, G. J., Keller, C. H., and Heiligenberg, W. (1987). "Ancestral" neural mechanisms of electrolocation suggest a substrate for the evolution of the jamming avoidance response. *J. Comp. Physiol. A* **160**, 491-500.

Saunders, J., and Bastian, J. (1984). The physiology and morphology of two types of electrosensory neurons in the weakly electric fish *Apteronotus leptorhynchus*. *J. Comp. Physiol. A* **154**, 199-209.

Scheich, H. (1974). Neural analysis of wave form in the time domain: Midbrain units in electric fish during social behavior. *Science* **185**, 365-367.

Scheich, H. (1977). Neural basis of communication in the high-frequency electric fish *Eigenmannia virescens* (Jamming Avoidance Response). *J. Comp. Physiol.* **113**, 181-255.

Scheich, H., Bullock, T. H., and Hamstra, R. H. (1973). Coding properties of two classes of afferent nerve fibers: High frequency electroreceptors in the electric fish, *Eigenmannia*. *J. Neurophysiol.* **36**, 39-60.

Suga, N. (1982). Functional organization of the auditory cortex. Representation beyond tonotopy in the bat. *In* "Cortical Sensory Organization" (C. N. Woollsey, ed.), Vol. 3, pp. 157-218. Humana Press.

Suga, N. (1984). The extent to which biosonar information is represented in the bat auditory cortex. *In* "Dynamic Aspects of Neocortical Function" (G. M. Edelman, W. E. Gall, and W. M. Cowan, eds.), pp. 315-373. Wiley, New York.

Sullivan, W. E., and Konishi, M. (1984). Segregation of stimulus phase and intensity coding in the cochlear nucleus of the barn owl. *J. Neurosci.* **4**, 1787-1799.

Sullivan, W.E., and Konishi, M. (1986). Neural map of interaural phase difference in the owl's brainstem. *Proc. Natl. Acad. Sci. U.S.A.* **83**, 8400-8404.

Takahashi, T., Moiseff, A., and Konishi, M. (1984). Time and intensity cues are processed independently in the auditory system of the owl. *J. Neurosc.* **4**, 1781-1786.

Tinbergen, N. (1951). "The Study of Instinct." Oxford Univ. Press, London.

# Behavioral Adaptations to Aquatic Life in Insects: An Example

ANN CLOAREC

LABORATOIRE D'ETHOLOGIE, CNRS, UA 373
UNIVERSITÉ DE RENNES I
CAMPUS DE BEAULIEU
35042 RENNES CEDEX, FRANCE

## I. Introduction

Aquatic insects are remarkably diverse, representing almost half the orders of the class, although relatively few of the one million known insect species live in or on water and those that do are mainly found in or on fresh water. (Usinger, 1956, counted 1,057 aquatic insect species in California, Bertrand, 1954a,b, 633 in Europe.)

The few species in salt water have colonized only the intertidal zones. This implies special behavioral adaptations to regular periods of submergence which follow lunar rather than circadian rhythms. Behavioral data concerning these insects are anecdotal and therefore they are not considered here.

Although paleontological data are scarce, all present-day aquatic insects have undoubtedly evolved from terrestrial ancestors following two main radiation patterns. The first group, sometimes called the *primary aquatic group*, includes closely related families which have no doubt diversified in the aquatic environment after invading it (e.g., all Odonata which spend their larval lives in water or, exceptionally, in damp environments). In the second case, single families or genera (e.g., *Nymphulea*, Lepidoptera) have colonized the aquatic habitat independently and are considered to be secondary invaders (Hynes, 1984). The first group usually appears more closely adapted to their habitat.

Aquatic and terrestrial insects have to deal with different physical constraints which have induced divergent morphological, physiological, ecological, and behavioral adaptations. The main differences concern the following environmental features:

1. Temperature. The amplitude of daily and seasonal temperature variations is less in water, especially still water, than it is on land. Annual

water temperature fluctuations are more highly predictable from one year to the next. Thermoregulation therefore requires much less energy in water.
2. Hygrometry. Environmental hygrometry in the aquatic habitat is obviously constant except in temporary water bodies. However, migration and behavioral adaptations to drying out of the habitat are not considered here. Nevertheless, aquatic insects need the protection of hydrofuge cuticle or hair to prevent their bodies from being invaded by water.
3. Density. The density of water is greater than that of air; locomotion is probably the behavior most affected by this and it is often modified in consequence.
4. Turbidity. All water bodies are more or less turbid, due to suspended sediment, for example. Light is rapidly absorbed as it penetrates water. As a result, vision is somewhat impaired in aquatic insects compared to their terrestrial relations.
5. Current. In running waters, unattached animals can easily be carried along by the current.
6. Oxygen. Probably the most important environmental difference between aquatic and terrestrial habitats is oxygen pressure, which is highly variable in water but constant in the atmosphere of a given terrestrial habitat. Aquatic insects present many diverse respiratory adaptations, though most retain a tracheal system.
7. Propagation of vibrations. Vibrations propagate much faster in air than in water or over the water surface. However, aquatic insects use both surface and underwater vibrations to communicate. The analysis of acoustic communication of aquatic insects has been neglected except for one or two cases (e.g., Corixidae, Theiss, 1982), although several species are known to produce underwater sounds.

Since the mid-1970s there has been an increase in interest in aquatic entomology, but behavioral studies of aquatic insects as such are still few. Much of the available data are anecdotal and unfortunately have been reported only from either the angler's or the fish's point of view.

The aim of this article is not to present an exhaustive or systematic review of aquatic insect behavior but rather to illustrate the main behavioral adaptations involved with a selection of examples mainly from the stick insect *Ranatra linearis*. By a behavioral adaptation I mean a behavior pattern which has evolved because, either alone or associated with another feature, it has improved the chances of survival and/or reproductive success of the individual which possesses it and of its descendants. In addition I hope to show that insect behavior differs from that of a mechanical automaton because conditions during postembryonic development can influence subsequent performance, and that the study of behavioral adaptations in aquatic insects is essential to understanding their biology and the functioning of aquatic ecosystems.

## II. Respiratory and Locomotory Adaptations to Aquatic Life

### A. Respiratory Constraints

The unpredictable variations of oxygen pressure and the absence of gaseous oxygen in water have been some of the harshest constraints on aquatic insects. Behavioral adaptations to facilitate gas exchange are highly diverse and although a great majority of aquatic insects have retained a tracheal system, a wide variety of techniques facilitate respiration. Aquatic insects acquire oxygen in three main ways: from submerged plant organs (e.g., some coleopteran larvae), directly from the surrounding water by diffusion, or from atmospheric air.

Oxygen can be acquired by diffusion from water either through unspecialized cuticle or through specially modified structures like the gills of Ephemeroptera, or through an air bubble or a thin layer of gas that adheres to the greater part of the body surface and is held in position by an unwettable hair structure called a *plastron*. The difference between the partial pressure of oxygen in the plastron and in the water enables extraction of oxygen from solution in the water. Modified spiracles open into the plastron. Animals that acquire oxygen directly by diffusion from water possess no respiratory openings, and some aquatic insects do not have any tracheal system at all but rely on gas exchange directly between water and their blood through their cuticle. Presence of hemoglobin in blood facilitates this type of exchange.

As the partial pressure of oxygen in the tracheal system is often very low, the rate of oxygen uptake is primarily controlled by its concentration in the water. However, this concentration declines rapidly in the immediate vicinity of the respiratory surfaces and therefore the rate of diffusion also declines if the external supply is not renewed.

Different species have solved this problem in different ways. Some live only in well-aerated running waters; others use behavioral ventilation to increase the movement of water around their bodies and so increase the oxygen gradient and avoid having to move to a more oxygenated area. Thus plecopteran nymphs wag their abdomens, and trichopteran and dipteran larvae undulate their abdomens and thereby create a continuous flow through the solid case which surrounds their body. According to Klyuge *et al.* (1984), who have described the movements and postures during swimming, submerging, and breathing in baesoid ephemeropteran larvae, species with or without gills that make either horizontal or vertical abdominal respiratory movements are less primitive than those that rely mainly on gill movements.

A few dipteran species have developed behavior allowing them to use the oxygen in submerged plants, and so have the coleopteran larvae of *Donacia*; they stab plants with their daggerlike terminal spiracles and thus they can reach the air trapped in spaces between the roots of a plant (Grassé, 1976).

### B. Insects That Breathe Atmospheric Air

The majority of insects that remain in the water all their lives (Coleoptera, Heteroptera) breathe atmospheric air and obtain it at the water surface by contacting the atmosphere with a specialized part of their body. This is generally the posterior end of the abdomen. This technique is usually associated with a reduction in the number of functional spiracles, and sometimes only the posterior abdominal pair, which are nearly always the most important, remain functional. There is often an additional mechanism around these spiracles for breaking the water surface, a mechanism which can vary from a few specialized hydrofuge hairs (e.g., the last two abdominal segments which are covered with unwettable hairs in Dytiscidae) to the typical siphon in Nepidae or Belostomatidae. The larvae of Eristalinae possess a telescopic extension which contains two breathing tubes whose openings can reach the surface from up to 75 mm below it without the larva having to move or being influenced by oxygen pressure.

Breathing atmospheric air at the surface implies periodic contact with the air–water interface and the ability to store some air. Exceptionally, this contact can be permanent: Some stratiomydous larvae always hang head down from the surface, while their abdominal spiracles, protected by a circle of hairs, remain dry. Other insects come to the surface periodically. After exhalation, insects obtain fresh air and store it on or around their bodies more often than in them for use while submerged. In adults the main air stores are under their wings. In addition, air in *plastron* or air-bubble air stores that vary in size and distribution from one species to another, trapped by long hydrofugous hairs, is often exposed to the water and can also be used to extract dissolved oxygen. These air stores are said to act as "physical gills," as they are in direct contact with functional spiracles.

Structural modifications appear to reflect differences in modes of respiration. In Coleoptera, the subelytral cavity acts as an air store during submergence and as a connection between the dorsal spiracles and the atmosphere during gas exchange at the air–water interface. *Dytiscus marginalis* hangs head down while air exchange occurs between head and thorax, and *Hydrophilus* rises to the surface headfirst and uses a modified antenna to conduct air to reservoirs where it remains trapped among fine hairs. However, in aquatic Heteroptera the abdominal spiracles are ventral, so there is no simple way of connecting the tracheal system with the atmosphere. This group has overcome this difficulty in several ways (Parsons, 1974, 1976; Popham, 1960).

Corixidae contact the water surface anterodorsally, storing air ventrally as their spiracles open below air stores situated between two rows of hydrofuge hairs; *Notonecta* and the coleopteran *Berosus* press and stroke their abdomens with their hind legs and thus manipulate the air layer covering their bodies and accelerate gas exchange. These movements have been interpreted as pumping movements supplying air to the tracheae (Dahm, 1972; Faucheux, 1977). Similarly, submerged straliomyidous larvae present periodic contractions and extensions of the last abdominal segment, thus facilitating gas exchanges with their air bubble. In *Nemotelus* this cycle lasts 3 s. The majority of insects that breathe atmospheric air, however, contact the surface posterodorsally. Breathing positions in turn influence general posture. *Nepa* can also extract a limited amount of oxygen from water (Vlasblom, 1970).

C. Breathing Sequence in *Ranatra*

In vegetation, *Ranatra* usually clings to a plant head downward, and the body axis usually forms an angle of between 5 and 30° with the vertical. Before a respiratory ascent, the siphon–abdomen angle changes from 180° to 150° so that the siphon points more vertically toward the water surface and the forelegs are straightened (Fig. 1A). Then the animal starts climbing slowly backward along the support while the vertical inclination of its abdomen decreases. A 25 cm ascent takes about 1 min, including pauses between movements. When *Ranatra* reaches the water surface, contact is made between the siphon and the atmospheric air, and gas exchanges take place (Fig. 1B). These last an average of 40 s at 20° C under laboratory conditions before the animal crawls down to its previous resting place (Cloarec, 1972a). When conditions do not allow a climbing ascent, individuals, which are lighter than

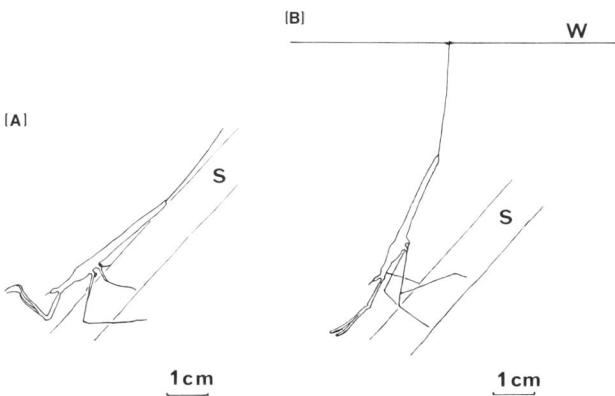

FIG. 1. (A), Precapture posture. (B) Breathing posture. S, glass support; W, water surface.

water, rise passively to the surface. They can also sometimes swim actively downward.

Similar behavior has been reported, but in less detail, for other aquatic insects like *Lethocerus cordofanus* (Belostomatidae), which surfaces for 1.25 to 1.5 min (Miller, 1977).

### D. Breathing Activity Cycles

In "siphon" and "air bubble" aquatic insects, air stores gradually deplete in volume and must be periodically renewed at the water surface. For example, the volume of *Corixa dentipes'* air bubble varies between 45 and 10 mm$^3$ (Theiss, 1982). Plastron air stores, with most of their air exposed to water do not diminish in volume under optimal conditions; for example, *Aphelocheirus* can remain permanently submerged (Parsons, 1974).

Like other regulatory behaviors which are associated with the more or less constant metabolic needs of either active or resting animals, breathing behavior shows some regularity over time. These cycles vary greatly from one species to another. Under laboratory conditions, outside the reproductive period, *Ranatra* individuals surface regularly every 40 min at 20° C (Cloarec, 1972a), and *Lethocerus* every 30 min (Miller, 1977), although intervals between surfacing vary from one individual to another and, for a given subject, from one day to another. *Belostoma flumineum* stay longer underwater and spend less time renewing their air stores at the surface than the other two aquatic Heteroptera, but show similar regularity (Parsons, 1972).

A correlation of intervals between two successive surfacings and duration of surfacing was found in *Ranatra* ($y = 1.4x - .3$; $r = .93$; Cloarec, 1972a). Other atmosphere-breathing insects also show regular surfacing but few cases have been well documented. In *Aedes detritus* larvae, both submergence and gas exchange last on average 15 s (Faucheux, 1977), and *Stratiomyidae* larvae surface for 5 min after 8 min under water.

On the scale of seconds rather than minutes, regularity of respiratory behavior unrelated to surfacing has been documented for anisopteran larvae. Their gills are inside a specialized rectal chamber where dissolved oxygen is absorbed from water. A normal ventilation cycle includes first expulsion of water from the rectal chamber followed by the entry of an equivalent volume of water, followed by a pause. This cycle includes anal valve and sternal movements. Electromyograms give detailed information on neuromuscular relationships (Pickard and Mill, 1974), and reveal regular cycles over relatively long periods. The duration of the active part of the cycle varies between 0.5 and 1.4 s according to the species and about the same for the following pause (Hughes and Mill, 1966).

E. Factors Modifying Breathing Activity

Any factor which causes an increase in metabolic demand may also induce an increase in ventilation rate. The most-documented factor is oxygen pressure, although many aquatic insects can show respiratory rates that remain independent of declining oxygen levels over a wide range of pressure values down to very low levels (Macan, 1962). Local migration is a common response to below normal pressures. Mayfly larvae can survive months under anoxic conditions in Norwegian humic ponds by migrating to the underside of the ice along the shore, the only place where oxygen concentrations are predictably high enough to allow survival (Brittain and Nagell, 1981). Elsewhere other mayfly larvae have been observed to move away from sheltered places to nearby positions more exposed to current (Wiley and Kohler, 1980) as oxygen pressure declines.

Another response to variations in oxygen levels is to modify respiratory rates. These rates increase rapidly at first with declining oxygen saturation and then more slowly (Klekowski and Kamler, 1968; Lawton, 1971; Swain et al., 1977), while a periodically sharp increase in amplitude of respiratory movements and a subsequent slow decline have also been observed. When dissolved oxygen levels are very low, *Anax* larvae modify their ventilation cycle, and a secondary inspiration and expiration is observed. This second cycle of lesser importance occurs consistently prior to the major cycle (Swain et al., 1977).

Contrary to what would be expected, respiratory rates ($\mu$l/h) of *Pyrrhosoma* larvae declined with decreasing oxygen tensions (Lawton, 1971) whereas respiratory frequency (in cycles/s) increased in *Anax* larvae (Swain et al., 1977). In addition, *Pyrrhosoma* larvae usually remain stationary near the ground in oxygen-saturated waters but, at reduced oxygen pressures, move toward the water surface, spread out their caudal lamellae and wave their abdomens, seemingly renewing their air stores in contact with the atmospheric air. There has been considerable debate over the function of the caudal lamellae of Zygoptera; Corbet (1962) favored a primarily respiratory function, and regular lateral movements of the abdomen have been interpreted as ventilatory movements. However, according to Rowe (1985), these movements are intraspecific agonistic displays and not ventilatory movements. No doubt they could serve either function according to circumstances.

Temperature variations also affect respiratory rates directly, as well as indirectly, through their influence on oxygen pressure and metabolic rates. Generally, respiratory rates increase with increasing temperature (Lawton, 1971). Because all these factors interact, the correlation between temperature and respiratory rates is not linear in dragonfly larvae (Petitpren and Knight, 1970) or in *Nepa* (Waitzbauer, 1974). Average interval between two successive surfacings in *Ranatra* decreases from over 3 hr at 13° C to 80 min at 16° C and 40 min at 20° C.

The intervals between two successive surfacings remain regular over longer periods when the intervals are longer. A *Ranatra* which surfaces every hour is likely to continue to show that rhythm for over 12 hr, but the rhythm of a *Ranatra* that surfaces every quarter of an hour or so will often be modified after 3 to 5 hr (Cloarec, 1969b). Rates vary between individuals from 15 surfacings/24 hr to 60/24 hr (mean = 34/24 hr). No significant differences between sexes were found. Activity also modifies ventilation frequency; in dragonfly larvae it increased from 40 cycles/min when the larvae were quiescent to 100 cycles/min while swimming for *Libellula* and reached 210 cycles/min for *Anax* and *Aeshna* larvae (Mill and Hughes, 1966). This frequency declines between meals, especially during the first 4 hr of fasting in *Aeshna* larvae, but then remains almost stable if fasting continues (Lacombe, 1974). Metabolic rates and therefore respiratory frequencies also tend to increase with increasing food intake, independently of other changes.

Under controlled conditions, a diel respiratory rhythm was demonstrated in *Aeshna grandis* (Berezina, 1959), although no significant variations in respiration rates related to diel variations were found in other odonatan larvae such as *Aeshna cyanea* (Lacombe, 1974) or *Pyrrhosoma* (Lawton, 1971). In water with rich vegetation, *Nepa* visit the surface more frequently during the night than during the day (Vlasblom, 1970). By contrast, under laboratory conditions, *Ranatra* ascend to the water surface significantly more frequently during the day than during the night (1.54 times/hr during the day, 1.08/hr during the night, Wilcoxon, $P < .01$).

Oxygen consumption in nepids undergoes seasonal and physiologically caused variations, for example, during overwintering and reproduction (Waitzbauer, 1978). Brood-caring male belostomatids spend longer in the air-acquisition position (mean 5 min) than females and non-egg-caring males (mean 2 min) (Venkatesan, 1983).

F. Variations of Breathing during Postembryonic Development

The most important modifications in breathing activity during postembryonic development occur when aquatic larvae become adults, with all the difficulties involved in changing to the tracheal system of the terrestrial adult. Sometimes even when the adult remains in the same aquatic habitat as the larvae, respiratory changes occur. For example, coleopteran larvae (Elmidae) use rectal tracheobranchies, whereas adults use plastrons. First instar *Aphelocheirus* larvae in well-aerated water depend almost entirely on cutaneous gas exchange, whereas adults use plastron respiration (Thorpe and Crisp, 1947). Other changes have also been reported during development. Respiratory rates increase during an instar in *Aeshna* larvae (Lacombe, 1974).

When oxygen pressure declines, aeshnid larvae can replace normal ventilation by "gulping" and "chewing" movements (Pickard and Mill, 1974). Generally the respiratory efficiency of the body surface declines gradually as insects grow, but most aquatic insects that breathe atmospheric air become gradually more independent of surface breathing. However, this aspect is poorly documented. Duration of submergence (i.e., intervals between two successive surfacings) increases during larval development in *Buenoa* (Gittelman, 1977) and gradually but significantly from one instar to another in *Ranatra* (Cloarec, 1972b); see Table I.

In *Ranatra*, time at the water surface does not vary significantly from one instar to another during the first four instars, but increases slightly after the fourth and last larval moult, and again more significantly after the imaginal moult (Table II). These increases correlate with the increase in air storage capacity and with morphological structures ($r = .89$ for body length; $r = .93$ for larval wing pads).

Diel variations do not appear to influence respiratory activity at any larval stage. No significant differences were found between the light and dark periods, nor during an instar from one day to another. Behavior changes were recorded during postembryonic development in *Ranatra*. A larval respiratory sequence is simpler than that of adults because, among other features, their caudal siphon cannot move independently of their abdomen. Just before contact is made with the surface, they raise their abdomen (the thorax-abdomen angle changes from 140 to 125° in first instar larvae) and they extend their meso- and meta-thoracic legs, but the foreleg posture of younger larvae (first to third instars) is not modified, contrary to what is observed in adults.

First and often second instar larvae usually cling to vegetation just below the water surface, so movement of the abdomen is generally sufficient to make contact with atmospheric air and no other movement is necessary. Older larvae are usually found in deeper water and they usually have to crawl backward along a support to reach the water surface. Fourth and fifth instar larvae straighten their forelegs slightly before and during gas exchange. Quiescent

TABLE I
MEAN DURATION OF INTERVALS BETWEEN TWO
RESPIRATORY SURFACINGS[a]

|  | Instar | | | | | |
| --- | --- | --- | --- | --- | --- | --- |
|  | 1 | 2 | 3 | 4 | 5 | Adult |
| Mean | 1:55 | 2:16 | 3:04 | 5:56 | 9:39 | 40:00 |
| SE | ±9 | ±8 | ±9 | ±27 | ±41 | ±4 |

[a] Minutes:seconds.

TABLE II
MEAN DURATION OF PRESENCE AT WATER SURFACE[a]

|  | Instar | | | | | Adult |
|---|---|---|---|---|---|---|
|  | 1 | 2 | 3 | 4 | 5 | |
| Mean | 13.7 | 14.0 | 13.2 | 13.4 | 19.9 | 40.0 |
| SE | ±2.7 | ±2.4 | ±2.7 | ±2.8 | ±3.3 | ±5.2 |

[a] Duration measured in seconds.

animals indicate that they are about to go to the surface either by side-to-side body movements or by straightening their forelegs or, even in adults, by grooming their siphon and expelling an air bubble.

Time spent breathing, as measured by the time the tip of the siphon remains in contact with the air–water interface, decreases significantly after the first instar and again after the imaginal moult (Fig. 2A). Adult *Ranatra* spend approximately 3.35% of their time at the surface. This is comparable to the data given by Miller (1977) for the belostomatid *Lethocerus*, which spends 4% of the daytime at the surface. Giller (1982) showed that the proportion of time different notonectid species spent at the surface varied between complex and simple environments.

### G. ORIENTATION TO WATER SURFACE

This regularity with which atmospheric air-breathing aquatic insects surface raises the problem of orientation and recognition of the area just below the air–water interface. Surfacing mechanisms must have been present before the insects invaded water for the first time in their evolutionary history so as to prevent them from being swept away by the current or wandering to a depth where their tracheal system might be flooded.

### 1. *Variations of Oxygen Pressure*

It has long been known that oxygen shortage induces insects to swim upward. If air stores are not renewed regularly, insects become in danger of losing their physical gill by consuming the oxygen from it while the nitrogen diffuses from it into the water. Vlasblom (1970) suggests that this danger is countered by the insect's tendency to surface and to renew air stores in response to a change in its mean specific gravity. As the proportions of the different gases in the air stores change, insects can be passively and hydrostatically raised to the surface (e.g., *Nemotelus* larvae, Faucheux, 1977). Many species use this buoyancy. Nepidae can survive without a physical gill only at the very low

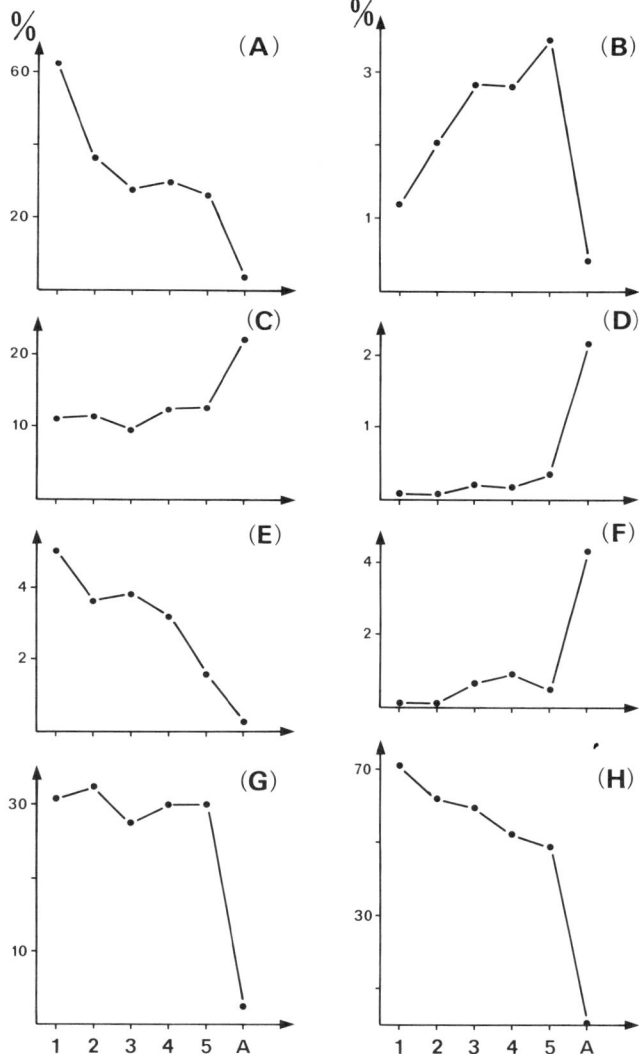

FIG. 2. Variations of *Ranatra*'s time budget during postembryonic development, in percentage of total time. (A), Contact with the water surface (breathing). (B), Ascents and descents to and from the water surface during a breathing sequence. (C), Foreleg and body readjustment movements, without modification of spatial position. (D), Crawling not associated with a breathing sequence. (E), Grooming. (F), Swimming not associated with a breathing sequence. (G), Foraging. (H), Proportion of time spent eating in contact with the water surface in relation to total time spent eating. These behavioral categories are not all mutually exclusive, for example, foraging and breathing.

temperatures at which oxygen requirements are also very low (Vlasblom, 1970). Toward the end of a dive, electromyograms reveal that fast axons become tonically active and their activity has been correlated with surfacing behavior in Belostomatidae (Miller, 1977). It is thought that hypoxia and/or reduction of air store volume can initiate surfacing.

## 2. Light

However, if variations in oxygen concentration most often seem to initiate surfacing, light rather than oxygen pressure appears to be the most commonly used directional cue for orientation and position changes related to respiratory behavior (Wiley and Kohler 1984). Gravity as well as light can be used to orient toward the surface. The specialized leg mechanoreceptors and proprioceptors involved in gravity-oriented movements have been reviewed by Horn (1975). Special pressure gravity-sensitive organs associated with spiracles have been described in Belostomatidae and in Nepidae (Baunacke, 1912; Parsons, 1972). Their exact mechanism has yet to be discovered.

Corixidae are normally negatively phototactic but become positively phototactic when deficient in oxygen (Popham, 1960), and likewise mayfly larvae have been reported to change from being negatively phototactic at high oxygen pressures to positively phototactic at low oxygen pressures (Brittain and Nagell, 1981; Scherer, 1965).

## 3. Dorsal Reaction to Light in Adult Ranatra

Many aquatic invertebrates possess a dorsal orientation to light (Schöne, 1962) which can only be demonstrated experimentally. Quiescent adult *Ranatra* react to a light, presented under their transparent tanks after at least 12 hr in the dark, by gradually straightening their forelegs in the minute after lights on. Their whole reaction to an unexpected direction of light is a complex behavioral sequence. Following foreleg extension they start crawling slowly down their support while at the same time turning round it. After 215 s on average their bodies are in a vertical position, head downward. They continue their slow turning movement and reach a horizontal position with their backs toward the light 330 s after lights on. This movement ceases when they are positioned on the underside of the support in a posture similar to their initial one, but back toward the light and head toward the surface, completely upside down, a mean of 435 s after lights on.

This is a relatively slow reaction to change of direction of light, but the great majority of *Ranatra* react in the same way. If a *Ranatra* is swimming when lights are switched on, the sequence is shorter (180 s on average). However sometimes adults do not react to light from below and keep their usual position. In this case, they are always observed breathing at the surface within 300 s. After renewing air stores at the surface, under these conditions, adults descend gradually and start turning round between 300–330 s after leaving the surface. The duration of the subsequent orientation sequence does not differ significantly from the one described above. Under these experimental conditions, the position of adult *Ranatra* when contacting the atmosphere does not differ from their normal position with lighting from above. Before surfacing they follow the orientation sequence in reverse.

## 4. Dorsal Reaction to Light in Larval Ranatra

Larval *Ranatra* show a similar dorsal reaction to light. They can turn over either around their longitudinal axis like adults or around a horizontal axis head first. They react quicker to a change in the direction of light than adults. But the delay before the first movement is recorded increases for both active and quiescent larvae as they grow older (Table III).

Unlike adults, larvae with their respiratory siphon in contact with atmospheric air also turn over after a slightly longer delay. The balance between orientation to light and orientation to the water surface changes during larval development; first, second, and third instar larvae, whether swimming or resting, orient toward light even during gas exchanges at the surface. Active, but not quiescent, fourth instar larvae also orient toward light while breathing, but fifth instar larvae, like adults, do not. First and second instar larvae can rise to the surface with their backs still toward light. However, once they contact the surface, they turn over and breath in the usual position.

These behavioral differences between adults and larvae are probably related to the importance of pressure receptors which are present only in adult nepids (Baunacke, 1912).

## H. Locomotory Adaptations

After behavioral modifications due to constraints related to breathing, the most important adaptations to the aquatic habitat in insects concern locomotion. These adaptations are remarkably diverse. In most cases, buoyancy

TABLE III
MEAN DURATION OF DELAY IN ASSUMING NEW
ORIENTATION AFTER ILLUMINATION FROM BELOW[a]

|  | Instar | | | | | |
| --- | --- | --- | --- | --- | --- | --- |
|  | 1 | 2 | 3 | 4 | 5 | Adult |
| Active | 2.0 | 2.5 | 3.0 | 9.5 | 9.5 | 180.0 |
| Quiescent | 13.5 | 14.4 | 16.0 | 24.0 | 25.0 | 420.0 |
| Breathing | 14.8 | 18.0 | 20.0 | 27.0 | — | — |

[a] Duration measured in seconds.

associated with large air stores reduces the effect of gravity and therefore less energy is required to support their weight, but generally movement in water is more costly than movement in air in terms of energy. Some insects can rise hydrostatically to the surface as soon as they lose contact with a support. Body density of adult *Ranatra* is usually just below that of pond water, so they usually float passively up to the surface to breathe after having let go of their support, but they have to swim actively down. This adaptation helps prevent drowning.

Morphological locomotory adaptations include streamlining of the body (e.g., hydrodephagan beetles) and diverse modifications of the legs, such as long hair fringes which are used as paddles (e.g., in notonectids). Many aquatic larvae swim with undulating movements of the body, either from side to side (stonefly and damselfly larvae), up and down (mayfly larvae), or curl and jerk (midges). Anisopteran larvae have developed a special locomotory ability: jet propulsion following contraction of their rectal chamber. Aquatic Heteroptera with modified raptorial forelegs use only their middle and hind legs when swimming and crawling. Their coordination of leg movements differs from the usual hexapod pattern, as both legs of a pair move simultaneously while swimming.

A low mechanical advantage value (length of metathoracic trochanter/ length of metathoracic leg) and a high leg length/body length ratio ($>1$) are considered to be adaptations increasing mobility and allowing sustained but weak movements. The reverse indicates stronger action in the form of short bursts of rapid acceleration (Alexander and McNeill, 1971). These ratios are .43 and .91 (for body length minus siphon) respectively for adult *Ranatra*, indicating a type of locomotion intermediate between these two types.

*Ranatra*'s motor activities in the aquatic environment include moving up and down from the water surface (by crawling, swimming, or floating up), readjusting posture on a perch (without changing spatial position) by leg movements or body movements, crawling along plants, pond bottom, or other supports, and swimming. Crawling and swimming not associated with surfacing for breathing together account for less than 1% of time at any larval stage (Fig. 2D,F). All categories of locomotory activities not associated with breathing increase significantly after the imaginal moult. However, most of *Ranatra*'s locomotory activity is associated with surfacing for breathing and returning to rest site. This is the only locomotory activity which varies significantly during postembryonic development: It increases gradually from the first instar to the fifth as larvae become gradually more independent of the water surface for breathing and colonize deeper layers of the water body. As there is an important increase in breathing autonomy after the imaginal moult, surfacings become rarer and the total amount of time adults spend in moving to breathe decreases, although each surfacing and following descent take longer (Fig. 2B).

Other motor activities, especially moving one leg without changing spatial position, account for an important part of all the observed activities after the imaginal moult (Fig. 2C). They appear associated with readjusting postures, but in adults these movements usually occur just before or just after a change in spatial position whether or not related to breathing.

I. Variations of Specific Locomotory Activity

*Ranatra* overwinter as adults, and when they become sexually mature the following spring their general level of activity increases significantly. From the end of March until the end of June, adults show a daily period of intense swimming activity around midday (beginning approximately 4 hr 45 min after lights on under a 12:12 light regime) that lasts approximately 3 hr (Cloarec, 1969b) (Fig. 3). Similar activity peaks at around midday have been reported in notonectids, which are active again in the evening at around 9:30 (Dahm, 1972).

An intense swimming session is often preceded by several surfacings at shorter and shorter intervals. Outside the reproductive period, adults move more during the photophase than during the scotophase, partly because they are nearer the surface during the night and surfacings are rarer during the night. Kosicki (1966) reported general activity in *Ranatra* to be low in February as compared to November or April and presumed that this variation was correlated to temperature variations. No diel variations in general locomotory activity have been observed at any stage of larval development (Cloarec, 1969b). By contrast, many aquatic predators (Odonata, *Anax*, Cloarec, 1975b; Blois, 1988) are more active at dusk and dawn, when potential prey species, for example, *Chaoborus* larvae, are also reported to be active or to show vertical migrations (Lewis, 1977). Typically the third and fourth instar larvae of

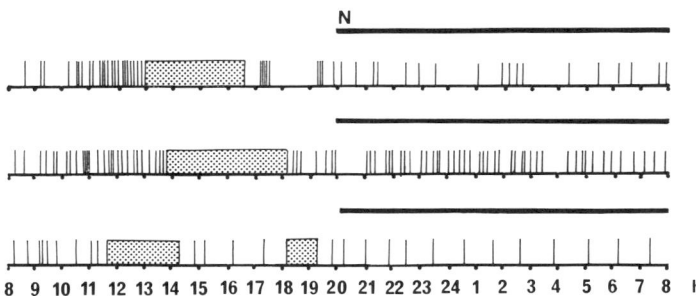

FIG. 3. Examples of actograms recorded during the reproductive season. Vertical bar, a respiratory ascent and descent; stippled blocks, intense swimming activity; h, hour; *N* over horizontal bar, darkness under a 12:12 light regime.

*Chaoborus* are benthic during the day and emerge from the sediment shortly after sunset to begin their migration into the upper layers of the water body; shortly before dawn these larvae begin their descent and they reenter the sediment before sunrise. The diel and seasonal changes in timing of these migrations appear to be controlled by subsurface illumination. Light intensity also appears to be the control factor for larval emergence from the sediment, but other factors (especially low oxygen pressure) determine vertical migration. The absence of food delays for 1–2 hr the time after termination of the light phase when the greatest percentage of larvae are planktonic. Lower temperatures decrease the percentage of planktonic larvae (LaRow, 1970).

## III. Spatial Distribution

Microdistribution of aquatic insects is poorly documented. The long intervals between two successive renewals of air stores in adult *Ranatra* ensures a relative independence if the water surface. This in turn influences their spatial distribution. *Ranatra* is one of the atmospheric breathing species that can be found farthest (over 5 m) from the water surface (Landsbury, 1981). However, as it is rather difficult to study their spatial distribution in detail in the field, only experimental laboratory data are available.

### A. Vertical Distribution of Adult *Ranatra*

The aquatic environment is special in the sense that physical factors (light intensity, oxygen pressure, temperature, etc.) change sharply along a vertical gradient. Spatial distribution of *Ranatra* has been studied along this gradient. Vertical distribution of adults was not random, but showed diel variations (Fig. 4) (Joly and Cloarec, 1988). During the photophase, significantly more individuals were observed nearer the substrate, in the lower quarter of the aquarium, and during the scotophase they were found significantly nearer the surface, in the upper quarter of the aquarium (mean 2.8 cm from the surface, $t$-test, $p < .05$). In an aquarium with 25 cm of water, the mean amplitude variation between day and night depths was 13.7 cm. When the water was deeper, diel mobility was greater.

Changes in vertical distribution coincide with the natural changes of light intensity: The animals rise to the surface at dusk and descend at dawn. As light intensity decreases, predator risk probably decreases. Birds that capture prey at or just under the water surface, and most predatory fish forage visually. Blinn *et al.* (1983) have already reported diel variations in spatial distribution of another *Ranatra* (*R. montezuma*) in the field. These diel variations were also related to changes in light intensity, but the "migrations" occurred in a horizontal plane, *Ranatra* leaving the border vegetation at dusk to swim out into the open water.

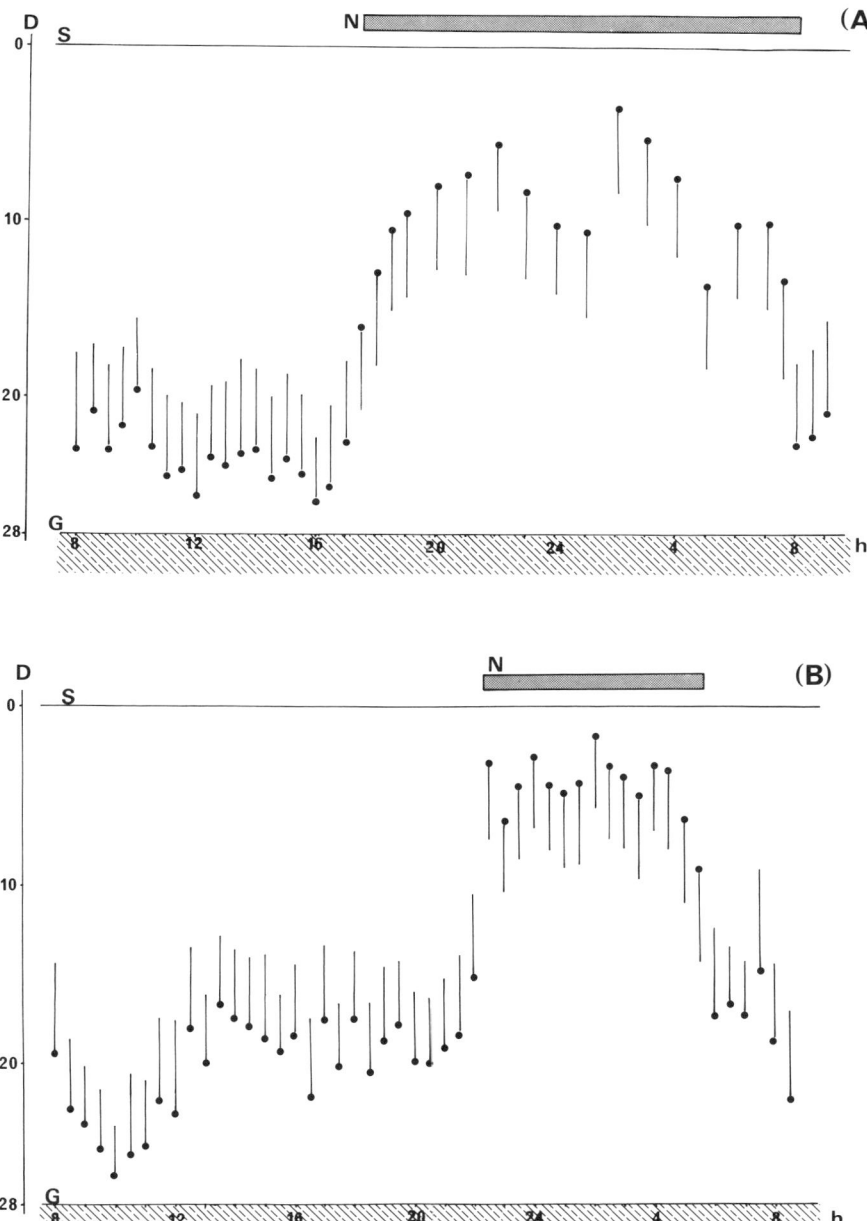

FIG. 4. Diel variations of mean depth (+SE) of adult *Ranatra* in a 28-cm deep aquarium under natural photoperiod. (A), in winter. (B), in summer. D, depth in cm, calculated from the water surface; G, substrate; h, time; N, night; S, surface.

## B. Variations of Vertical Distribution during Larval Development

Vertical spatial distribution of *Ranatra* was significantly different from random at all developmental stages ($x^2, p < .001$ for each larval instar). The great majority of first, second, third, and even fourth instar larvae were always found very close to the water surface, within the top 2 cm. No distribution outside this zone could be observed for first and second instar larvae. Third instar larvae descended exceptionally as deep as 10 cm. As *Ranatra* grew older, more and more animals were observed deeper and deeper in the aquarium (Fig. 5). The majority of fifth instar larvae, like adults, were found near or on the bottom of the aquarium during the day. The whole migration process was very gradual and no significant differences concerning vertical distribution could be found between two consecutive instars (Joly, 1984). Similarly, *Buenoa* larvae swim deeper as they mature, and duration of dive increases during larval development (Gittelman, 1977).

## C. Influence of Light Intensity on Spatial Distribution

Because the nightly rise to the surface by adults was related to changes in light intensity, the influence of light intensity and direction on the spatial distribution of *Ranatra* during postembryonic development was tested. Given a choice between three differently lighted sections of an aquarium (normal daylight, shade, and completely covered and dark) larvae of all developmental stages were significantly more often in the daylight section than in the other sections (Fig. 6). By contrast, adults preferred the dark section. This change in preference is not gradual like that in vertical distribution but occurs after the imaginal moult (Joly, 1984).

The distribution of *Ranatra* in a horizontal light gradient over 100 cm varied significantly from one instar to another: First instar larvae were found near the lighter end, whereas adults were mainly observed near the darker end. Second to fifth instar larvae showed no particular preference. First, second, and third instar larvae significantly preferred the lighted side of perches which were planted perpendicularly to the direction of the light, contrary to adults which preferred the darker side.

This different spatial distribution in relation to direction of light and to the water surface induces a spatial segregation between individuals of different developmental stages. Similarly, two sympatric *Buenoa* species select different depth distributions and thus avoid competition (Gittelman and Bergtrom, 1977). Differential reactions to light in *Ranatra* contribute among other factors to avoidance of proximity between individuals of different developmental stages, thereby reducing the risk of cannibalism, which has often been recorded in the laboratory when precautions have not been taken

# BEHAVIORAL ADAPTATIONS TO AQUATIC LIFE IN INSECTS

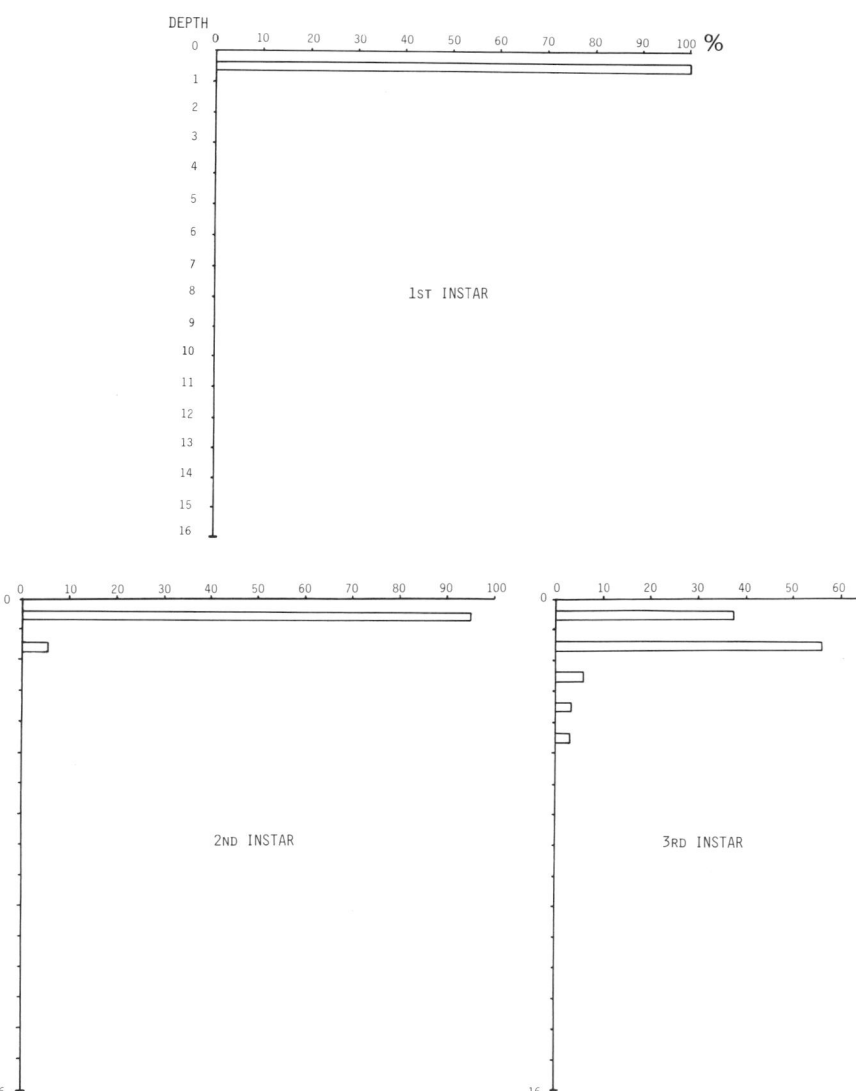

FIG. 5. Variations of vertical distribution during postembryonic development in a 16-cm deep aquarium. Proportion of *Ranatra* observed in relation to depth. (*Continued.*)

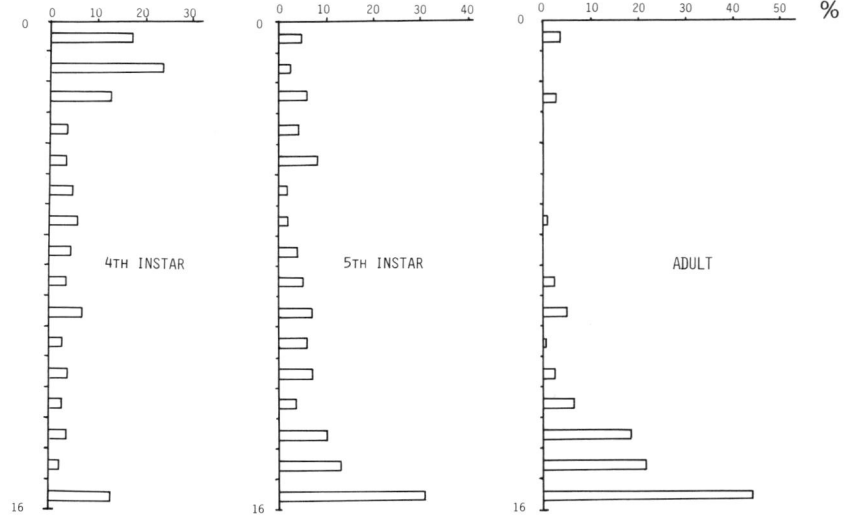

FIG. 5. (*Continued.*)

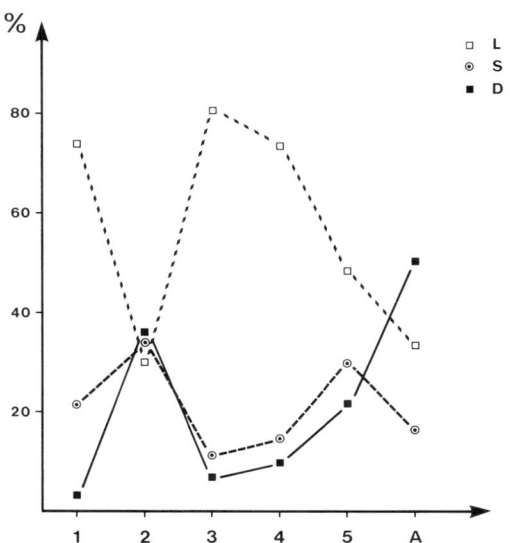

FIG. 6. Variations of distribution in relation to light intensity. L, light part of the aquarium; S, shaded part; D, dark part; 1–5: instar number; A, adult.

to avoid it. It seems that in this species which has evolved towards a cryptic antipredator strategy, younger larvae would not be protected from conspecifics if there were no spatial segregation.

Murdoch and Sih (1978) suggested that spatial distribution of younger notonectids (first to third instar larvae) was heavily influenced by the need to avoid predation. In spite of these differences in spatial distribution, young *Ranatra* have very low survival rates. Waitzbauer (1976) estimated that total mortality in the field from hatching until oviposition was approximately 99% for *Ranatra*. In spite of fairly synchronized hatching and first moult at least, in *Ranatra* some overlap of individuals of different developmental stages, and therefore sizes, exists: In the field hatching is spread over 3 weeks and the first instar can last as little as 5 days. This overlap could favor cannibalism when there is spatial proximity as in notonectids (Fox, 1975).

Dispersal of newly hatched larvae occurs in the first 24 hr after hatching. These larvae usually remain on the vegetation in which the eggs had been laid for 3 to 4 hr while their cuticle darkens slightly and hardens. Then they move gradually away (Blois and Cloarec, 1988). By Day 3 after hatching their distribution over the aquarium surface is random in relation to the hatching site.

D. CHOICE OF REST SITE

We have seen so far that behavioral adaptations of *Ranatra* to high and variable predation pressure include maximum immobility compatible with breathing, and slow movement. The efficiency of other antipredator adaptations such as cryptic coloring and sticklike shape depend on where they rest. The physical characteristics of preferred perches have been tested. A change in color preference occurred gradually during larval development: Lighter first instar larvae chose green supports 90% of the time whereas the darker adults preferred brown supports. Older larvae preferred wider supports, but adults do not avoid 3–4 mm ones completely (Joly, 1984). At all stages of development they preferred reeds (*Phragmites*) to rushes (*Juncus*) in the laboratory (Joly, 1984) (Fig. 7) and in the field (Waitzbauer, 1976). Our laboratory observations did not confirm *Ranatra*'s preference, reported by Waitzbauer (1976), for vertical structures: Inclination of support did not influence spatial distribution in the laboratory.

The inclination of the support influenced adult *Ranatra*'s posture (Fig. 8). When resting on the ground, their longitudinal axis generally formed an angle between 0 and 30° with the horizontal plane (21% were parallel to the substrate). Perched on an artificial vertical support, their body axis formed an angle of between 0° and 20° with the vertical plane (30% were parallel to the support). In vegetation without any particular structure (*Elodea*) their

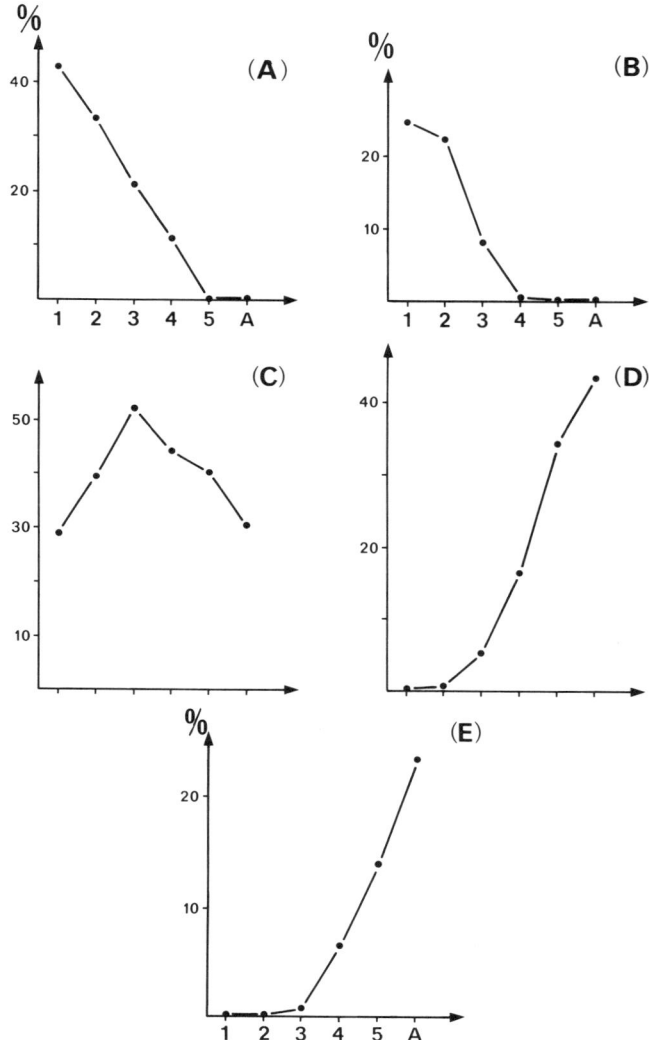

FIG. 7. Distribution of *Ranatra* of different developmental stages on different natural supports. (A), *Lemna*. (B), Grass, mean diameter 1 mm. (C), *Elodea*. (D), Reeds, mean diameter 10 mm. (E), Substrate.

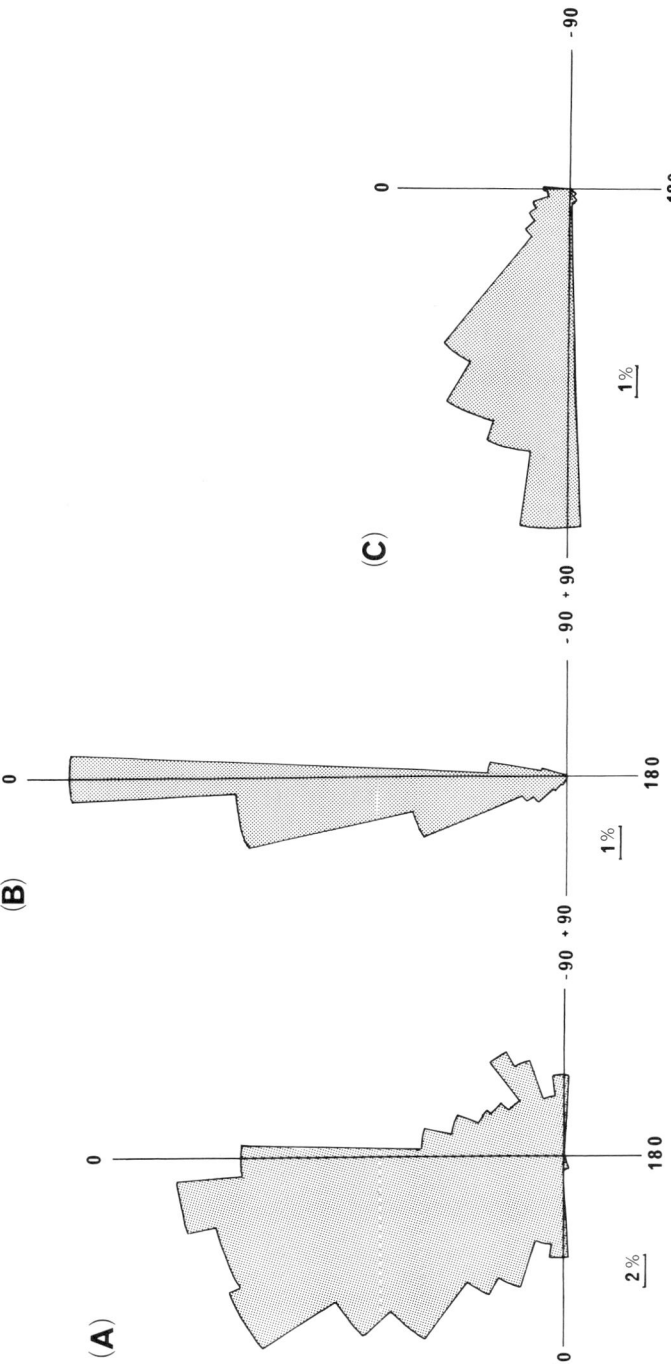

FIG. 8. Distribution of angles between adult *Ranatra*'s longitudinal axis and the axis of the support. Observations divided into 10° classes. (A), In nondirectional vegetation (*Elodea*). (B), On artificial vertical supports. (C), On substrate, no supports available.

position in relation to the vertical plane varied greatly from $-90°$ (ventral side toward the surface) to $+90°$ (dorsal side toward the surface) with, however, a majority of subjects observed forming an angle of between 0 and 30° with the vertical plane.

Waitzbauer (1976), during a mark and recapture study, noted that *Ranatra* were often recaptured at the same place. Continuous observations revealed that *Ranatra* generally return to the same spatial position they occupied prior to surfacing. The proportion of subjects returning to the same position after breathing decreased during postembryonic development as the distance to the surface increased (Fig. 9).

Notonectids have been reported to return to the same perch after a successful capture, but their choice of perch site varies with the species and with environmental features: For example, *Notonecta obliqua* prefer deeper perches in a complex environment but remain longer just under the surface in a simpler one (Giller and McNeill, 1981). In *Notonecta maculata*, selection of perch site appears related to prey distribution (Giller and McNeill, 1981). There are several indications that ambush predators change sites more often when conditions become less favorable, but this tendency has not been documented for aquatic insects. When conditions become really unfavorable in summer (ponds drying up, etc.), adult *Ranatra* have been reported to migrate. In addition, position changes are often associated with increase in activity rates (Elliott, 1968, 1970; Bailey, 1981).

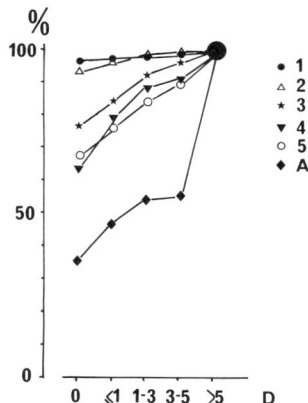

FIG. 9. Proportion of returns to same position after a respiratory surfacing in relation to developmental stage. Cumulative data. Black dot, 100%; 0, exactly the same place; <1, within 1 cm; 1–3, within 3 cm; 3–5, within 5 cm of the previous perch site; >5, farther than 5 cm from the previous perch site.

## E. INFLUENCE OF TEMPERATURE

The high specific heat of water promotes thermal stability; diel and seasonal variations in temperature are considerably damped in static water bodies. Nevertheless temperature, although not a factor with a major influence on the behavior of aquatic insects, is used to locate favorable sites by ephemeropteran larvae which select significantly higher temperatures during darkness than during daytime (Brittain and Nagel, 1981).

## IV. TIME BUDGET OF *RANATRA*

### A. INTERACTIONS BETWEEN BREATHING AND FORAGING

Breathing involves considerable muscular activity in aquatic insects and it is often energetically costly. For some aquatic species, gas exchange cannot be carried out simultaneously with activities such as foraging, or other motor activities such as building or repairing cases in Trichoptera.

Hungry adult *Ranatra* change sites more often after surfacing, and move farther, in a poorer trophic environment (Cloarec, 1988). All larval *Ranatra* spend approximately the same proportion of time ingesting prey while in contact with the water surface as below the surface (Fig. 2G,H). Adults, however, never remain at the surface during a meal. After a successful capture, the interval between two surfacings decreases, as adults usually surface within 10 min after a capture, whatever the time lapse since the previous intake of air (Fig. 10). This is no doubt related to the high cost of a predatory strike. On the other hand, adults do not react to a potential prey item during a breathing sequence. An adult *Ranatra* which is prevented from contacting the atmospheric air after a capture starts swimming in all directions under the surface and usually discards its prey after less than 30 min unsuccessful search, during which it does not ingest any food. This rejection of prey is not related to satiety, as the animal will capture and eat prey immediately after it has been able to contact atmospheric air, but shows that all feeding activities are interrupted until respiratory requirements have been satisfied.

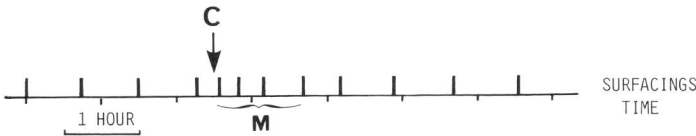

FIG. 10. Modifications of surfacing intervals after a successful capture (C) by an adult. M, duration of feeding.

Postures associated with breathing differ generally from those associated with feeding in aquatic insects (Wiley and Kohler, 1984). Another indication of conflicting demands between breathing and foraging in *Ranatra* is to be found in adult foreleg postures. *Ranatra* straighten their forelegs before ascending to the surface and only resume the capture posture after they have returned to their perch. Foreleg posture has been shown to be a good indicator of gut clearance and willingness to respond to prey. Adults do not react to a potential prey item when their forelegs are straightened (Cloarec, 1974). Larvae show less variety in foreleg postures and retain the capture posture during a breathing sequence. Although postures become more diversified as larvae grow older, fourth and fifth instar larvae can still seize a prey item and initiate feeding during a breathing sequence; when this occurs during an ascent, a pause is usually observed before surfacing.

## B. Grooming

At all developmental stages, grooming in *Ranatra* usually precedes or follows a breathing sequence or locomotory activity. Grooming is particularly common in adults before a phase of intense swimming. Outside the reproductive period, the proportion of time spent grooming decreases after the first instar and again after the fourth and fifth instars. Adults groom significantly less than larvae (Fig. 2E). Time spent grooming correlates with both time spent breathing and developmental stage (Table IV). In insect predators, grooming is usually more closely associated with feeding activities than with any other category of activities; *Ranatra* is unusual in that this is not so,

TABLE IV
INTERACTIONS OF GROOMING AND OTHER BEHAVIORS

|  | Developmental stage | | | | | |
| --- | --- | --- | --- | --- | --- | --- |
|  | 1 | 2 | 3 | 4 | 5 | Adult |
| Grooming movements (%) | | | | | | |
| Before breathing | 13.7 | 18.8 | 29.7 | 34.6 | 28.3 | 10.0 |
| During breathing | 29.8 | 39.1 | 11.3 | 14.9 | 13.5 | 2.5 |
| After breathing | 37.9 | 25.8 | 38.9 | 28.5 | 35.0 | 49.1 |
| Total | 81.4 | 83.7 | 79.9 | 78.0 | 76.8 | 61.6 |
| Toilet movements associated with feeding (%) | 8.3 | 8.2 | 9.2 | 4.8 | 7.3 | 2.5 |
| Toilet movements associated with locomotory activity (%) | 0 | 0 | 0 | 0 | 0 | 22.5 |

although it may occasionally clean both its mouthparts and eyes after a meal (Bailey, 1986a).

C. INTERACTIONS BETWEEN LOCOMOTORY ACTIVITIES AND FORAGING

An important aspect of predation strategies is efficiency in locomotion. Depending on specific foraging strategies, locomotion either enhances an animal's chances of encountering prey or is incompatible with feeding. Active predators should show an ability for sustained efficient locomotion with minimal energy expenditure. The notonectid *Martarega* swims against the current while waiting for prey stranded on the water surface to be carried within reach. Because the prey are immobile, *Martarega* has not developed the capacity for rapid acceleration in the pursuit of prey and has reduced in size its prey-restraining appendages and increased its ability to maintain its position in a current (Gittelman, 1974).

By contrast, ambush predators that pursue prey should maximize rapid acceleration from a stationary position. Morphometric analysis indicates that a higher mechanical advantage should be an adaptation for rapid acceleration after prey. *Notonecta* and *Buenoa* live in static water and sit and wait for potential free-swimming prey possessing good capacity for escape. These two species have evolved large fore- and mid-legs capable of prey restraint; they are able to sustain the effort necessary to lunge from a stationary position and accelerate rapidly to capture their prey (Gittelman, 1974). The adjustment of locomotory capacity to fit different predatory strategies has been accomplished by changing the mechanical advantage of the metathoracic legs in swimming.

Just as there is mutual inhibition between breathing and foraging in adult *Ranatra*, there is incompatibility between locomotion and foraging: An adult when swimming will never react to prey and, even when a claw accidentally closes over one, it is always discarded rather than eaten. This inhibition does not exist in larvae. In addition, during spring, periods of intense swimming activity are suppressed in satiated mature adults on the day of, or following, a large meal (Cloarec, 1969b). The variations in the amount of a standard-size prey item eaten coincide with variations of locomotory activity (Cloarec, 1975a). Food deprivation usually increases the general level of activity in actively foraging insects. In *Phormia regina*, general activity increases as a function of deprivation time and leads to starvation and death after a short period (Barton-Browne and Evans, 1960). On the other hand, food deprivation in ambush predators such as *Aeshna* larvae induces a decrease in all movements that lead to a change in visual input. This decrease cannot be attributed to a state of exhaustion; rather, food deprivation specifically inhibits the larva's readiness to move (Etienne, 1972).

As larval *Ranatra* grow older, they can survive gradually longer periods of starvation, and adults can survive several weeks without showing any significant modification in locomotory activity except for more frequent changes of perch after a breathing sequence. Small anisopteran larvae do not show any diel variations of food intake, but a biphasic feeding rhythm develops as larvae grow larger (Blois and Cloarec, 1988). The feeding rhythm of *Chaoborus* is strongly related to the rhythm of vertical migration of their cladoceran prey (Lewis, 1977). Thus the coincidence of predator feeding rhythms and prey activity rhythms may suggest that individual predatory rhythms have been modified to match those of the hunted species (Fedorenko, 1975a,b).

In *Ranatra*, time spent feeding is very variable from one day to another and from one individual to another at all stages of development, depending mainly on the rate of predator–prey encounters. Under conditions of superabundant food supply, larvae spend at least 40% of their time eating, but outside the reproductive period adults spend only about 4.6% of their time feeding (Fig. 2G). No diel variations could be found in food intake or in any other activity category observed (Fig. 11).

At low temperatures (4–5° C), maximum feeding rates in damselfly larvae (*Pyrrhosoma*) were depressed more than predicted either from the effects of temperature on the gut-clearance time or from respiratory rate (Lawton, 1971).

### D. Predation Risk

A common situation where conflicting behavioral demands are observed is between foraging and predator vigilance: A high feeding rate, especially by actively foraging predators can rarely be attained without also a high risk of predation. The time-budget data outlined above indicate an antipredator strategy based on maximum immobility compatible with fundamental needs, slow movement, cryptic coloring, and shape, causing *Ranatra* to resemble a twig.

Experiments with model threat stimuli revealed two main defense responses in *Ranatra dispar* (Bailey, 1986b): (1) foreleg extension and remaining motionless, thus enhancing crypsis (Fig. 12), or (2) escaping from ambush site and swimming to the bottom. If a threat occurs during a meal, the prey is usually abandoned. An individual's response is correlated with the time since the last meal. The longer the deprivation, the more likely it is that the predator will risk remaining in a prey-capture position when a threat appears.

Similarly, damselfly larvae (*Ischnura elegans*) that are at a significant risk from predators when swimming remain at their ambush site even when threatened by starvation (Lawton, personal communication, in Hassell and Southwood, 1978).

According to the few reports available, the natural predators of *Ranatra* include other *Ranatra* (Radinovsky, 1964), notonectids, dragonfly larvae and dytiscid beetles (Bailey, 1986b), fish, and birds, but the extent of this predation is not known.

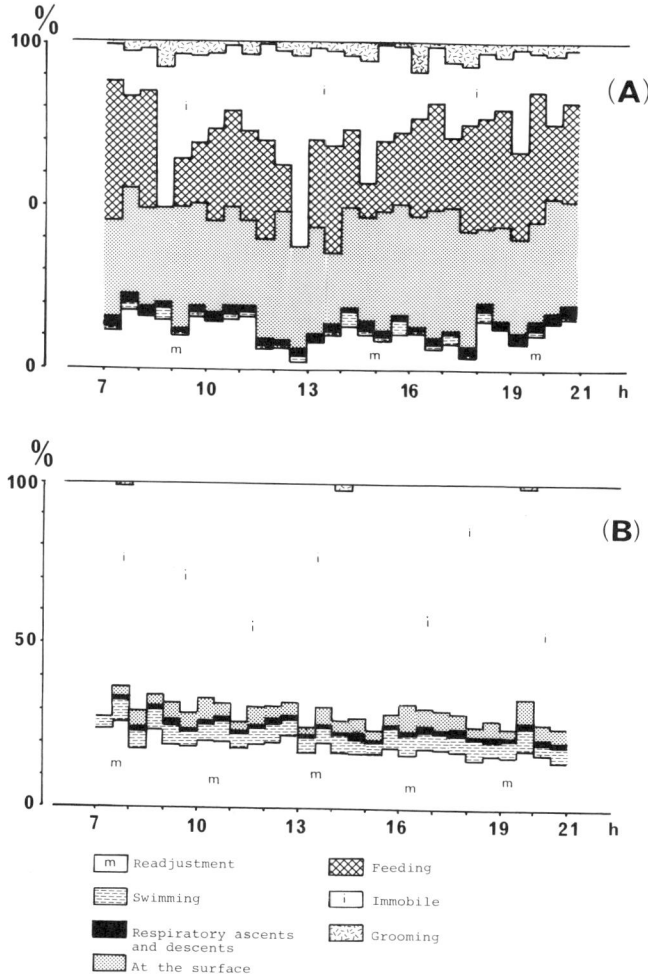

FIG. 11. Time budgets of fourth instar larvae (A) and adults (B). Feeding has been omitted from (B). Since breathing at the surface and feeding are not mutually exclusive in larvae, only feeding below the surface is represented here.

### E. Conflicting Demands

For *Ranatra*, balancing conflicting demands between remaining in a prey capture position or not when a threat is present involves a complex decision-making process. Both the defensive and the evasive responses inhibit reactions to potential prey. The outcome is made more complicated when one takes into account the hunger level and the energy costs involved in performing the response (Bailey, 1986b).

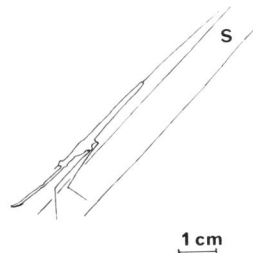

Fig. 12. Defensive posture. S, support.

Ydenberg and Houston (1986) investigated how great tits balance feeding requirements with the demand for vigilance. Another well-documented case of conflicting behavioral demands is courtship in newts (Halliday, 1977). Clearly there is a cost associated with breathing during courtship, but the reduction of a male newt's oxygen supply affects his sexual behavior. The time he can remain underwater without taking in a fresh supply of air is limited and limits the time available for sexual behavior.

The data outlined above for interactions between different activities in *Ranatra* indicate that adaptive allocation of time and energy among various daily activities is functionally important. Conflicting demands from other behavior patterns (for food, air, protection against predators) must be taken into account when considering one behavior.

Both oxygen supplies and food stores usually deplete gradually in aquatic insects, thereby inducing a steady rise in the level of the corresponding internal factors. Our experimental data suggest that, although there is competition between activities, there are also well-established dominance relationships between activities. A dominant activity is considered here not in terms of the behavior that is expressed after an experimental interruption of the ongoing activity (McFarland, 1974) but, following Evans and Downie (1986), as an activity that can interrupt and replace another activity as the ongoing behavior as the result of a change in its associated level of causal factors. Although predator–prey encounters are highly unpredictable in *Ranatra*, breathing can replace feeding or inhibit capture even when the next meal is uncertain and the last one is a long time ago. Clearly, regular renewal of air supplies is dominant. Besides, perch-site selection and locomotion associated with surfacing are affected by predator risk.

## V. Comparisons between Aquatic and Terrestrial Ambush Predators

Schiodte (1870) pointed out *Ranatra*'s affinities with terrestrial forms, and *Ranatra*'s forelegs clearly bring to mind the raptorial forelegs of mantids. There are also obvious similarities between their predatory behaviors, and particularly between the dynamic components of strikes of mantids (Mittelstaedt, 1962; Holling, 1964; Gray and Mill, 1983) and those of *Ranatra* (Cloarec, 1969a). However, because of differences in density between air and water, a strike in water is more energy consuming than a strike in air. This selection pressure could explain the streamlining of *Ranatra*'s forelegs compared to mantid forelegs.

A. ADULT PREDATORY BEHAVIOR

Under normal circumstances, the effects of visual and mechanical stimuli combine during different phases of predatory behavior in *Ranatra*, and particularly before a strike is elicited (Cloarec, 1976). *Ranatra* waits in ambush for prey and strikes at any prey item that moves within attacking distance. Nevertheless, a prey in the main part of an adult's perceptual sphere usually elicits a strike visually. Precise localization of a prey item before striking is particularly important because, although predatory movements of the forelegs cover several millimeters and do not necessitate aiming exactly at one given spot, *Ranatra* never pursue a prey item if it escapes a predatory attempt. They can only aim and capture prey which come within striking distance. However, in the laboratory they show a high rate of successful captures (82% of all attempts led to grasping an item) (Cloarec, 1969a).

Reactivity (i.e., the proportion of predatory movements in relation to the number of presentations of prey items) and strike efficiency (i.e., the proportion of successful captures in relation to all predatory attempts) of intact mantids (Maldonado *et al.*, 1967) and of intact *Ranatra* (Cloarec, 1979) decrease similarly with increasing predator–prey distances. However, unlike mantids, there is no decrease in reactivity for *Ranatra* for shorter distances. Performance of *Ranatra* is particularly good up to 60–80 FD[1], and hits are efficient up to 100 FD, which is farther than in mantids.

Mantids compensate this poorer performance with a "lunge," a forward movement of the body. *Ranatra* stay still during a strike: The only movements of the body associated with predatory behavior occur while orienting toward prey before a strike is elicited. Predatory movements before a strike concern mainly the forelegs, and never the head.

B. VARIATIONS OF PREDATORY BEHAVIOR DURING
   POSTEMBRYONIC DEVELOPMENT

During development, predatory behavior undergoes several modifications (Cloarec, 1969a):

---

[1]FD is a relative measure of predator–prey distances which uses the individual predator's foreleg as the unit of measure, thus allowing comparison of performance between different-sized predators.

1. General strike efficiency increases from 22.5% for first instar larvae to 82% for adults. There are no significant differences among the daily scores for a given instar, although they improve rapidly from one instar to the next, with sudden changes due to their discontinuous growth.
2. More foreleg postures become possible after each moult as the femur-coxa angle increases its range.
3. Orientation phases prior to a strike can only be observed after the third instar.
4. Forelegs gradually lose their independence of movement during a strike.
5. The proportion of complex predatory movements gradually increases during development. Predatory movements have been divided into four categories according to their complexity (Cloarec, 1969a) (Fig. 13).
6. Visual detection increases while the importance of mechanoreception decreases.

The relationship between striking and hitting distances and foreleg length do not remain constant throughout larval development (Cloarec, 1980a). Reactivity and strike efficiency improve gradually after each moult for each distance tested. Maximum reactive distance and maximum hit distance increase with

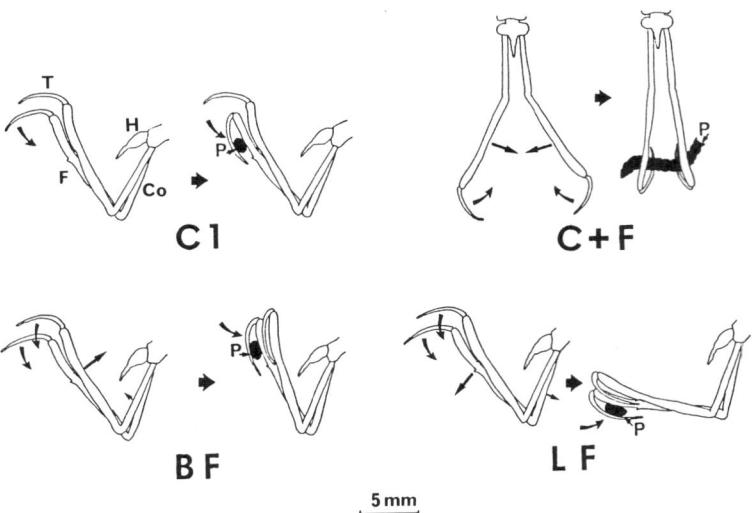

FIG. 13. Predatory movements. C1, side view, one or both claws close, no other foreleg movement; C+F, top view, both prothoracic femurs move simultaneously in a horizontal plane; BF, side view, both femurs move backward toward the head; LF, side view, femurs lowered; on the left, precapture posture of forelegs; on the right, position at the end of strike; P, prey item; Co, coxa; F, femur; H, head; T, tibiotarsal claw.

age, proportionally faster than the forelegs increase in length. Hits are impossible with prey items presented at distances equal to total foreleg length before adulthood. Strikes at prey items presented at 100 FD can only be observed by fourth instar and older larvae.

Balderrama and Maldonado (1973) followed up their study of distance estimation in adult mantids by studying its ontogeny. For mantids, the number of strikes and hits decreased with increasing distances up to a relative distance (80 FD) the same for all instars, beyond which no strikes or hits were recorded. Sixth and seventh instar larvae and adult mantids do not strike at prey items beyond 80 FD but first to fifth instar larvae strike at prey items up to 100 FD. By contrast, in *Ranatra*, the fall was gradual and occurred at different relative distances for different instars: Younger larvae do not strike at items so far away, but older larvae and adults strike at items much farther away even when the probability of seizing them is zero.

For mantids there is no agreement between the distance at which hits and strikes fell abruptly. Balderrama and Maldonado (1973) postulated that there is a double component to mantid strikes: a static component (movement of predatory legs without movement of body), and a dynamic component or lunge (movement of body). The lunge can cover a distance of up to 40 FD for younger larvae and up to 20 FD for older ones. This dynamic component is absent in the predatory behavior of *Ranatra* at all stages of development. The static component of mantid strikes seems to include an invariant relationship between maximum strike distance and foreleg extension for all stages of development. No such relationship has been found in *Ranatra*. However, for both mantids and *Ranatra* there seems to exist a precise estimation of catching distance at all developmental stages, although it improves with age in *Ranatra*. Strikes are not elicited with the same probability at the same relative distances for all stages. Therefore the details of distance estimation differ between mantids and *Ranatra* during postembryonic development (Cloarec, 1980a). Nevertheless, there appears to be a greater convergence between mantids and *Ranatra* when adult predatory behavior is considered: Two different routes of behavioral development lead to analogous adult behaviors which are in addition related to morphophysiological analogies. These points raise two main questions: First, how does the animal achieve accurate distance estimation, and second, how are readjustments made after each moult?

C. Visual Mechanisms Related to Distance Estimation in Adult *Ranatra*

The high rate of capture success observed for adults implies accuracy of attack and precise estimation of predator-prey distance before a strike is elicited. It is generally accepted that, in insects with highly developed compound eyes and important overlapping frontal visual fields, distance estimation is accomplished by some sort of binocular method. This conclusion is mainly based on studies by Baldus (1926) on *Aeshna* larvae, Friederichs (1931) on cicendelid beetles, Chmurzynski (1963) on *Bembex*, and Maldonado and Levin (1967) on mantids. Binocular vision has been demonstrated in mantids by Rossel (1983).

Visual mechanisms concerned with distance estimation have been investigated in *Ranatra* (Cloarec, 1979). Mechanoreceptors play a relatively more important part in prey capture during the first instar. Thereafter, the increasing part played by eyes and the decreasing part played by mechanoreceptors probably explain some specific developmental differences, but nothing corresponding to the increasing mobility of *Ranatra*'s forelegs has been reported for mantids. The importance of visual mechanisms in distance estimation in adult *Ranatra* has been tested by unilaterally blinding some individuals and comparing their performance to that of intact subjects.

The decrease in reactivity after unilateral blinding is not so great in *Ranatra* as in mantids. Maximum strike distance for adult monocular *Ranatra* is 120 FD (compared to >200 FD) and maximum hit distance is 80 FD (compared to 100 FD). Range of striking remains relatively greater in monocular *Ranatra* than in mantids, but nevertheless monocular subjects are incapable of hitting normal distances. During strikes, forelegs remain well coordinated contrary to those of monocular mantids whose predatory movements were generally atypical.

Maldonado and Barros-Pita (1970) showed that a particular region in the mantid eye, the fovea, was involved in prey fixation and distance estimation. There is no visible fovea in the *Ranatra* eye, but ommatidia in the anterodorsal part of the eye have significantly smaller interommatidial angles (mean 4°) than those in other parts of the eye (5-6°) (Cloarec, 1984). Reactivity and strike efficiency decrease when ommatidia outside this anterodorsal region are the only ones stimulated. Frontal ommatidia possess particular characteristics due to their position in the overlapping part of the visual fields, their relative position to the forelegs, and their optical characteristics. The relative importance of overlapping depends on the size of the compound eyes, their sphericity, their convexity, their relative position on the head, their spacing, and the number of converging ommatidia.

Central fixation of the prey is very important for insect predators before a capture. The 100° overlap of *Ranatra* visual fields is greater than that reported for most insects. Similar values for overlapping visual fields have been given for *Notonecta glauca* (94°, Von Buddenbrock, 1952) or for *Libellula quadrimaculata* (112°, Pritchard, 1966).

In *Ranatra*, fixation cannot be separated from arousal because they never follow prey movement visually and their heads are not very mobile, unlike mantids (Mittelstaedt, 1957; Rilling *et al.*, 1959; Maldonado and Levin, 1967).

To estimate position of prey it is necessary to distinguish between self-movement and movement of the object. However it should be remembered that, when they are moving, adult *Ranatra* do not react to potential prey.

Binocular distance estimation should be possible within the farthest and nearest limits perceived simultaneously with both eyes and determined by the theoretical analysis of insect vision presented by Burkhardt *et al.* (1973; Fig. 14). If all distances are related to the span between the eyes, the structure of the binocular field of vision and separation capacities depend mainly on the divergence angles of ommatidia. The range of possible binocular localization can be calculated. The nearest distance of binocular vision $C$ in a frontal plane is

$$OC = \frac{OA}{\tan a/2}$$

$OA$ is half the span between the optic centers of the eyes, $a$ is the angle at the intersection point of the axes of the innermost ommatidia and equals $100°$ in *Ranatra*. Therefore for adults, $OC = 0.9$ mm or approximately 4 FD. According to this calculation, binocular vision starts before the tip of the rostrum (Cloarec, 1984).

The farthest point of binocular vision, $E$, is given by the formula

$$E = OA \cot b/2,$$

where $b$ is the angle between axes of two neighboring ommatidia ($4°$ for frontal ommatidia). Thus $E$ equals 31.5 mm or 135 FD. This means that adult *Ranatra* can perceive binocularly objects up to and just beyond the tips of their forelegs (25 mm) along their midline. Intact adults react to objects farther away, but

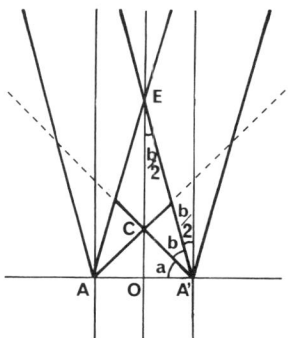

FIG. 14. Theoretical limits of binocular vision in insects (modified from Burkhardt *et al.*, 1973). A, A′, optic centers; a, angle at the intersection point of the axes of the innermost ommatidia; b, angle between axes of two neighboring ommatidia; C, the nearest distance of binocular vision; E, the farthest point of binocular vision.

there is a sharp drop in reactivity above 100 FD, which is the maximum catching distance, and again above 140 FD, which is beyond point $E$. As depth perception for all points beyond $E$ is impossible, distance estimation no longer relies on binocular vision and is not accurate.

$E$ comes nearer and nearer to the eyes the farther away the prey item is from the median plane. This could explain, in part at least, the poorer performance when prey is presented laterally; another reason is the structural relationship between eyes and forelegs. Before attempting to catch a prey, a predator generally orients so that the object to be localized is on or near its median plane where the range of binocular vision is the greatest. The analysis of Burkhardt *et al.* (1973) of insect vision helps to explain discrepancies between the point where prey elicit the most strikes (90 FD) and where they elicit the most hits (70 FD). There is less than 1° difference in intact subjects, but over 4° in monocular animals (60 FD and 40 FD respectively). Therefore objects at these two points probably do not stimulate the same ommatidia in monocular subjects (Cloarec, 1984).

Perceiving moving objects nevertheless sets special requirements on the visual analyzer that cannot all be explained by elementary optics. It is well known that there are several other types of information that can compensate, at least in part, for the absence of binocular information, such as angular size of object, its speed, linear perspective, absolute size differences, movement parallax, high contrast, and high flicker frequency. Some of these possibilities have been investigated in *Ranatra* in experiments on the role of visual discrimination of distance position, and size of targets.

### D. Distance Discrimination

Both monocular and intact *Ranatra* are able to discriminate between objects differing in absolute size but subtending the same angle, if they are presented at different distances from the head. Therefore it appears that *Ranatra* possess monocular mechanisms for judging depth. Distance estimation was nevertheless somewhat impaired by unilateral blinding as more aims were then nondirected or undershot.

Both monocular and intact *Ranatra* usually chose the target nearer to their foreleg claws and to the distance at which a prey is most likely to elicit a strike. Our experimental conditions do not allow us to infer the type of monocular cues actually used, although motion parallax would be a good candidate. As the performance of intact adults was significantly better than that of monocular animals, *Ranatra* probably normally use binocular cues in addition to monocular ones to estimate distances (Cloarec, 1986).

### E. Relative Positions of Targets

Position of targets in relation to the animal's midline was found to be an important factor influencing prey selection. Although symmetrical presentations of two identical targets to controls revealed no preference for one side, asymmetrical presentations of two identical targets revealed preference for the more central position: Controls always chose the target nearer their midline. Unilateral blinding modified this choice: Targets presented between 20° and 40° on the side of their intact eye were preferred, even when the second target was nearer their midline and well within their visual field. This emphasizes the importance of the specialized central zone of the eye within the binocular overlap (Cloarec, 1986). Ommatidia in the area covered by the projection of a centered prey usually have the best depth perception (Collett and Land, 1975; Bauer, 1981).

F. SIZE PERCEPTION

Retinal image size is also important in eliciting and controlling predatory behavior in *Ranatra*. Both monocular and intact subjects usually prefer the larger target within the experimental range (1–10°), even though monocular subjects chose the larger object less consistently. However targets subtending angles of 5 or 6° were nearly as attractive as 10° spherical targets whatever their presentation distance. This may be because a 10° target presented at 25 mm, that is at maximum catching distance, is difficult to handle as it has a 4.4 mm diameter compared to the 4.9 mm average length of a claw. It is therefore close to the maximum size that can be seized.

Although *Ranatra* can distinguish between targets differing by only 1° in diameter, there is no evidence that they can judge real size of objects in the way many vertebrates can. *Ranatra* do not seem to rely on image size to judge distance, but image size remains an important determinant of target choice. It would seem that retinal image size and distance act as two independent parameters to control probability of striking (Cloarec, 1986).

G. DOUBLE STRIKES

*Ranatra* can strike accurately at two prey at once. A high proportion of predatory movements were aimed at both targets simultaneously when they were presented symmetrically, whether they were of identical size or not. This occurred particularly when the angular distance between them was less than 60°, which corresponds to the angle formed by the two foreleg femurs when in the capture posture (Cloarec, 1974). Each claw closed over one target, even if *Ranatra* had to move both forelegs toward the midline. The same phenomenon was observed when the distance between the two targets was small (<10 mm). Complementary observations with live prey confirmed that this was not an experimental artifact. When presented with two similar live prey items under similar conditions, *Ranatra* caught both items simultaneously, one in each claw, at about the same rate as the dummies.

If *Ranatra* were using disparity information, one would expect them to be confused by two identical targets presented simultaneously and symmetrically. The fact that they usually respond correctly and simultaneously to both targets, even when the targets are at different distances, suggests an absence of confusion of the two targets or of their images, and the use of additional mechanisms, probably parallax. It must be stressed that monocular animals were also capable of seizing two targets simultaneously although they did it less frequently, but it is still obvious that different ommatidia were stimulated by each target.

These tests did not reveal any conditions under which intact animals presented with two targets responded to apparent rather than real images. Only monocular subjects misdirected strikes when two targets were presented simultaneously (Cloarec, 1986).

### H. Developmental Variations of Distance Estimation

Contrary to findings on mantids (Maldonado *et al.*, 1974), no constant relationship was found in *Ranatra* during postembryonic development between width of head, place of ommatidia involved in distance estimation, ocular prominence, ocular globe breadth, length of forelegs, and maximum striking or hitting distances (Cloarec, 1984; Fig 15). This could imply an automatic adaptation to the new maximum distances after a moult.

Values of maximum binocular vision were calculated for all developmental stages along the animal's midline in the same direction as the maximum distances had been estimated. Comparisons between observed and calculated values indicate that, for the first four larval instars at least, the theoretical limits of binocular vision and maximum hitting distance coincide. This suggests that these calculated limits of binocular vision correspond to some behavioral or perceptual reality, and that binocular vision limits *Ranatra*'s ability to respond to prey items presented at distances equal to foreleg length before the fifth instar. For fifth instar larvae and for adults, the theoretical limit is farther than maximum hitting distance, and therefore out of reach of the forelegs. This last value then limits catching ability. Burkhardt *et al.*'s (1973) theoretical analysis of insect vision helps to explain behavior in this case.

### I. Developmental Variations of Visual Receptors

In *Ranatra* the size of the eye increases both by increasing facet diameter and number of ommatidia. Improvement in visual acuity seems due essentially to the increase in facet diameter (Sherk, 1978a,b,c) and the decrease of interommatidial angle (Horridge and Duelli, 1979; Rossel, 1979).

*Ranatra* possess the typical eye of a visual sedentary predator according to criteria presented by Sherk (1978b). If the same ommatidia were involved in estimating maximum striking distance, for example, from one instar to another, the change in direction of the optical axes of these ommatidia should be equal to the angle subtending the new maximum striking distance, taking

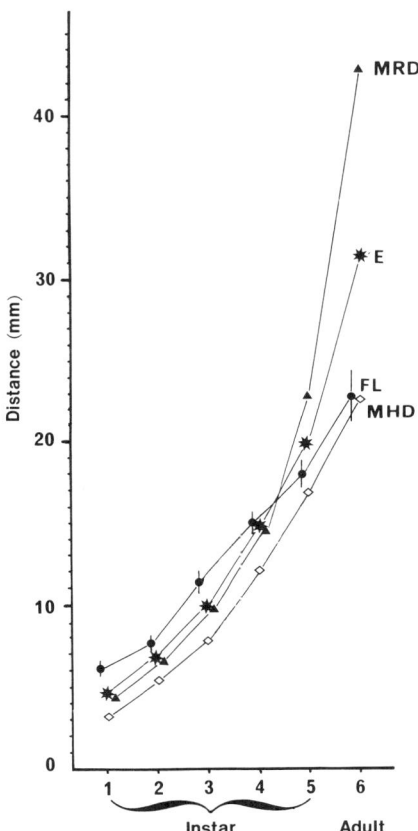

FIG. 15. Factors affecting maximum catching distance. E, theoretical limit of binocular vision; FL, foreleg length; MHD, maximum hitting distance; MRD, maximum reactive distance.

into account head growth and the developmental increase in maximum striking distance.

During postembryonic development, marked ommatidia diverge from one instar to another (10–30°) far more than the optimal calculated change of direction for the same ommatidia if they are to continue viewing maximum striking distance (0.6°), or even if it changes to view the new maximum striking distance after viewing maximum hitting distance (1.3°). New ommatidia view maximum striking and hitting distances after each moult. Therefore there is no constant relationship in *Ranatra* between predatory performance and position of stimulus, shape or position of receptors (eyes), and effector size (Cloarec, 1984; Table V).

TABLE V
SOME MEASURES OF RECEPTORS (EYES), EFFECTORS (FORELEGS),
AND PREDATORY PERFORMANCE[a]

|  | Instar | | | | | |
| --- | --- | --- | --- | --- | --- | --- |
|  | 1 | 2 | 3 | 4 | 5 | Adult |
| Angle between axes of two neighboring ommatidia | 8° | 7° | 6° | 5° | 4.5° | 4° |
| Distance between optic centers | 0.64 | 0.84 | 1.06 | 1.32 | 1.56 | 2.20 |
| Ocular prominence | 0.34 | 0.41 | 0.50 | 0.62 | 0.75 | 0.86 |
| Ocular width | 0.28 | 0.36 | 0.46 | 0.56 | 0.67 | 0.81 |
| Foreleg length | 6.2 | 7.7 | 11.4 | 15.0 | 18.0 | 23.2 |
| Maximum hitting distance | 3.7 | 5.4 | 7.8 | 12.0 | 16.5 | 23.2 |

[a] All measures are in millimeters except angle between axes of two neighboring ommatidia.

Several authors have found discrepancies between behavioral tests and visual acuity measurements. The apparent discrimination of patterns by small compound eyes with relatively few facets suggests that their spatial resolution is much better than would be expected from interommatidial angle measurements. *Velia* discriminates changes of 1° in the separation of disks although the mean interommatidial angle is 10° (Meyer, 1974). The optimal distance for eliciting attack by *Notiophilus* beetles corresponds to the intersection of ommatidia with the best depth and width perception. These minima, in turn, correspond approximately to the size of the smallest prey attacked (Bauer, 1981). In mantids (Maldonado and Barros-Pita, 1970; Barros-Pita and Maldonado, 1970), hoverflies (Collett and Land, 1975), and beetles (Bauer, 1981), projection of a centered prey covers ommatidia in an area next to the fovea, but not including it.

Sherk (1978c) argues that one possible reason why the greatest changes in larval eyes of Odonata occur in the regions with ommatidia viewing directions in which the larvae need the best vision is that individual ommatidia might be best adapted for the vision of the instar in which they become fully mature but are less-well adapted for vision in the following instars. This idea probably implies a mechanism for rearranging the underlying nervous pathways to neurons eliciting a strike. The underlying mechanisms are still unknown, but the intersection hypothesis, as far as it goes, can explain that some visual sedentary predators estimate predator–prey distance correctly simply because some of the ommatidia stimulated by an object near the midline are symmetrical.

Nevertheless, this analysis does not explain why there is a change after each moult in the relationship between foreleg length, receptor position, and predatory performance (maximum striking and hitting distances), nor how *Ranatra* adapt to the new relationship. During postembryonic development, maximum striking distance increases 6.3 times, proportionally faster than the forelegs increase in length (3.8 times).

## J. Adaptations to New Striking Distance after a Moult

These discrepancies between maximum striking and hitting distances and foreleg length raise the question of how, at the beginning of each instar, prey items out of reach during the previous instar could elicit a predatory movement. Maldonado *et al.* (1974) presented two hypotheses to explain the mechanisms underlying these readjustments which are made necessary because of discontinuous growth: (1) A reiterative learning process. Although hand-fed mantids miss more prey than controls with previous catching experience (Rilling *et al.*, 1959), it is impossible to determine whether in this case practice influences strike efficiency or correct distance estimation or both. (2) An automatic adaptation. Data on change of direction of ommatidial axes presented above indicate that this hypothesis, although adequate for explaining behavioral development in mantids, cannot apply to *Ranatra*.

Focal observations on *Ranatra* immediately after a moult revealed very unusual postmoult behavior (Cloarec, 1980b). The 4-hr period between moulting and cuticle darkening is characterized by slow opening and closing of claws and slow raising toward the head then lowering of foreleg femurs. This behavior pattern is very similar from one instar to another. The postmoult period has been divided into three phases on behavioral criteria:

Phase 1, lasting approximately 25 min: claws usually remain closed, very few foreleg movements.
Phase 2, lasting also approximately 25 min: forelegs stretched out in front, claws open, no foreleg movements.
Phase 3, lasting much longer (mean 205 min): many claw and femur movements.

Later during an instar no such movements are observed: Controls in the absence of prey items do not show any similar claw or femur movements. Developmental stage does not influence the duration of phases, but the rates of claw and femur movements during Phase 3 increase significantly with age. Phase 3 and the postmoult period end when all claw and femur movements cease in the absence of potential prey.

There is no reference in the literature to anything like this particular postmoult behavior. The main question that these observations raise concerns the function of this relatively complex and energy costly process for an insect, especially when duration of *Ranatra*'s larval development is considered, as instars are relatively short (from 5 to 15 days).

Proximity of moulting influences capture success (Cloarec, 1969a): On the first and last day of an instar the percentage of successful strikes is significantly less than on other days, and the proportion of simple strike movements in relation to all strike movements recorded is significantly higher.

Behavioral modification prior to moulting can be related to neurosensory changes; all the morphological and physiological evidence available indicates that sense organs are functional immediately after ecdysis is over. For example, moulting does not affect vibratory sensitivity in *Barathra* caterpillars until 1 or 2 hr before ecdysis, when the threshold of vibration sensitivity rises. However by the time ecdysis is over, all the new morphological structures have developed and the sense organs are functional immediately after the old cuticle is shed (Gnatzy and Tautz, 1977).

As the special foreleg movements in *Ranatra* cease when the cuticle has darkened and therefore hardened, maybe phenomena related to the hardening of the cuticle could stimulate such movements through reflexes elicited by receptors under the cuticle, particularly at the coxa–femur and femur-tibiotarsus articulations. This limb exercise presumably ensures that the cuticle has the right shape before tanning is complete and feeding starts. Slight deformations could well reduce strike efficiency. On the other hand, this exercise could be related to the lengthening of muscles readjusting to the new dimensions of the forelegs.

These postmoult movements involve considerable energy investment and increase the level of predator risk compared with the usual activity of *Ranatra*. It is reasonable therefore to think that they must have some special adaptive value. One hypothesis is that, as the relationships between foreleg length and performance change after each moult, these postmoult movements are involved in the adjustment of new foreleg length and new positions of ommatidia, thus facilitating the establishment of new links between receptors and effectors to enhance subsequent predatory performance. This could be possible, as there is a similarity between postmoult claw and femur movements and some acts of the predatory sequence (grasping prey and closing claws, establishing contact between prey held in the claws and rostrum before eating, and femur movements).

First instar larvae are most easily disturbed during Phase 1. Their usual reaction is then to swim away. Swimming is accompanied by claw and femur movements although these limbs do not actually participate in swimming. Their role is more for maintaining balance, therefore first instar larvae show higher rates of foreleg movements during Phase 1. This may be an adaptation, as eggs may not have been laid where food is plentiful. First instar larvae have little time to find their first meal: They must eat within 24 hr of hatching or they starve to death. On the other hand, older larvae moult where they were waiting in ambush for prey. If they moult, they must have found enough food to survive and grow at that place. It could be a disadvantage to move away, especially as movement would expose them to predators. However newly emerged adults are also easily disturbed during Phase 1 as well as during the remainder of the postmoult period; they are then more active than older larvae and they can stay underwater longer. Their requirements differ from those of larvae: Bigger prey items are preferred (Blois and Cloarec, 1983), mates and adequate oviposition sites must be found, and so on. Thus it may not be so advantageous for adults to remain at the place where they moulted.

An environmental factor such as the presence of potential prey can influence postmoult behavior by accelerating the whole process. Phases 1 and 3 last longer in the absence of potential prey than in their presence. Rates of claw and femur movements during Phase 3 are significantly higher in the presence of potential prey at all developmental stages. No spatial or temporal relationship between presentation of individual prey items and postmoult claw or femur movements could be found (Cloarec, 1980b).

### K. Exposure and Deprivation of *Ranatra* during Postmoult Periods

The influence of the differences in quantity of foreleg movements between subjects spending their postmoult periods "exposed" to potential prey and those "deprived" of potential prey on subsequent predatory performance was examined by Cloarec (1981).

*Ranatra* moulting in the absence of prey items did not appear to improve their predatory performance from one instar to another as much as those that moulted in the presence of prey. Strike efficiency was lower in deprived animals because: (1) their overall catching success was lower (Fig. 16), (2) their

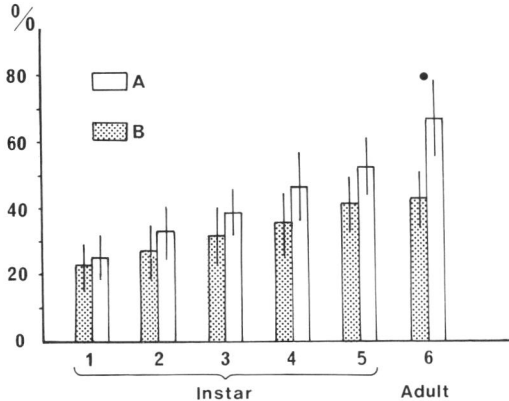

FIG. 16. Capture success. Percentage of hits in relation to the total number of strikes, for each developmental stage. A, exposed animals; B, deprived animals; black dot, significant difference ($p < .05$, Mann-Whitney) between values for Groups A and B; bars, *SD*.

maximum strike and hit distances were shorter (Fig. 17), (3) the proportion of their complex predatory movements was lower and therefore the space within which prey could be caught was reduced (Fig. 18), and (4) they seemed to react less accurately to prey and appeared to misjudge predator-prey distances, usually by undershooting.

Differences in general strike efficiency between subjects of the two groups were statistically significant only for adults, that is, only after six moults with or without prey present. There was also strong individual variation in performance. However, there were significant differences between the two groups for other measures of predatory behavior (strike and hit ranges, maximum strike and hit distances, the proportion of complex predatory movements) (Cloarec, 1981).

The effect of deprivation appears to be gradual and cumulative. The relative influence of postmoult periods at different stages of postembryonic development was tested, although only two cases of change of postmoult conditions (from deprivation to exposure and vice versa) were tested out of all the possible combinations: In one, conditions during the first postmoult period differed from conditions during later postmoult periods, and in the other the conditions were changed during the last postmoult period.

Each postmoult period is important, and a change of conditions from one instar to the next immediately modifies subsequent predatory performance. Not all postmoult periods had the same effect. A change after the first period

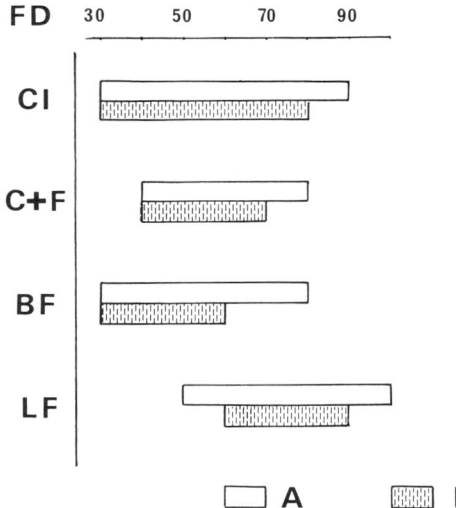

FIG. 17. Hit ranges for the four predatory movement categories. A, exposed animals; B, deprived animals; Cl, C+F, BF, LF, predatory movement category; FD, relative measure of predator-prey distance.

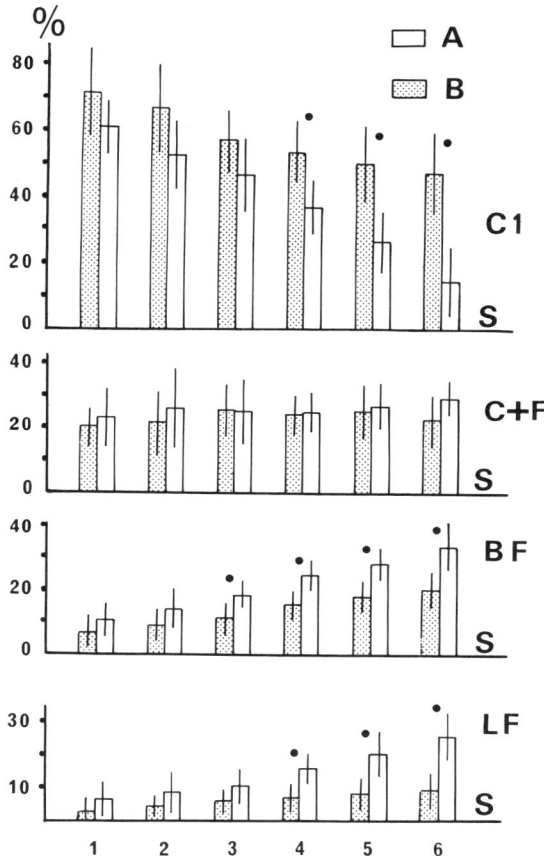

FIG. 18. Distribution of strikes as a function of predatory movement categories, shown as a percentage of each type of strike movement in relation to the total number of strikes. A, exposed animals; B, deprived animals; C1, C+F, BF, LF, predatory movement category, see Fig. 13; black dot, significant difference ($p < .05$, Mann-Whitney) between values for Groups A and B; bars, SD.

did not influence subsequent adult predatory performance significantly, but it did affect survival rate. Nevertheless, total compensation for deprivation during the first postmoult period appeared impossible, as adult predatory performance was then still poorer.

When the change in postmoult conditions occurred for the last (imaginal) postmoult period, adults showed a predatory performance intermediate between that of totally deprived subjects and that of continuously exposed ones: Conditions during the last postmoult period appear to influence predatory performance as much as those during all the preceding postmoult periods (Cloarec, 1983).

The effect persisted during adult life. However, predatory performance of both exposed and deprived *Ranatra* improved significantly with time: Capture success, hit and strike ranges, and the proportion of complex predatory movements all increased, but values of these parameters for subjects of the deprived group never reached the level of those for the exposed group (Cloarec, 1985).

The presence or absence of potential prey items during Phase 3 of the postmoult periods, when the foreleg claw and femur movement occur, and only during that phase, had exactly the same effect on subsequent predatory performance as the presence or the absence of potential prey during the entire postmoult period (Cloarec, 1982a).

The absence of potential prey during the postmoult periods appears to deprive *Ranatra* of some kind of stimulation necessary for the successful estimation of predator-prey distance. It seems reasonable to hypothesize from these observations that less stimulation and fewer foreleg movements during postmoult periods impair subsequent predatory performance and that these movements afford *Ranatra* some sort of exercise or experience and stimulate the animal in some way that influences predatory capacities, perhaps by increasing proprioceptive input and familiarization with new foreleg position and length.

Within the limits of specific constraints, earlier experience with potential prey (i.e., the amount of foreleg, claw, and femur movements) affects the development of a behavior pattern and hence increases individual variation in adult behavior. The greater rate of movement during Phase 3 of the postmoult period has a certain adaptational value in that exposed larvae develop quicker and survive better than deprived animals do, no doubt due to higher subsequent capture success.

It is not the lack of opportunity to find food just after moulting that increases death rate, because immediately after the postmoult periods all animals were given surplus prey, but probably the poorer predatory performance of deprived subjects. Presumably fewer deprived larvae manage to catch enough prey to survive.

These observations seem to indicate that the foreleg movements that occur during the postmoult periods help *Ranatra* to establish a new relationship between receptors, effectors, and performance at the beginning of each instar, and ensure appropriate development of the catching mechanism. In addition, genetic factors may influence these changes that occur during development, and the higher rates of movement during the postmoult periods may facilitate a maturational process such as shaping the foreleg articulations while the cuticle is hardening.

Further investigations into the mechanisms underlying variability of postmoult behavior looked at the separate effects of visual and mechanical stimuli received from potential prey during the postmoult periods and evaluated their influence on subsequent predatory performance. Under normal conditions, information through mechanoreceptors and eyes combine to elicit a predatory attempt (Cloarec, 1976). Deprivation of visual cues during the postmoult periods impaired subsequent predatory performance, but not to the same extent as the absence of both visual and mechanical cues.

Postmoult mechanical stimulation improves the accuracy of simple strikes only, whereas visual stimulation improves the subsequent accuracy of more complex movements (Cloarec, 1982b). Mechanical stimulation alone cannot compensate completely for the absence of visual stimulation. It seems, therefore, that during the postmoult periods *Ranatra* receives multichannel information which is used in readjustment associated with the estimation of predatory–prey distance.

## VI. Discussion

It has been possible to show that in an insect like *Ranatra* individual experience (i.e., the amount of foreleg, claw, and femur movements during the postmoult periods) can affect the development of a behavior pattern and hence increase individual variation in adult behavior.

Such influences of experience have hardly been analyzed before in insects. In their study on the ontogeny of mantid predatory behavior, Balderrama and Maldonado (1973) did not consider the influence of experience on distance estimation. By comparing the predatory behavior of mantids raised on live flies with that of isolated hand-fed animals, Rilling *et al.* (1959) showed that the stimulus–response relations of acts following catching prey can be quantitatively modified during the life of an individual. Nevertheless, it is not known whether in this case practice influenced grasping efficiency, correct distance estimation, or both.

The phenomenon described here could be more common in insects than we know; several cases showing that insects may be susceptible to certain environmental variables only during restricted periods have already been described. Some phytophagous insects may change their preference after exposure to certain plants (Jermy *et al.*, 1968; Schoonhoven, 1977; Traynier, 1986). Exposure to cocoons during the first week after emergence is a critical requirement for the development of cocoon nursing in *Formica polyctena* ants (Jaisson and Fresneau, 1978). In the ant *Cataglyphis cursor*, early imaginal experience merely attenuates, but does not reverse, brood preference. The main process affecting colony-brood recognition then seems to occur during larval life (Isingrini *et al.*, 1986). This is a rare case in insects that shows that experience at two different times during development can influence subsequent behavior. However, the present case of repeated exposure-sensitive periods is unusual if not unique among insects. Nevertheless, it may be unusual only because ontogeny of insect behavior has not been investigated from this angle yet.

Some problems insects have to face in an aquatic environment are very different from those facing terrestrial insects, for example those concerning respiration and thermoregulation, but others such as foraging are not. Comparisons of development of predatory behavior in *Ranatra* with what is known of similar developments in terrestrial predatory insects revealed two different developmental patterns, but many analogies between adults. I have concentrated on a single species and have described different interactions among various mechanisms, factors, and behavior in *Ranatra* with a view to elucidating the place of this species in its community. I have revealed several highly specialized adaptations with which *Ranatra* cope with its complex environment, although the picture is not complete, if indeed it ever will be.

*Ranatra* show several adaptations that can hardly be considered primitive. Torre-Bueno (1916) suggested that "aquatic Hemiptera were a series that displays so many highly specialized (and therefore not primitive) adaptations to a very special environment." Among aquatic Heteroptera, *Ranatra* is considered one of the more advanced Nepidae (Landsbury, 1981). The first Heteroptera (no doubt terrestrial) appeared during the upper Triassic, and the family Nepidae has been traced back to the upper Jurassic (Grassé, 1976).

Analysis of ontogenetic history is necessary to understand individual variations in behavior and the presence of alternative tactics which confer unequal fitness on their bearers. I have presented here two different development patterns: (1) an age-related variation in spatial distribution that is closely bound to respiratory requirements, and (2) a developmental mechanism that appears responsible for alternative predatory tactics and that influences survival rate directly. It must not be forgotten that spatial distribution and capture success are not independent: Perch site influences prey-encounter rate.

More investigations are needed to understand the evolution of the marked energetic investment in foreleg, claw, and femur movements during the postmoult periods which no doubt increase predation risk, as movement is the commonest cue to finding prey, when *Ranatra* is most vulnerable (the cuticle has not hardened). In addition, *Ranatra* react to a disturbance during the postmoult period by swimming away and not by death-feigning, as at other times. Apart from this exception, the other behavior patterns appear to be a good compromise between different constraints.

### References

Alexander, R., and McNeill, S. (1971). "Animal Mechanics." Sidgewick & Jackson, London.
Bailey, P. C. E. (1981). Diel activity patterns in nymphs of an Australian mayfly *Atalophlebioides sp.* (Ephemeroptera: Leptophlebiidae). *Aust. J. Mar. Freshwater Res.* **32**, 121-131.

Bailey, P. C. E. (1986a). The feeding behaviour of a sit-and-wait predator, *Ranatra dispar* (Heteroptera: Nepidae). Description of behavioural components of prey capture, and the effect of food deprivation on predator arousal and capture dynamics. *Behaviour* **97**, 66-93.

Bailey, P. C. E. (1986b). The effect of predation risk on the predatory behaviour of a sit-and-wait predator *Ranatra dispar* (Heteroptera: Nepidae), the water stick insect. *J. Ethol* **4**, 17-25.

Balderrama, N., and Maldonado, H. (1973). Ontogeny of the behaviour in the praying mantis. *J. Insect Physiol.* **19**, 319-336.

Baldus, K. (1926). Experimentelle Untersuchungen über die Entfernungslokalisation der Libellen (*Aeschna cyanea*). *Z. Vergl. Physiol* **3**, 472-505.

Barros Pita, J. E., and Maldonado, H. (1970). A fovea in the praying mantis eye. II: Some morphological characteristics. *Z. Vergl. Physiol.* **67**, 79-92.

Barton-Browne, L., and Evans, D. R. (1960). Locomotor activity of the blowfly as a function of feeding and starvation. *J. Insect Physiol.* **4**, 27-37.

Bauer, T. (1981). Prey capture and structure of the visual space of an insect that hunts by sight on the litter layer (*Notiophilus biguttatus* F., Carabidae: Coleoptera). *Behav. Ecol. Sociobiol.* **8**, 91-97.

Baunacke, W. (1912). Statische Sinnesorgane bei den Nepiden. *Zool. Jahrb. Abt. Anat. Ontogen. Tiere* **34**, 179-346.

Berezina, N. A. (1959). Energetic balance of the larvae of the dragonfly *Aeshna grandis* L. *Tr. mosk. tekhnol. Inst. ryb. Prom. Khoz.* **10**, 58-61 (in Russian).

Bertrand, H. (1954a). Les insectes aquatiques d'Europe *Encycl. Entomol* **30**, 1-566.

Bertrand, H. (1954b). Les insectes aquatiques d'Europe. *Encycl. Entomol.* **31**, 1-547.

Blinn, D. W., Pinney, C., and Sanderson, M. (1983). Nocturnal planktonic behavior of *Ranatra montezuma* Polhemus (Nepidae: Hemiptera) in Montezuma Well, Arizona. *J. Kansas Entomol. Soc.* **55**, 481-484.

Blois, C., and Cloarec, A. (1983). Density dependent prey selection in the water stick insect *Ranatra linearis* (Heteroptera). *J. Anim. Ecol.* **52**, 849-866.

Blois, C. and Cloarec, A. (1988). Diel variations of food intake in *Anax imperator* and *Aeshna cyanea* larvae. *Biol. Behav.*, in press.

Brittain, J. E., and Nagell, B. (1981). Overwintering at low oxygen concentrations in the mayfly *Leptophlebia vespertina*. *Oikos* **36**, 45-50.

Burkhardt, D., Darnhofer-Demer, B., and Fischer, K. (1973). Zum binokularen Entfernungssehen der Insekten. I. *J. Comp. Physiol.* **87**, 165-188.

Chmurzynski, J. A. (1963). Some remarks on the optics of the *Bembex rostrata* (L.) eye (Hymenoptera: Sphegidae). *Zool. Pol.* **13**, 111-135.

Cloarec, A. (1969a). Etude descriptive et expérimentale du comportement de capture de *Ranatra linearis* au cours de son ontogenèse. *Behaviour* **35**, 84-113.

Cloarec, A. (1969b). Contribution à l'étude des rythmes d'activité locomotrice de *Ranatra linearis* (Insecte Hétéroptère aquatique). *Rev. Comp. Anim.* **3**, 11-25.

Cloarec, A. (1972a). Activité respiratoire de *Ranatra linearis* (Insecte, Hétéroptère aquatique). *Bull. Soc. Zool. Fr.* **97**, 729-736.

Cloarec, A. (1972b). Variations du comportement respiratoire au cours du développement larvaire de *Ranatra linearis*. *Rev. Comp. Anim.* **6**, 237-244.

Cloarec, A. (1974). A study of the postural variations of the foreleg of *Ranatra linearis* (Insect, Heteroptera). *Behaviour* **48**, 89-110.

Cloarec, A. (1975a). Variations quantitatives de la prise alimentaire chez *Ranatra linearis* L. (Hétéroptère aquatique carnivore). *Ann. Nutr. Aliment.* **29**, 245-257.

Cloarec, A. (1975b). Variations quantitatives circadiennes de la prise alimentaire des larves d'*Anax imperator* Leach (Anisoptera: Aeshnidae). *Odonatologica* **4**, 137-147.

Cloarec, A. (1976). Interactions between different receptors involved in prey capture in *Ranatra linearis* (Insect Heteroptera). *Biol. Behav.* **1**, 251-266.

Cloarec, A. (1979). Estimation of hit distance by *Ranatra*. *Biol. Behav.* **4**, 173-191.

Cloarec, A. (1980a). Ontogeny of hit distance estimation in *Ranatra*. *Biol. Behav.* **5**, 97–118.
Cloarec, A. (1980b). Post-moult behaviour in the water-stick insect *Ranatra linearis*. *Behaviour* **73**, 304–324.
Cloarec, A. (1981). Effect on predatory performance of the presence of prey after moulting in the water stick insect *Ranatra linearis*. *Physiol. Entomol.* **6**, 241–249.
Cloarec, A. (1982a). Predatory success in the water stick insect: the role of visual and mechanical stimulations after moulting. *Anim. Behav.* **30**, 549–556.
Cloarec, A. (1982b). Influence of the duration of deprivation on the predatory performance of the water stick insect. *Z. Tierpsychol.* **58**, 217–230.
Cloarec, A. (1983). Deprivation of prey during development of the water stick insect *Ranatra linearis*. *Biol. Behav.* **8**, 141–157.
Cloarec, A. (1984). Mechanismes intervenant dans l'estimation des distances prédateur-proie chez *Ranatra*. *Behav. Processes* **9**, 123–133.
Cloarec, A. (1985). Persistance of deprivation effects in the water stick insect. *Biol. Behav.* **10**, 279–289.
Cloarec, A. (1986). Distance and size discrimination in a water stick insect *Ranatra linearis* (Heteroptera). *J. Exp. Biol.* **120**, 59–77.
Cloarec, A. (1988). Variations of behavioural patterns during development in the water stick insect. In preparation.
Collett, T. S., and Land, M. F. (1975). Visual control of flight behaviour in the hoverfly *Syritta pipens*. *J. Comp. Phsyiol.* **99**, 1–66.
Corbet, P. S. (1962). "A Biology of Dragonflies." Witherby, London.
Dahm, E. (1972). Zur Biologie von *Notonecta glauca* (Insecta: Hemiptera) unter besonderer Berücksichtigung der fischereilichen Schadwirkung. *Int. Rev. gesamten Hydrobiol.* **57**, 429–561.
Elliott, J. M. (1968). The daily activity patterns of mayfly nymphs (Ephemeroptera). *J. Zool. (London)* **155**, 201–221.
Elliott, J. M. (1970). The diel activity patterns of caddis larvae (Trichoptera). *J. Zool. (London)* **160**, 279–290.
Etienne, A. S. (1972). The behaviour of the dragonfly larva *Aeschna cyanea* M. after a short presentation of a prey. *Anim. Behav.* **20**, 724–731.
Evans, S. M., and Downie, P. J. (1986). Decision making processes in the polychaete *Platynereis dumerilii*. *Anim. Behav.* **34**, 472–479.
Faucheux, M. (1977). Contribution à l'étude de la respiration et de la nutrition chez quelques insectes aquatiques des marais salants: *Stratiomyia, Nemotelus, Ephydra, Aedes* (Diptères), *Berosus* (Coléoptère), *Sigara* (Hétéroptère); importance des soies hydrofuges et des appareils filtrants. *Soc. Sci. Nat. Ouest Fr.* **75**, 56–68.
Fedorenko, A. Y. (1975a). Instar and species-specific diets in two species of *Chaoborus*. *Limnol. Oceanogr.* **20**, 238–249.
Fedorenko, A. Y. (1975b). Feeding characteristics and predation impact of *Chaoborus* (Diptera: Chaoboridae) larvae in a small lake. *Limnol. Oceanogr.* **20**, 250–258.
Fox, L. R. (1975). Some demographic consequences of food shortage for the predator, *Notonecta hoffmanni*. *Ecology* **56**, 868–880.
Friederichs, H. F. (1931). Beiträge zur Morphologie und Physiologie der Sehorgane der Cicindelinen (Col.). *Z. Morphol. Okol. Tiere* **21**, 1–172.
Giller, P. S. (1982). Locomotory efficiency in the predation strategies of the British *Notonecta* (Hemiptera: Heteroptera). *Oecologia* **52**, 273–277.
Giller, P. S., and McNeill, S. (1981). Predation strategies, resource partitioning and habitat selection in *Notonecta* (Hemiptera: Heteroptera). *J. Anim. Ecol.* **50**, 789–808.
Gittelman, S. H. (1974). Locomotion and predatory strategy in backswimmers (Hemiptera: Notonectidae). *Am. Midl. Natl.* **92**, 496–500.
Gittelman, S. H. (1977). Leg segment proportions, predatory strategy and growth in backswimmers (Hemiptera: Pleidae, Notonectidae). *J. Kansas Entomol. Soc.* **50**, 161–171.

Gittelman, S. H., and Bergtrom, G. (1977). Depth selection in two species of *Buenoa* (Hemiptera: Notonectidae). *Ann. Entomol. Soc. Am.* **70**, 469–476.

Gnatzy, W., and Tautz, J. (1977). Sensitivity of an insect mechanoreceptor during moulting. *Physiol. Entomol.* **2**, 279–288.

Grassé, P.-P. (1976). L'appareil respiratoire. *In* "Traité de Zoologie. VIII: Insectes. 4: Splanchnologie, phonation, vie aquatique, rapports avec les plantes/publ. sous la dir. de P.-P. Grassé," Vol. 8, pp. 93–204. Masson, Paris.

Gray, P. T. A., and Mill, P. J. (1983). The mechanics of the predatory strike of the praying mantid *Heirodula membranacae*. *J. Exp. Biol.* **107**, 245–275.

Halliday, T. R. (1977). The effect of experimental manipulation of breathing behaviour on the sexual behaviour of the smooth newt *Triturus vulgaris*. *Anim. Behav.* **25**, 39–45.

Hassell, M. P., and Southwood, T. R. E. (1978). Foraging strategies of insects. *Annu. Rev. Ecol. Syst.* **9**, 75–98.

Holling, C. S. (1964). The analysis of complex population processes. *Can. Entomol.* **96**, 335–347.

Horn, E. (1975). The contribution of different receptors to gravity orientation in insects. *Fortschr. Zool.* 1–20.

Horridge, G. A., and Duelli, P. (1979). Anatomy of the regional differences in the eye of the mantis *Ciulfina*. *J. Exp. Biol.* **80**, 165–190.

Hughes, G. M., and Mill, P. J. (1966). Patterns of ventilation in dragonfly larvae. *J. Exp. Biol.* **44**, 317–333.

Hynes, H. B. N. (1984). The relationships between the taxonomy and ecology of aquatic insects. *In* "The Ecology of Aquatic Insects" (V. H. Resh and D. M. Rosenberg, eds.), pp. 9–23. Praeger, New York.

Isingrini, M., Jaisson, P., and Lenoir, A. (1986). Influence of preimaginal experience on the social adult ants and the importance of fellow in nest mate recognition. *In* "The Individual and Society" (L. Passera and J. P. Lachaud, eds.), pp. 49–53. Privat, Toulouse.

Jaisson, P., and Fresneau, D. (1978). The sensitivity and responsiveness of ants to their cocoons in relation to age and methods of measurement. *Anim. Behav.* **26**, 1064–1071.

Jermy, T., Hanson, F. E., and Dethier, V. G. (1968). Induction of specific food preference in lepidopterous larvae. *Entomol. Exp. Appl.* **11**, 211–230.

Joly, D. (1984). Essai de caractérisation du site d'affût chez *Ranatra linearis*. Diplôme d'Etudes Approfondies, Rennes (unpublished).

Joly, D., and Cloarec, A. (1988). Choice of perch by the water stick insect. In preparation.

Klekowski, R. Z., and Kamler, E. (1968). Flowing water polarographic respirometer for aquatic animals. *Pol. Arch. Hydrobiol.* **15**, 121–144.

Klyuge, N. Y., Novikova, E. A., and Brodsky, A. K. (1984). Movements of larve of the Ephemeroptera during swimming, respiration and cleaning. *Zool. Zh.* **63**, 1345–1354 (in Russian).

Kosicki, S. (1966). The mobility of *Ranatra linearis* L. and its thermal background. *Ann. Univ. Mariae-Curie-Sklodowska Sect. C. Biol.* **21**, 75–106.

Lacombe, H. (1974). La respiration de la larve d'*Aeschna cyanea* (Odonate, Anisoptère). Diplôme d'Etudes Approfondies, Lyon (unpublished).

Landsbury, J. (1981). Aquatic and semi-aquatic bugs (Hemiptera) of Australia. *Ecol. Biogeogr. Aust.* **43**, 1197–1211.

LaRow, E. J. (1970). The effect of oxygen tension on the vertical migration of *Chaoborus* larvae. *Limnol. Oceanogr.* **15**, 357–362.

Lawton, J. H. (1971). Ecological energetics studies on larvae of the damselfly *Pyrrhosoma nymphulae* (Sulzer) (Odonata: Zygoptera). *J. Anim. Ecol.* **40**, 385–423.

Lewis, W., Jr. (1977). Feeding selectivity of a tropical *Chaoborus* population. *Freshwater Biol.* **7**, 311–325.

Macan, T. T. (1962). Ecology of aquatic insects. *Annu. Rev. Entomol.* **7**, 261–288.

McFarland, D. J. (1974). Time sharing as a behavioral phenomenon. *Adv. Study Behav.* **5**, 201–225.

Maldonado, H., and Barros-Pita, J. C. (1970). A fovea in the praying mantis eye. I: Estimation of the catching distance. *Z. Vergl. Physiol.* **67**, 58–78.
Maldonado, H., and Levin, L. (1967). Distance estimation and the monocular cleaning reflex in praying mantis. *Z. Verg. Physiol.* **56**, 258–267.
Maldonado, H., Levin, L., and Barros-Pita, J. C. (1967). Hit distance and the predatory strike of the praying mantis. *Z. Vergl. Physiol.* **56**, 237–257.
Maldonado, H., Rodriguez, E., and Balderrama, N. (1974). How mantids gain insight into the new maximum catching distance after each ecdysis. *J. Insect Physiol.* **20**, 591–603.
Meyer, H. W. (1973). Differenzierte Orientierungsleistung und räumliche Organisation des Insektenauges. *Fortschr. Zool.* **21**, 294–306.
Mill, P. J., and Hughes, G. M. (1966). The nervous control of ventilation in dragonfly larvae. *J. Exp. Biol.* **44**, 297–316.
Miller, P. L. (1977). Motor responses to changes in the volume and pressure of the gas stores of a submerged water-bug *Lethocerus cordofanus*. *Physiol. Entomol.* **2**, 27–36.
Mittelstaedt, H. (1957). Prey capture in mantids. In "Recent Advances in Invertebrate Physiology" (B. T. Scheer, ed.), pp. 51–71. University of Oregon.
Mittelstaedt, H. (1962). Control systems of orientation in insects. *Annu. Rev. Entomol.* **7**, 177–198.
Murdoch, W. W., and Sih, A. (1978). Age-dependent interference in a predatory insect. *J. Anim. Ecol.* **47**, 581–592.
Parsons, M. C. (1972). Respiratory significance of the thoracic and abdominal morphology of *Belostoma* and *Ranatra* (Insecta: Heteroptera). *Z. Morphol. Tiere* **73**, 163–193.
Parsons, M. C. (1974). Anterior displacement of the metathoracic spiracle and lateral intersegmental boundary in the prothorax of Hydrocorixae (Aquatic Heteroptera). *Z. Morphol. Tiere* **79**, 165–198.
Parsons, M. C. (1976). Respiratory significance of the thoracic and abdominal morphology of three Corixidae *Diaprepocoris, Micronecta* and *Hesperocorixa* (Hemiptera: Heteroptera: Hydrocorisae). *Psyche* **83**, 132–179.
Petitpren, M. F., and Knight, A. W. (1970). Oxygen consumption of the dragonfly *Anax junius*. *J. Insect Physiol.* **16**, 449–459.
Pickard, R. S., and Mill, P. J. (1974). The effects of carbon dioxide and oxygen on respiratory dorso-ventral muscle activity during normal ventilation in *Anax imperator* Leach (Anisoptera: Aeshnidae). *Odonatologica* **3**, 249–255.
Popham, E. J. (1960). On the respiration of aquatic Hemiptera Heteroptera with special reference to the Corixidae. *Proc. Zool. Soc. London* **135**, 209–242.
Pritchard, G. (1966). On the morphology of the compound eye of dragonflies, Odonata: Anisoptera, with special reference to their role in prey capture. *Proc. Entomol. Soc. London* **41**, 1–8.
Radinovsky, S. (1964). Cannibal of the pond. *Nat. Hist.* **11**, 16–24.
Rilling, S., Mittelstaedt, H., and Roeder, K. D. (1959). Prey recognition in the praying mantis. *Behaviour* **14**, 164–184.
Rossel, S. (1979). Regional differences in photoreceptor performance in the eye of the praying mantis. *J. Comp. Physiol. A* **131**, 95–112.
Rossel, S. (1983). Binocular stereopsis in an insect. *Nature (London)* **302**, 821–822.
Rowe, R. J. (1985). Intraspecific interactions of New Zealand damselfly larvae. 1: *Xanthocnemis zealandica, Ischnura aurora* and *Austrolestes colensonis* (Zygoptera: Coenagrionidae: Lestidae), *N. Z. J. Zool.* **12**, 1–15.
Scherer, E. (1965). Zur Methodik experimenteller Fliesswasser-Okologie. *Arch. Hydrobiol.* **61**, 242–248.
Schiodte (1870). Quoted in: Torre Bueno, J. R., de la (1916). *Ann. Nat. Hist.* **4**, 225.
Schoonhoven, L. M. (1977). On the individuality of insect feeding behavior. *Proc. K. Ned. Akad. Wet. C* **80**, 341–350.

Schöne, H. (1962). Optisch gesteuerte Langeänderungen: Versuche an Dytiscidenlarven zur Vertikalorienterung. *Z. Vergl. Physiol.* **45**, 590–604.
Sherk, T. E. (1978a). Development of the compound eyes of dragonflies (Odonata). II: Development of the larval compound eyes. *J. Exp. Zool.* **203**, 47–60.
Sherk, T. E. (1978b). Development of the compound eyes of dragonflies (Odonata). III: Adult compound eyes. *J. Exp. Zool.* **203**, 61–80.
Sherk, T. E. (1978c). Development of the compound eyes of dragonflies (Odonata). IV: Development of the adult compound eyes. *J. Exp. Zool.* **203**, 103–200.
Swain, W. R., Wilson, R. M., Neri, R. P., and Porter, G. S. (1977). A new technique for remote monitoring of activity of freshwater invertebrates with special reference to oxygen consumption by niaids of *Anax sp.* and *Somatochlora sp.* (Odonata). *Can. Entomol.* **109**, 1–8.
Theiss, J. (1982). Generation and radiation of sound by stridulating water insects as exemplified by the corixids. *Behav. Ecol. Sociobiol.* **10**, 225–235.
Thorpe, W. H., and Crips, D. J. (1947). Studies on plastron respiration. *J. Exp. Biol.* **24**, 227–328.
Torre-Bueno, J. R., de la (1916). Aquatic Hemiptera: A study in the relation of structure to environment. *Ann. Entomol. Soc. Am.* **9**, 353–365.
Traynier, R. M. M. (1986). Visual learning in assays of sinigrin solution as an oviposition releaser for the cabbage butterfly *Pieris rapae*. *Entomol. Exp. Appl.* **40**, 25–33.
Usinger, R. L., ed. (1956). "Aquatic insects of California with keys to North American genera and California species." Univ. of California Press, Berkeley.
Venkatesan, P. (1983). Male brooding behaviour of *Diplonychus indicus* Venk & Rao (Hemiptera: Belostomatidae). *J. Kansas Entomol. Soc.* **56**, 80–87.
Vlasblom, A. G. (1970). The respiratory significance of the physical gill in some adult insects. *Comp. Biochem. Physiol.* **36**, 377–385.
Waitzbauer, W. (1974). Die Larvalentwicklung einiger aquatischer Wanzenarten (Insecta; Heteroptera: Hemiptera): *Naucoris cimicoides, Ranatra linearis, Notonecta glauca. Anz. Oesterr. Akad. Wiss. Math. Naturwiss. Kl.* **1**, 77–102.
Waitzbauer, W. (1976). Energieumsatz aquatischer Hemipteren *Naucoris cimicoides* L., *Notonecta glauca* L., *Ranatra linearis*. *Oecologia* **22**, 179–209.
Waitzbauer, W. (1978). Studies in energetics and population dynamics of the water scorpion *Nepa rubra* L. (Insecta: Hemiptera). *Oecologia* **33**, 235–253.
Wiley, M. J., and Kohler, S. L. (1980). Positioning changes of mayfly nymphs due to behavioral regulation of oxygen consumption. *Can. J. Zool.* **58**, 618–612.
Wiley, M. J., and Kohler, S. L. (1984). Behavioral adaptations of aquatic insects. *In* "The Ecology of Aquatic Insects" (V. H. Resh and D. M. Rosenberg, eds.), pp. 101–133. Praeger, New York.
Ydenberg, R. C., and Houston, A. I. (1986). Optimal trade-offs between competing behavioural demands in the great tit. *Anim. Behav.* **34**, 1041–1050.

# The Circadian Organization of Behavior: Timekeeping in the Tsetse Fly, A Model System

JOHN BRADY

DEPARTMENT OF PURE AND APPLIED BIOLOGY
IMPERIAL COLLEGE OF SCIENCE AND TECHNOLOGY
LONDON SW7 2AZ, ENGLAND

## I. INTRODUCTION

Behaviorists generally treat the circadian rhythm of their experimental animal as an inconvenience to the timetabling of their observations; as a phenomenon to be taken account of rather than studied for its own sake. Circadian physiologists, on the other hand, are usually little concerned with the niceties of their animal's behavior; they simply select a species with a good rhythm and concentrate on the underlying clock, either physiologically or, more commonly, phenomenologically.

In reality, an animal's circadian periodicity—in the guise of its sleep-wakefulness cycle—probably causes the greatest and most predictable changes in its "motivational" level. Nevertheless, few species have had their behavior studied from a circadian point of view. The most obvious case is man, in whom many psychomotor rhythms have been measured, mainly for applied medical reasons (see Aschoff, 1982). But the circadian organization of man's behavior is highly complex, subject to numerous social and other inputs that modify its timekeeping, and thus difficult to generalize from. Other notable cases are water snails, in which Morgan and Last (1982) and Chaudhry and Morgan (1983) measured five different behaviors through several circadian cycles; zebra finches, in which Ollason and Slater (1973) measured the changes in six different behaviors; and house flies, in which Parker (1962) performed a rather similar study. Alternatively, there has been the approach of Jones and Gubbins (1978) and Chiba *et al.* (1985), who examined in mosquitoes the circadian effects of different behavioral inputs (feeding, mating, oviposition) on a single rhythmic output (locomotion).

The work on the tsetse fly, however, is unique. In no other animal has a study been made not only of several different circadian behavioral rhythms, but also of the rhythm-modulating effects of both behavioral and nonbehavioral inputs. This review therefore analyses what is known of the circadian organization of the tsetse's behavior, in the hope that it may serve as a paradigm for other species' behavioral timekeeping. It reveals much of general interest about the interplay between circadian "clocks" and behavioral integration.

## II. Bouting of Flight

### A. Physiological Background

Tsetse flies, especially bush-savannah species such as *Glossina morsitans*, flourish in hot, arid habitats in Africa at remarkably low densities; for example, with minimum populations of around 50 pairs $km^{-2}$ (Glasgow, 1963) and with less than 10-fold seasonal population changes (Jordan, 1974). Their adaptations are comparably striking. The problem of nutrition in a dry climate is solved by the adults living exclusively on vertebrate blood and by total viviparity for the larvae (each adult female depositing every 10 days or so one fully grown larva which immediately buries itself and pupates). Since a 25-mg female must be able to carry a 20–30-mg larva, and both sexes may take 50-mg blood-meals, the cost of this lifestyle is a severe weight problem. That is solved in part by having a large flight musculature, ca. 40% of the body weight, or twice that of most other Diptera (Hargrove, 1975), and in part by burning the amino acid proline as flight fuel, which provides 0.52 moles ATP $g^{-1}$ as against 0.18 moles ATP $g^{-1}$ for carbohydrates (Bursell *et al.*, 1974).

This metabolic dependence on proline has profound consequences for the way tsetse flies distribute their activity in time. For *Glossina morsitans*, 2 min of flight exhausts most of the free proline in the thorax, and flight thereafter can only be sustained with difficulty, by the slow mobilization of proline from the abdominal fat body (Bursell *et al.*, 1974; Bursell, 1978). Long before the thoracic proline is burned up, however, wing-beat frequency and lift are already rapidly declining (Hargrove, 1975). Presumably as a response to this metabolic stress, flights in nature rarely last longer than 1 min (Bursell and Slack, 1969; see Brady, 1972b, p. 275), even though they can be forced for longer when the flies are supported on flight mills (Hargrove, 1975; Bursell, 1978).

### B. Flight Structure in the Laboratory

In actograph cages, tsetse flies are active in similar short bursts (Fig. 1; Brady, 1970), with each burst typically consisting of about thirty 2-s flights, interspersed with brief rests of ca. 2 s, bouts of preening (ca. 5 s), and one or two short walks (ca. 1 s) (Nichols, 1979). These flight bursts are strikingly

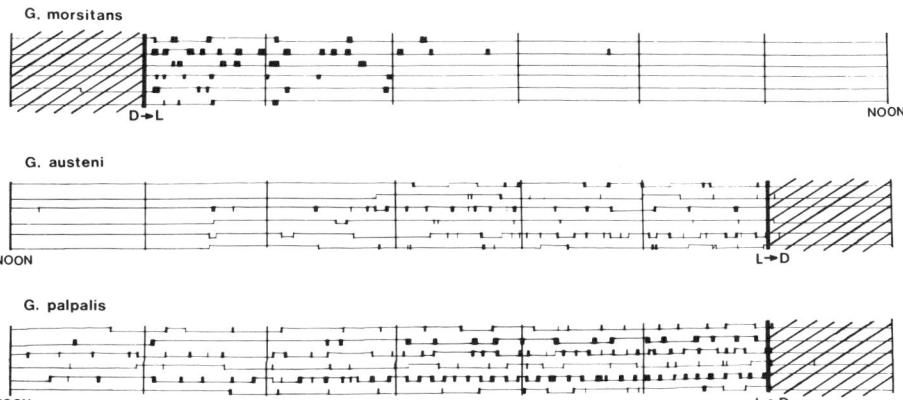

FIG. 1. Spontaneous flight patterns of 18 immature male tsetse flies of three different species recorded in rocking cage actographs. Each horizontal line is the record of the six most active hours of one fly: for *Glossina morsitans* from lights-on to midday, for *austeni* and *palpalis* from midday to lights-out. Note that activity, shown by vertical excursions of the trace, occurs exclusively in short bursts of flight, mostly lasting < 60 s (see Tables I and II). (After Crump and Brady, 1979.)

consistent for any one individual or species: For a typical group of immature male *G. morsitans* they have a mean recorded duration of about 50 s, with a coefficient of variation of only 35% (though direct observation indicates that the real length of a burst can be up to twice this, Nichols, 1979).

The actographs used are small (ca. 15 × 8 body lengths × 4 high), but the daily number of flight bursts in them is nevertheless about the same as in a large arena (ca. 85 × 50 body lengths × 50 high). However, the duration of each burst in the arena is less than half that in actographs, even though the individual flights, rests, preens, and walks within the burst are all about twice as long. With much greater flight space, therefore, the flies make the same number of flight bursts, but each burst consists of fewer, longer, separate actions (Nichols, 1979).

The daily pattern of flight bursts is modulated by a steep rise in activity from day to day in response to increasing food deprivation (Brady, 1975a). This evidently applies to all tsetse regardless of sex, age, or species (Crump and Brady, 1979). Mature male *G. morsitans*, for example, are some five times more active 5 days after a blood-meal than they are 24 hr after it (Figs. 3A and 6). This dramatic modulation of activity level, as with the modulation due to the circadian rhythm, occurs exclusively as a result of changes in the frequency of flight bursts; no significant change in mean burst duration takes place (Tables I and II), although changes in the internal structure of a burst may occur (Nichols, 1979). Modulation of activity level, due to whatever cause, therefore occurs by changing the probability of a flight burst occurring,

TABLE I

Changes Relative to Starvation Level in Duration of Flight Bursts in Male Tsetse Flies (Mean ± SE in sec)[a]

|  | Days unfed since emergence | | |
| --- | --- | --- | --- |
|  | Day 1 | Day 2 | Day 3 |
| G. morsitans | 49 ± 6 | 44 ± 5 | 48 ± 7 |
| G. austeni | 32 ± 3 | 28 ± 2 | 29 ± 2 |
| G. palpalis | 34 ± 2 | 37 ± 2 | 42 ± 2 |

[a] No within-species differences are significant ($p > .05$); $n = 25$–$28$ days per mean.

and whenever flight occurs it does so for a relatively fixed period (whether spontaneous or stimulus-evoked, see Brady, 1972b, Figs. 3 and 5; Nichols, 1979).

Much of animal behavior is performed through this phenomenon of *bouting*, that is, activity in effect occurring as unitary points separated by variable gaps (Slater, 1975). It has, however, been largely overlooked in circadian research, except by Nichols (1979) and Peterson (1980), presumably because the active phases of popular experimental animals such as rats, finches, and cockroaches are so intense that any bouting is obscured. Peterson's analysis shows that although the minute-by-minute distribution of activity in mosquitoes is largely stochastic, the daily structure is subject to

TABLE II

Changes Relative to Time of Day in Duration of Flight Bursts in Male Tsetse Flies (Mean ± SE in sec)[a]

|  | Dawn[b] | Noon[c] | Dusk[d] |
| --- | --- | --- | --- |
| G. morsitans | 50 ± 5 | 46 ± 6 | 45 ± 6 |
| G. austeni | 27 ± 2 | 26 ± 2 | 29 ± 2 |
| G. palpalis | 39 ± 6 | 37 ± 3 | 38 ± 3 |

[a] Means (sec) of first three unfed, postemergence days; no within-species differences are significant ($p > .05$); $n = 25$–$28$ days per mean.
[b] Mean of first 2 hr of photophase.
[c] Mean of middle 6 hr.
[d] Mean of last 2 hr.

a rhythmic modulation of the probability of transitions from rest to flight. The rhythm therefore arises by the circadian control of the durations of the bouts of inactivity.

The same is clearly true also for tsetse although—as an apparent consequence of rapid fuel consumption in flight alternating with slow regeneration at rest—the activity sometimes exhibits quasirhythmic episodes, with periods in the range of several minutes to an hour or two (as in the last two lines of Fig. 1 above; and Brady, 1970). This is evidently not an uncommon phenomenon in animal behavior (e.g., Jones *et al.*, 1967, p. 506; Clopton, 1984, fine detail of Fig. 1; Daan and Aschoff, 1981); there is, nevertheless, no evidence that any such metabolic relaxation oscillation participates in the circadian timing of the tsetse's behavior.

It is thus important to realize that, except for Fig. 1, the figures presented below (and previously, Brady, 1988 *et ante*) are misleading in one behaviorally significant respect. They are form estimates of an individual's activity pattern, compiled by averaging the records of several individuals. This gives the impression that activity level changes smoothly across the day, in a way which does not exist in the individual. Thus, a male *G. morsitans* may perform only five or six widely separated flight bursts over its entire first 24 hr of adult life, and even the most active of flies (Fig. 3A, Day 4) are totally inactive for at least 95% of the time. Flight bursts are rare and, except in the occasional high-frequency episodes, sporadic. It is not possible to predict precisely when one will occur. In the individual they are controlled stochastically, and the curves in the figures represent the mean (low) probability of flight occurring in any one hour.

III. Activity Pattern in Nature: Temperature Effects

In the field, tsetse activity is usually measured by the number of flies that can be caught per hour at some sort of host animal (e.g., man, ox) or in a trap (usually a simple conspicuous visual target, sometimes odor-baited). Published analyses of such catches indicate, with varying precision and detail, the daily pattern of activity of 19 species or subspecies of *Glossina*. Eighteen follow a pattern showing activity mostly in the morning and/or evening, relative inactivity through the middle of the day, and almost total inactivity at night (Crump and Brady, 1979). Over 90% of all the approximately 100 published figures for day-long catches that show clear patterns for male *G. morsitans*, *G. pallidipes*, and *G. palpalis* reveal either U-shaped activity patterns in this form, or else a single build-up to an evening peak (for females the score is over 70%).

The diel patterns of these flies are of course strongly affected by environmental conditions, especially temperature (e.g., Pilson and Pilson, 1967; Dean et al., 1969; van Etten, 1982). In cool seasons in central Africa, the air temperature may fall below 10° C by dawn and not rise much above 20° until near midday, only to fall again soon afterwards. Tsetse are reluctant, or unable, to fly at much below about 18° (Brady, 1974a), so under these circumstances their activity is inevitably restricted to the middle of the day. In hot seasons, on the other hand, the dawn temperature may already be above 20° and the afternoon close to 40°. Under these circumstances, the midday high temperature switches on photonegative, shade-seeking behavior (Pilson and Pilson, 1967; Vale, 1971; Huyton and Brady, 1975), and the flies come to baits or traps only near dawn and in the late afternoon.

Activity level is thus positively correlated with temperature over the lower half of the habitat's range, but is negatively correlated with temperature above about 28° C. This relationship can also be demonstrated for spontaneous flight under constant temperature in the laboratory (see Brady and Crump, 1978, Fig. 6).

These field observations have given rise to a tradition that the pattern of tsetse's activity is largely controlled by the air temperature. Closer examination of the published records shows that this is too simple an interpretation, however. If all the day-long catches of *G. morsitans* are converted to standard units by expressing each hour's catch as a percentage of its respective day's total catch, the different records can be aggregated into one large set of over 500 data points. It is then possible to collate all the hourly catches that happened to occur at a particular temperature and follow the activity level across the day for any given temperature, as if it were at "constant" temperature. When this is done (Fig. 2), it is immediately apparent that the activity pattern has a morning and evening peak plus a broad middle-of-the-day trough regardless of the temperature, at all likely temperatures (at least from about 20 to 34° C). Gaps at the "front" and "back" of the graph are not due to the absence of flies but to the absence of the relevant temperatures at these times (J. W. Hargrove, personal communication, has data for up to 40° which essentially continue the time curves in Fig. 2).

The activity of *G. morsitans* in the field is therefore U-shaped without the intervention of any effects of environmental temperature cycles; and van Etten's (1982) data indicate a similar situation in *G. pallidipes* (though in this case each hour covers too small a temperature range for the curves to be so clear).

Moreover, although this U-shape is, of necessity, measured in populations in the field, so that the morning and evening peaks and the midday trough involve different flies which might come from different populations, it has also been amply demonstrated in individuals in constant conditions in actographs (see Section IV). The U-pattern is therefore evidently endogenously generated; indeed, Brady and Crump (1978) argue that around 80% of the

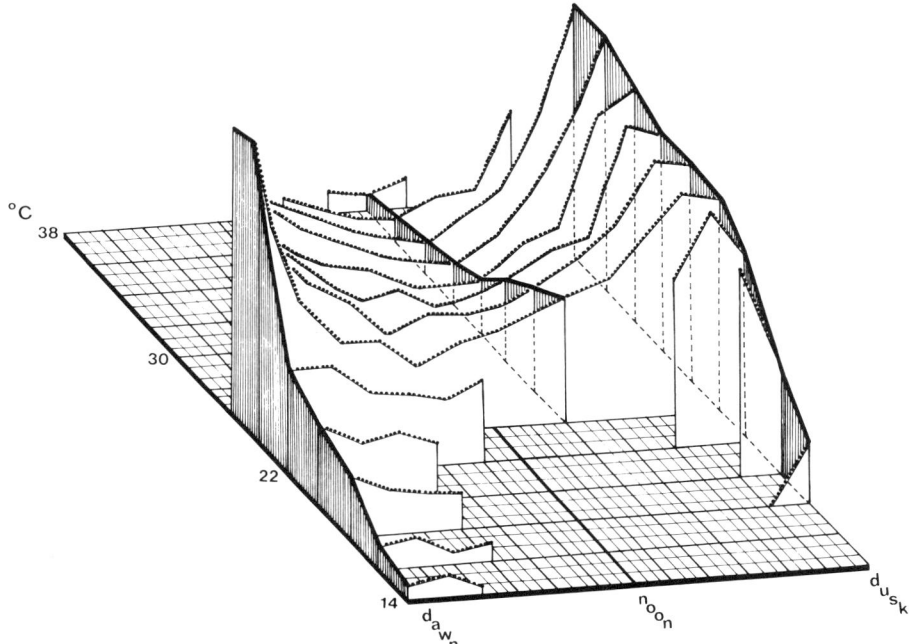

FIG. 2. Activity of *Glossina morsitans* in nature in relation to time of day and temperature (males caught on bait oxen in Zimbabwe). Vertical axis shows mean relative activity level (hourly catches as percentage of each day's total catch). $x$ axis shows time of day of the catch; $z$ axis, air temperature at the time of catch. Planes along $x$ axis show correlation of activity with time of day at different "constant" temperatures; planes along $z$ axis show correlations with temperature at different times of day. The gaps in the curves arise from the absence of the relevant temperatures at particular times. Note that though the data are entered as mean percentage units to reduce the variance, similar curves arise from the geometric means of the raw catches. (After Brady and Crump, 1978.)

U-pattern in nature may be due to endogenous rather than environmental control.

Nevertheless, Fig. 2 also shows that there is a correlation between activity in the field and air temperature, although this is more complicated than the simple positive correlation up to 28° and negative above that. The relationship is, in fact, itself strongly dependent on the time of day. Around dawn it is positively correlated with temperature at all observed temperatures, and also at dusk up to at least 34° C (Brady and Crump, 1978; van Etten, 1982), although somewhere above this the correlation probably turns negative (J. W. Hargrove, personal communication). So at dawn and dusk there is little evidence for normal high temperatures either inhibiting activity or switching on the photonegative response described by Pilson and Pilson (1967) and others (see above). That appears mainly during the afternoon, when a negative correlation occurs over much of the same temperature range (from about 24° upwards). The situation in *G. pallidipes* is virtually identical (van Etten, 1982).

Thus, although activity level in nature is certainly affected by temperature, not only is its diel pattern set up largely independently of that effect, but the effect itself is subject to time-of-day control.

## IV. Diel Pattern of Activity in the Laboratory

Under constant temperature and in a 12hr light:12hr dark cycle (LD 12:12), *G. morsitans* in actographs almost invariably exhibit morning and evening peaks of spontaneous flight with little activity around noon and none in the dark. In mature flies that are food-deprived and therefore relatively active, the morning and evening peaks are roughly equal, but in less-active flies the evening peak is much lower than the morning's (Fig. 3A). For unfed, recently emerged flies, even when their day's total activity is as high as mature flies' maximum, the evening's peak is never more than about 30% of the morning's, so that it is much like that of mature flies when recently fed (see Fig. 8A; Brady, 1972a; Brady and Crump, 1978, Fig. 3).

In the field, however, the most frequent pattern is with the evening peak much higher than the morning peak. Most of this difference must be due to the changing temperature that field flies are exposed to. Since early morning in the field is invariably much colder than the evening (typically by well over 10° C), there will inevitably be more individuals flying in the second half of the day than in the first.

In *G. austeni* in LD 12:12 under constant conditions, the spontaneous flight pattern in similarly U-shaped, but with the evening peak higher than the morning's (Crump and Brady, 1979); little is known of its field pattern. In *G. palpalis*, the activity rises steadily throughout the day from shortly after lights-on until lights-out, just as its usual field pattern does (Crump and Brady, 1979). Likewise in *G. pallidipes* (the only species investigated simultaneously in both laboratory and field, van Etten, 1982), activity typically rises more or less steadily through the day, in both natural and constant temperature conditions.

Since all of these daily rhythms occur under constant temperature, light (during the photophase), odor, humidity, noise, and so on, they must be controlled across the day endogenously (i.e., both genetically and physiologically). They must also be superimposed on the day-to-day increase in mean activity level with increasing starvation. In *G. morsitans* this occurs in the form shown in Fig. 3A, and it occurs in similar ways in the other species examined (Crump and Brady, 1979; van Etten, 1982).

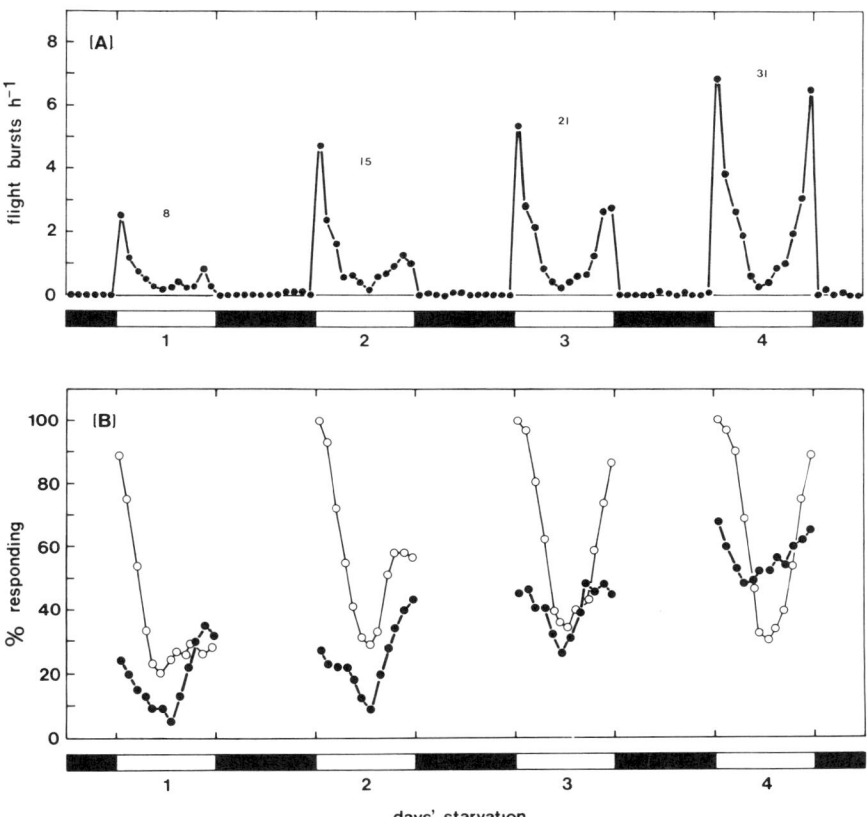

FIG. 3. (A), Diel rhythm of spontaneous flight activity of mature male *Glossina morsitans* in LD 12:12 expressed as the mean number of flight bursts per fly per hour (recorded as for Fig. 1; after Brady, 1981); figures above curves, mean flight bursts per 24 hr; abscissa, days since last fed. (B), Open circles, percentage of the males in A flying spontaneously each hour; closed circles, percentage of similar males responding to a slow-moving visual stimulus (tested as in Fig. 5F).

## V. Circadian Rhythm in the Laboratory

### A. Lack of Bimodality

As the diel activity pattern is endogenously controlled, one would expect it to be built into the fly's circadian clock and therefore to be demonstrable as a free-running rhythm in constant darkness or constant light. To some extent this does indeed occur in the four species in which it has been investigated (Barrass, 1962; Brady, 1972a; Crump and Brady, 1979), although in constant light the rhythm rapidly damps out (Brady, 1972a). There is one curious feature about this free-running rhythm, however. In neither *G. morsitans* nor *G. austeni* has a persistent bimodal U ever been demonstrated in constant darkness (or constant light), notwithstanding that in *G. moristans* a 12-hr-wide U persists when the photophase is extended to 18 hr (see Section V,F). (As the diel rhythms of *G. palpalis* and *G. pallidipes* are effectively unimodal in LD 12:12 anyway, the persistence of their activity as single free-running peaks is, by contrast, to be expected.)

The difficulty in analyzing these rhythms stems from tsetse's extreme inactivity in darkness (often <5 flight bursts 24 $hr^{-1}$), which makes it impracticable to present free-running records of the usual chronobiological raster type: No rhythm is ever apparent by visual inspection of a single fly's record in constant darkness. The best one can do is to show form estimates of the rhythm's pattern from the average of several individuals' records.

In young unfed *G. morsitans*, with their activity averaged in this way over several days, only a single, broad peak of activity fills the subjective photophase in the free-running rhythm (Brady, 1972a, 1974a). Even when just the first 3 days in constant darkness are examined this is still true for both *G. morsitans* and *G. austeni* (Crump and Brady, 1979). We concluded then that what persists into the free run for *G. morsitans* is in effect the morning peak of the U (since that is almost always the higher of the two peaks in LD 12:12), and for *G. austeni* the evening peak (likewise the higher).

B. Change in Endogenous Timing

Extensive further trails have revealed an unexpected and more significant feature of the free-running rhythm: It *is* unimodal, but it shows a marked phase jump during maturation (Brady, 1988). For young unfed flies, it is indeed the subjective morning peak that persists in constant darkness (Barrass's, 1970, single 24-hr records also suggest this). For mature flies, however, it is the evening peak that persists both in constant darkness and in constant light; little activity occurs between subjective midnight and subjective noon (Fig. 4).

This change in phase-setting is evidently a consequence of taking a bloodmeal, since in constant darkness young unfed flies continue with their morning setting until death, but a single blood-meal switches the peak to the evening phase (Fig. 4). This occurs even though one meal is not nearly enough to complete a fly's physiological maturation (Bursell and Kuwengwa, 1972), which suggests that the phase resetting is not switched by maturation per se, but is a more direct result of the ingestion of food, presumably as a consequence of the hormonal events that follow feeding (Langley, 1966; Gee, 1975; see also Anderson and Finlayson, 1978).

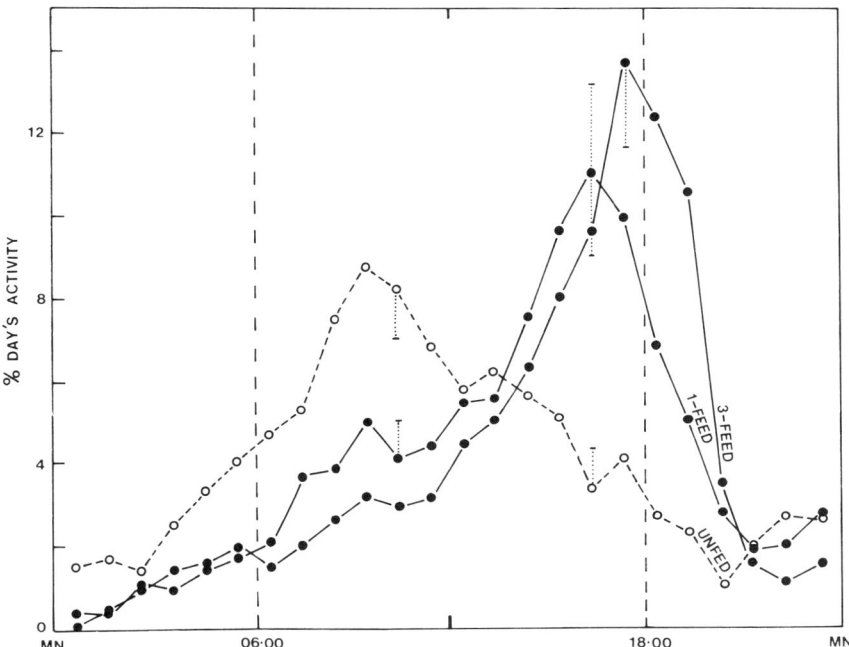

FIG. 4. The different phase-settings of the circadian rhythm of immature unfed male *Glossina morsitans* (open circles) and mature fed males (closed circles) in constant darkness; the mean of each hour's spontaneous flight bursts per fly is expressed as a percentage of the fly's total bursts that day. Unfeds, 1–2 days old postemergence; once-feds, 5–6 days old; thrice-feds, 15–16 days old ($n$ = 14, 12, and 8 fly-days, respectively). All curves are means of first 2 days in DD, smoothed with 3-point sliding means; key *SE* bars are dotted in. Note that the once-fed and thrice-fed curves are statistically indistinguishable, but their peaks are highly significantly greater than the activity level of the immatures at 17.00–18.00 h (and vice versa at 09.00–11.00 h). (After Brady, 1988.)

## C. Comparison with Field Behavior

It is clear that in the field, except in very hot weather, the maximum activity of *G. morsitans* occurs more commonly in the evening than in the morning (Pilson and Pilson, 1967; Dean *et al.*, 1969). This may therefore be the adaptive reason for mature flies having the evening component endogenously timed. That does not explain why the unfed immature flies (so-called tenerals) peak endogenously in the morning, however, though this may be associated with their extreme need for a first blood-meal (see Brady 1972b, 1988). There are no published field data differentiating between catch times of teneral and mature flies, but there is at least some evidence that teneral *G. morsitans* have a tendency to be more active earlier in the day than mature flies (Brady, 1988; see also Section VII,C).

The loss of the mature flies' morning peak in constant darkness or constant light, and their performance of a bimodal U pattern in 24-hr light cycles (whether natural or artificial) could, in principle, be due to the evening peak being endogenously generated by the circadian clock, and the morning peak being a perseverating response to the arrival of light at dawn, especially since dawn is apparently the rhythm's main *zeitgeber* (Section V,D). On the other hand, this explanation does not help identify the origin of the tenerals' evening peak, though it must be due to their response to the light cycle, since it occurs only in that.

### D. Entrainment of the Circadian Rhythm

The infrequent and sporadic nature of tsetse flies' activity makes it unsuitable for the normal types of experiment used to demonstrate the entrainment of circadian rhythms. However, in young male *G. morsitans*, the phase resetting effect of 6-hr shifts in *zeitgeber* time, combined with increasing the length of the photophase from LD 12:12 to LD 18:6, have been tested to see whether "dawn" or "dusk" is the principal *zeitgeber* (Brady and Crump, 1978).

When lights-on is advanced 6 hr, both arms of the U move forward to the new *zeitgeber* time taking two or three transient cycles to re-entrain fully, but when lights-out is delayed 6 hr, no phase shift of either arm occurs. In both 18-hr photophases, the two arms of the U remain clear and about 12 hr apart.

It must, therefore, be lights-on (dawn) that is the principal *zeitgeber*, since the U advances toward an earlier lights-on but does not delay toward a later lights-out. Furthermore, since both arms of the U remain 12 hr apart, advance together to the earlier *zeitgeber*, and take several cycles to do so, it seems that both are entrained and both persist (at least in a changed light cycle) at an endogenously controlled phase angle of 12 hr to each other, even though only one peak persists in constant darkness (Section V,B).

### E. Dusk Activity

The response to the sudden onset of darkness in a square-wave light cycle is clear: Before all spontaneous activity ceases for the night, there is first a brief flurry of flight. It was assumed that this was a direct photokinetic response to the lights suddenly going out, and thus an artifact of using a square-wave light cycle. It was therefore excluded from published records in the past (Brady and Crump, 1978, *et ante*). However, when a square-wave cycle is replaced by a regime that includes a smooth 30-min "dusk," a similar burst of flight still occurs, during the last few minutes of dim light before the final onset of absolute darkness (Brady, 1987a). This happens at a mean critical light intensity of about 350 mW m$^{-2}$, regardless of how quickly that intensity is reached in an artifical dusk, and whether it is reached via a linear or logarithmic dusk, or whether the initial (photophase) light intensity is 900 or 2500 mW m$^{-2}$.

This response to an absolute illumination level rather than to either a relative intensity or a rate of intensity change is apparently the same as that shown by moths in the entrainment of their circadian flight rhythm (Dreisig, 1980). The critical intensity is, however, affected by the flies' physiological state, since it is considerably lower in recently fed or newly emerged flies (50–100 mW m$^{-2}$) and is also lower (ca. 200 mW m$^{-2}$) if a "dusk" is presented at midday.

Intensities of this range occur in typical tsetse habitats within a few minutes of sunset. The burst of activity, therefore, seems not to be an artifact but rather a natural behavior pattern, apparently associated with the flies' habit of moving at dusk to the ends of twigs and onto leaves before settling for the night (Brady, 1987a).

## VI. Diel Pattern of Other Behaviors

### A. In-Phase Behaviors

Ten different types of behavior in *G. morsitans* have been measured across the day in controlled conditions in the laboratory. The diel patterns of these are summarized in Fig. 5, and compared there with a typical warm-season field catch of males on a bait ox (Curve C).

Eclosion (Curve B), though certainly under circadian control (Dean *et al.*, 1968), is a unique event that occurs only once in the life of each individual (i.e., a gated, "Type I" rhythm, see Brady, 1974, p.76), and is thus both functionally distinct and temporally separated from the rest of the animal's behavioral repertoire. Larviposition (Curve A), which females do once about every 10 days, may be similarly separated from the normal repertoire; it concerns not only the mother's behavioral timing but her larva's gated emergence behavior as well (Denlinger, 1983; see Section VII,G). In any event, these two discrete acts are timed to peak in the latter part of a 12-hr photophase. All the other behaviors—those of the more usual, ongoing, daily-repeated type like locomotor activity (Curve D)—are timed to follow a more or less U-shaped bimodal pattern over the day.

Curves D to K follow similar patterns with closely similar phase settings which, like the spontaneous activity, must be endogenously controlled since they occur across the 12-hr light phase in the constant conditions of an artifical LD 12:12 cycle (Curve F has actually been shown to persist, briefly, in constant light, Brady, 1975b, Fig. 2).

Man (Aschoff, 1982) and water snails (Morgan and Last, 1982; Chaudhry and Morgan, 1983) are probably the only other species in which a range of behaviors has been demonstrated to be cophasic in this way. The data from

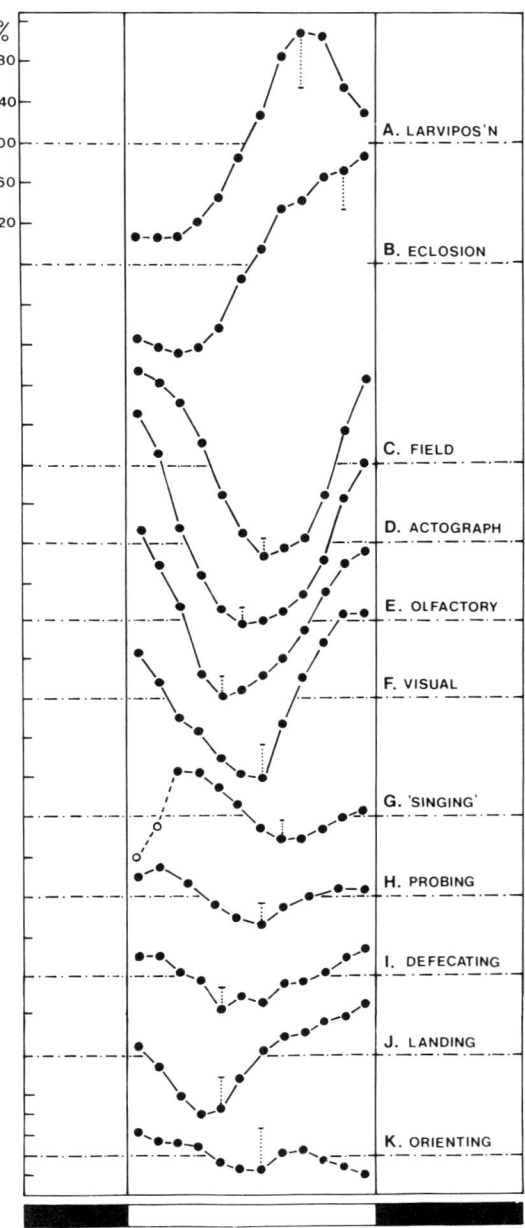

other species that have had cophasic rhythms demonstrated in them suffer from one of two defects. In the first, the stimuli for the measured responses are present continuously so that the rhythms may merely reflect the inevitable variation in stimulus frequency or intensity as the animal's activity level changes (e.g., Parker, 1962; Ollason and Slater, 1973; Morgan, 1983). This defect possibly applies to Curve J here, and almost certianly to Wall's report (1988) on the tsetse's rhythm of mating, since that was measured in a cage of fixed dead females, encounters with which must have paralleled the spontaneous flight frequency (there was no daily pattern of mating duration). In the second defect, the behavior(s) in fact concern only a single form of motor act in response to different stimuli, for example, locomotion under different conditions, as in Jones and Gubbins' mosquitoes (1978), Morgan's snails (*l.c.*), and here in Curves D, E, and F.

Fig. 5 thus presents an apparently unique circadian profile, covering not only so-called spontaneous activities (actograph flight and defecation) and responsiveness to externally applied stimuli (odor and visually evoked flight and probing), but also behaviors involving different sensorimotor systems (take-off for Curves D, E, and F; the wing muscles in a different mode for Curve G; the gut for Curve I; and the legs and head for Curve H), as well as rhythms in orientational responses (Curves K and perhaps J) which must be generated by changing levels of integration in the central nervous system.

Only Morgan's work on snails covers the same kind of range: Spontaneous locomotion, light-evoked locomotion, feeding (in response to ever-present stimuli), and egg-laying are all diurnal and cophasic (the first two involving the same behavior, but the last involving two different sensorimotor systems);

---

FIG. 5. Circadian behavioral profile of *Glossina morsitans*. The diel patterns of 11 behaviors measured in LD 12:12 (abscissa) with hourly levels expressed as percentage of mean level (marked as broken horizontal lines at 100% for each curve); curves smoothed with 3-point sliding means, and on same ordinate scale as A (except K = scale × 4). All peaks and troughs are highly significantly different from 100% (except K, where noon trough is significantly less than dawn and predusk peaks, $P <.02$); key 95% CI bars dotted in; phase settings of midday troughs in C–K do not differ significantly. A. Frequency distribution of larviposition (after Denlinger and Ma, 1974). B. Frequency distribution of eclosion (after Dean *et al.*, 1968). C. Biting activity in nature; male flies caught on bait oxen in hot season, Zimbabwe (after Dean *et al.*, 1969). D. Spontaneous flight activity in actographs (mean flight bursts per hour by 3-4-day-starved males). E. Responsiveness to human body odor (number of males flying in 60 s of odor stimulation). F. Responsiveness to a moving visual stimulus (number of males flying when stimulated for 60 s by a 5°-wide vertical black stripe moving horizontally at 14° s$^{-1}$). G. Number of males "singing" in each hour, first day after a blood-meal (after Saini, 1981a). H. Responsiveness to a probing stimulus (number of tethered males probing a warm sponge ball) (J. Nondo, personal communication). I. Defecation frequency of tethered males. J. Preference of males for landing on a backlit window rather than elsewhere in a darkened chamber. K. Attraction to a moving visual target (proportion of males flying toward the moving stripe in F). Curves D–F and I–K after Brady (1975b).

defecation is nocturnal. Egg-hatch is also rhythmic but belongs to that separate class of once-in-a-lifetime behaviors like the tsetse's eclosion. These snail rhythms are especially interesting in that, unlike most of the tsetse's, all have been shown to free run in constant darkness or light. They do not, however, include orientational responses, nor the effects of other physiological inputs described in the next section.

B. OUT-OF-PHASE BEHAVIORS

Evidently, not all of an animal's different behaviors can be modulated across the day in exact parallel. Some, like activity and rest, are mutually exclusive and must therefore run in antiphase (rest, not shown in Fig. 5, is the inverse of Curve D). More subtly, it is the nature of behavior to be organized in a dynamic hierarchy (see, e.g., Hinde, 1970, p. 608; Barnard, 1983, p. 63), with one behavior giving way to another of higher priority, and with different levels of behavior associated with different arousal states (see, e.g., Andrew, 1974). Thus, as general arousal waxes and wanes with the circadian cycle across the day, there will be changing tendencies for lower-level behaviors to break through as higher-level behaviors decline.

Such is evidently the case in *Eugaster* grasshoppers in which stridulation peaks daily together with locomotion in young males but gradually displaces locomotion in the peak as the males mature sexually (Nielsen, 1974). It is also apparent in the differential timing of flight activity and proboscis-extension responsiveness in blowflies (Hall, 1980b) and in the timing of feeding and oviposition in *Oncopeltus* (Caldwell and Rankin, 1974), *Anopheles* (Jones and Gubbins, 1978), and crickets (Loher, 1979). It may be the basis, as well, for the small phase differences in tsetse behavior shown in Fig. 5 (e.g., G vs J), and in the changing balance between locomotor activity (Fig. 3) and "singing" (Saini, 1981b).

It is important to recognize, however, that the switching from one behavior to another is not total. What typically happens is an alternation between the competing behaviors, with one successively taking up more time at the expense of the other, as is well illustrated for singing and walking in *Teleogryllus* by Sokolove (1975). Averaged form estimates of the kind shown in Fig. 5 (and, e.g., Caldwell and Rankin, 1974) obscure this fine detail, which more accurately depicts actual behavior.

VII. PHYSIOLOGICAL INPUTS THAT AFFECT THE DIEL PATTERN OF BEHAVIOR

A. "HUNGER" AND SPONTANEOUS ACTIVITY

The most obvious day-to-day modulation of behavior in tsetse flies comes from the rise in level of activity with food deprivation (Fig. 6). Spontaneous activity (Brady, 1972a; van Etten, 1982), responsiveness to slow-moving visual

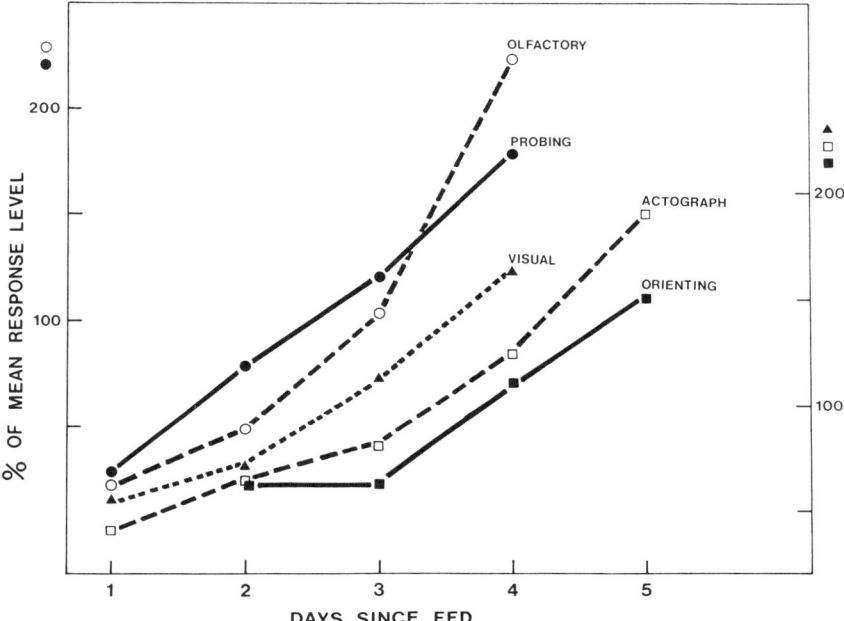

FIG. 6. Starvation-induced increases in various behaviors of mature male *Glossina morsitans* (see Fig. 5 for details). Levels expressed as percentage of mean levels over 4 or 5 days since last blood-meal.

stimuli (Brady, 1972b, 1975a), the degree of attraction to such movement (Brady, 1972b, Fig. 9), probing responsiveness (Brady, 1973; Chadd and Brady, 1982), and olfactory responsiveness (Brady, unpubl.) all increase steeply with increasing starvation, although singing declines (Saini, 1981b).

These increases by no means have a uniform effect on the U shape of the underlying diel pattern, however. Thus for the spontaneous activity of *G. morsitans*, whereas the morning peak roughly doubles over 4 days of starvation, the evening peak increases eightfold (Fig. 3A). There is in fact a strong positive relationship between the height of the evening peak and the total amount of activity performed through the day: For both sexes, the greater the overall activity level, the more of it occurs in the evening (Brady and Crump, 1978).

In the only other tsetse species whose spontaneous activity has been recorded, namely *G. austeni* and *G. palpalis* (Crump and Brady, 1979) and *G. pallidipes* (van Etten, 1982), starvation-induced pattern changes are less obvious, even though the mean activity levels increase markedly. *G. austeni* and *G. palpalis* have been studied only as young flies, however, and their lack of obvious pattern change may be due to their immaturity, since *G. morsitans* when young shows relatively little pattern change with starvation (Brady, 1972a, Fig. 1C; Crump and Brady, 1979, Fig. 2C).

Still more striking locomotor pattern changes caused by noncircadian inputs occur in other insects (see Brady, 1981, p. 128): in mosquitoes as a result of insemination and, to a lesser extent, the gonotrophic cycle (Jones, 1981; Jones and Gubbins, 1978; Chiba *et al.*, 1985); in silkmoths as a result of different rearing temperatures (Truman, 1973), as may also be the case in mosquitoes (Kon, 1985, 1986); and in many species in response to changes in illumination level (e.g., cockroaches, Lohmann, 1967) or photophase length (e.g., fruit flies, Tychsen, 1978). In mosquitoes and cockroaches, moreover, these marked pattern changes free run in constant light or darkness.

## B. "Hunger" and Other Behaviors

The diel pattern changes that occur in other behaviors as a result of starvation are not necessarily the same as those for spontaneous activity. In *G. morsitans*, as the visual responsiveness to movement increases day-by-day during starvation, all parts of the U increase together, as shown in Fig. 3B. The same is apparently true for its olfactory responsiveness (Brady, unpubl.) and for its probing responsiveness (Brady, 1973), and for probing in *G. austeni* (Chadd and Brady, 1982). Whereas the circadian control of spontaneous activity is strongly modulated by starvation, therefore, the circadian control of other behaviors may not be.

Underlying this difference between spontaneous activity and other behavior, for the visual response at least, is the fact that as more flies respond to stimulation, the number of responses (flights) made by each responder increases only linearly, scarcely doubling from two flights when approximately 20% of flies are responding, to about four when nearly all are (Fig. 7). For spontaneous flight, by contrast, once the level of about 70% active is reached, the increase in flights per flier is exponential. Moreover, this difference occurs in spite of the fact that the visual responses were measured in a small arena in which the flies often interact, whereas the spontaneous activity increase occurs in individuals isolated in actographs.

It seems that the coupling of the circadian "clock" to spontaneous flight control must be different from its coupling to a number of other responses, notwithstanding that both spontaneous activity and visual responsiveness actually involve the same motor act, that is, take-off and flight (see also Section VII,G).

Comparable pattern changes in nonlocomotor behavioral rhythms have been reported in only a few other insects. In *Drosophila*, the oviposition rhythm switches from being bimodal at 5 lux to being unimodal at 60 lux (Allemand, 1977), and shows even greater pattern changes in response to laying substrate and fly density (Allemand, 1983a,b). In male *Argyrotaenia*, the responsiveness to female pheromone peaks several hours earlier at 16° C than at 25° (Cardé

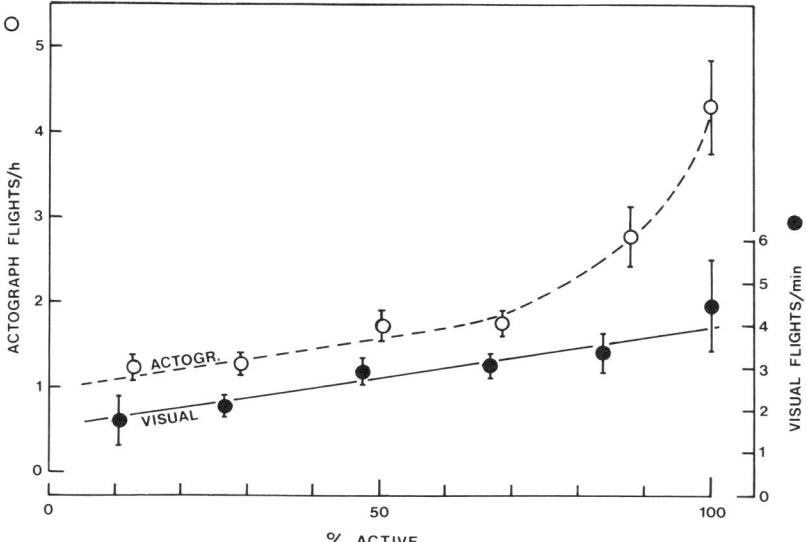

FIG. 7. Relationship for male *Glossina morsitans* between the number of flights made by individuals when unstimulated in actographs (open circles) or when responding to a moving visual stimulus (closed circles, tested as for Fig. 5F), and the proportion of the population active or responsive at that time (abscissa). Left ordinate, spontaneous flight bursts per hour per active fly; right ordinate, take-offs per responding fly per 60-s stimulation; bars show 95% CI, but note that the two scales are not directly comparable ($n$ per point = 20–50, except 100% visual = 9). The lack of the steep rise in the visual response is not due to saturation of the response in 60 s, because maximum flight levels were often 6 or 7, and there is no sign of a plateau.

*et al.*, 1975). In both these cases, however, the part played by locomotion in the recorded response was not analyzed.

C. MATURATION

There is a clear difference between young and mature tsetse in the phase-setting of their free-running unimodal activity rhythm in constant darkness (Section V,B, Fig. 4). A further difference due to maturation also arises in LD 12:12: There is a highly significant difference between young and mature *G. morsitans* in the distribution of their activity across the photophase (Fig. 8A). When the patterns are compared at equal overall activity levels, for every level except the lowest, mature males have much lower morning peaks (by at least 30%) and rather higher evening peaks than do young males (Brady and Crump, 1978, Fig. 3). Furthermore, for a given level of arousal (as indicated by the proportion of the population active), when a young fly is

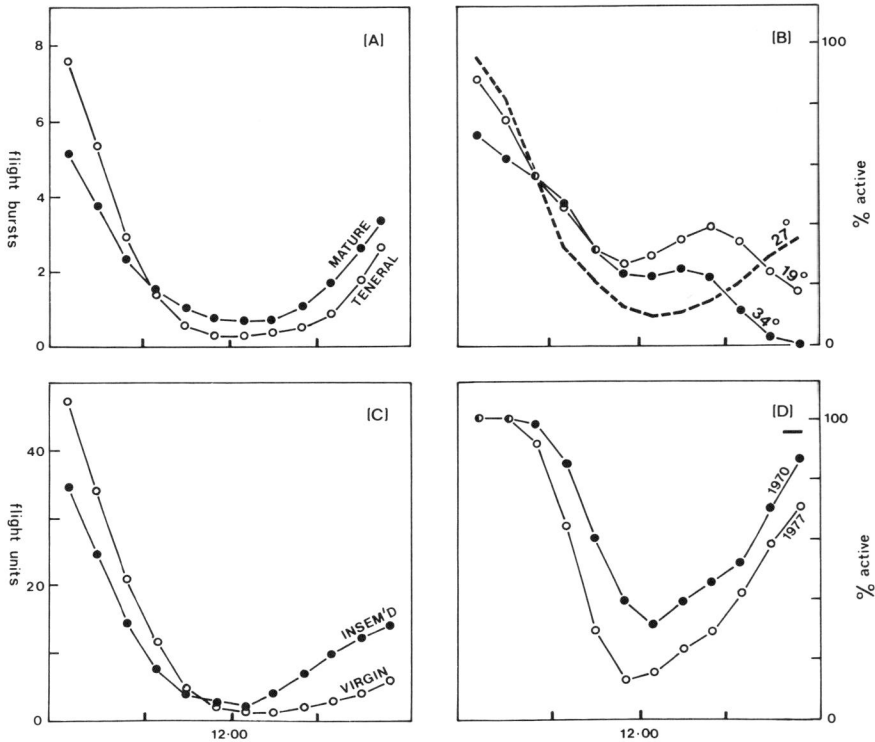

FIG. 8. Differential effect of various noncircadian inputs on the spontaneous activity rhythm's diel U-pattern in *Glossina morsitans*. For each pair of curves, the flies analyzed are in the same "bin" of activity level. (A), Effect of maturation and/or feeding in males (teneral = unfed newly emerged; mature, (ca. 10-day-old fed thrice). (B), Effect of three different constant temperatures on teneral males (27°, normal standard). (C), Effect of insemination in mature (fed thrice) females. (D), Effect of genotype or in-breeding in males from Langford colony (Kariba strain) tested in 1970 and 1977. Abscissa, time of day in LD 12:12. Ordinates in (A) and (C) show flight bursts (or minutes with activity) per fly per hour; ordinates in (B) and (D) show percentage of flies active each hour.

active it performs some 50% more activity than does an equivalent mature fly. No other behavior and no other tsetse species have been examined for this effect.

Not only does the circadian timing of the free-running activity rhythm in constant darkness thus switch its phase-setting after the fly has fed and starts to mature (Section V,B), but so also, though less dramatically, does the clock's modulation of activity level in a light cycle. These changes are apparently due to the manifold physiological consequences of having taken one or more blood-meals rather than to physiological maturation per se (Section V,B).

D. TEMPERATURE

Lowering the constant ambient temperature from the standard laboratory 27° to 19° C greatly lowers tsetses' overall activity level, and annihilates their evening peak (Brady, 1974a). It was assumed that this did not essentially change the circadian pattern but that the low temperature so depressed activity (to <1 flight 4 hr$^{-1}$ through most of the day) that the endogenous stimulus for the evening peak—whatever it was—never reached threshold. Subsequent analysis has revealed the situation to be not so simple, however.

Both low and high constant temperature do suppress activity—for young unfed male *G. morsitans* from a mean of about 20 flights day$^{-1}$ at 27° to 5 flights day$^{-1}$ at either 19 or 35° (Brady and Crump, 1978, Fig. 6). It is possible, however, to study the effect on activity pattern independently of this suppression, by comparing identical mean activity levels at different temperatures. When this is done, it is apparent that, for a given activity level, different behavior patterns emerge at 19, 27, and 35°: The evening peaks are annihilated at 19 and 35°, regardless of the overall activity suppression (Fig. 8B).

It thus appears that the coupling between the circadian clock and the control of spontaneous activity is set somehow differently at different temperatures. Although the differences from the normal (27°) behavior seem small, they are highly significant statistically and could have a marked effect on feeding patterns in nature. Van Etten's data (1982) suggest that a similar situation prevails in *G. pallidipes* at 24 and 30°.

Activity-pattern changes due to changes in constant temperature have also been found in other insects, most notably in silkworms, in which prolonged exposure of the post-diapause pupae to 12° C radically alters the adult's subsequent activity pattern (Truman, 1973); in mosquitoes treated similarly, lesser pattern changes occur (Kon, 1985, 1986). Similarly, constant low ambient temperature changes the balance between the morning and evening activity peaks in *Culex* mosquitoes (Chiba *et al.*, 1982), and advances *Argyrotaenia* males' responsiveness to female pheromone several hours (Cardé *et al.*, 1975).

E. GENETICS

It is a characteristic of the genus for tsetse flies to be most active at the ends of the day and to spend the middle of the day at rest (Section III). As one would expect, however, the different species have different pattern details (Crump and Brady, 1979). In this sense, therefore, there is obviously good evidence for genetic control of the circadian pattern of behavior in tsetse, but the evidence also extends to within-species differences. Van Etten (1982) has shown clear differences between populations of *G. pallidipes* from different parts of Kenya, differences that are consistent in both the field (as trap catches) and constant laboratory conditions (in actographs). One race has the typical *pallidipes* pattern of activity rising steadily from dawn up to a peak before dusk; the other has a steeper initial rise, a midday plateau, and no evening peak.

Less expected, perhaps, is the observation that over several years of laboratory in-breeding, the Langford (Bristol) colony of *G. morsitans* changed its activity pattern in two respects. First, the overall mean activity level declined by 25%, from a mean of 20 flight bursts per fly per day in 1970 to 15 per day in 1977. Second, and more interestingly, when compared at standardized activity levels, at every level the 1977 flies performed more of their activity in the morning peak than did the 1970 flies, representing a 25% increase in the first hour's activity and a 2% decrease in the other 11 hours (Brady and Crump, 1978, Table 4). The difference is even more marked in terms of the numbers of flies active in any one hour (Fig. 8D).

It appears, therefore, that small differences in the genetic make-up of tsetse alter the phase-setting of the circadian clock in LD 12:12, or its coupling to the control of spontaneous activity. Similar small genetically based differences in circadian timing have also been reported in other insects. Some especially relevant cases are the different emergence timings of the various races of the European intertidal midge, *Clunio marinus* (Neumann, 1976), and of *Drosophila littoralis* (Lankinen and Lumme, 1984), the different oviposition patterns of the different races of *Drosophila melanogaster* (Allemand and David, 1984), and the differences between the phase-angles of the first peaks of activity of four sibling species of *Anopheles gambiae* (Jones *et al.*, 1974). Very marked circadian period changes are, of course, well known in the behavioral mutants of *Drosophila* (Konopka, 1979, 1981).

F. Insemination

In female mosquitoes, insemination—or rather the transfer of male pheromone—removes the characteristic dusk peak of activity normally associated with swarming (Jones, 1981; Jones and Gubbins, 1978). In tsetse flies, the effect is less striking. Inseminated females over the first half of their first pregnancy cycle (i.e., while their larva is still very small) are consistently and significantly less active in the morning and more active in the evening than are virgins of similar age and feeding state (Fig. 8C). The difference is comparable to that due to maturation in males (Fig. 8A), although it occurs in females of identical "maturity." Whether the change is due to insemination per se (as it is in mosquitoes) or to the onset of early pregnancy is not known.

G. Pregnancy

Each fertile female tsetse deposits one fully developed third-instar larva every 10 days or so, and striking changes in her diel pattern of activity accompany this behavior for 3 days around the time of parturition (Brady and

Gibson, 1983). At other times, pregnant females' activity closely follows the mature males' pattern (Fig. 8A,C). Two days before larviposition, however, changes begin. Up to noon on this day (i.e., 48 hr before parturition), the females are 3 times more active than usual, and almost always feed if given the chance. Since this peak is so different from the behavior of the same females at the same apparent state of food deprivation earlier in pregnancy, it seems that it is a specially programmed adaptation for finding the last crucial blood-meal to complete the larva's development before parturition, rather than an expression of the normal development of "hunger."

Next day the females virtually cease to move: The morning peak is at most only one or two brief bursts of flight, and two-thirds of the flies perform no activity at all (Fig. 9, halved circles). It seems that this is a real change

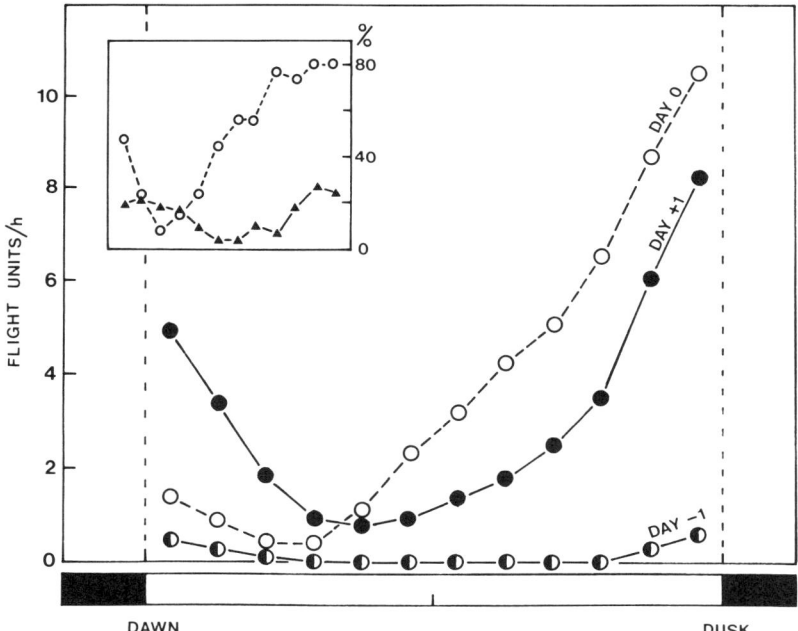

FIG. 9. Effects of pregnancy and larviposition on the diel behavior pattern of female *Glossina morsitans*. Day 0, day of larviposition; Day −1, day before larviposition; Day +1, day after larviposition showing the normal starved mature female U-pattern (as in Fig. 8C); $n = 29, 28$, and 37 fly-days respectively. Main figure shows mean units of activity per female per hour (units = minutes with some flight). Note that on the day before larviposition activity level is extremely low, and that on Day 0 it remains low till midday but then suddenly increases to double the normal starved, high activity level ($\overline{X}$ increase = 106% $h^{-1}$, $SE \pm 25\%$ relative to Day +1). Inset shows for Day 0 percentage of females active (circles) compared with percentage responding to a moving visual stimulus (triangles, tested as for Fig. 5F); note decoupling of activity pattern from usual U-pattern of visual response. (After Brady and Gibson, 1983; Abdel Karim and Brady, 1984.)

in circadian pattern, rather than merely an extremely low level of activity throughout the day, since it is very different from the pattern of barely active males, nearly all of whom participate in the morning peak (Brady, 1974a).

The day of larviposition itself opens with continued near zero activity (with the morning peak < 30% of normal), but there then ensues the most radical change of all in the endogenous U-pattern: Some time between noon and dusk each female performs a sharp 2–3-hr peak of activity (Brady and Gibson, 1983). In LD 12:12, an activity peak in the afternoon never occurs under any other circumstances, and it clearly represents a complete departure from the usual circadian control.

This atypical activity is apparently associated with the female's search for a larviposition site, since it stops as soon as parturition is complete. It also involves a complete change in behavior, from the usual sporadic about 1-min flight bursts (Fig. 1) to frequent short "flits" of a second or two (Abdel Karim and Brady, 1984). Afternoon parturition is typical also of several other tsetse species (see Brady and Gibson, 1983). Once larviposition is over, the daily activity pattern reverts to its normal U until the next larviposition is imminent (Fig. 9, solid circles).

The visual responsiveness of pregnant *G. morsitans* to a moving stimulus has also been measured, as for Fig. 5F (Abdel Karim and Brady, 1984). For most of the time, as in males, the visual response waxes and wanes in parallel with the females' spontaneous activity, implying a picture similar to that in Fig. 5. There are differences on the day of parturition, however. Here, when the spontaneous activity rises to its atypical afternoon peak, visual responsiveness remains low as usual (Fig. 9, inset), and even when the moving stimulus does evoke flight it is less attractive than usual. It is as if the larviposition-site-seeking females were "uninterested" in visual stimuli of the kind they respond to when "looking for" a host, and revert to that interest only when they have deposited their larva.

This all seems to imply that the later stages of pregnancy radically alter the coupling between the female's circadian clock and her behavioral control, but there is a major complication present in the form of the larva. Denlinger (1983) has shown that probably both mother and larva have inputs to the phase-setting of larviposition. It may thus be that the precise timing of parturition is due mainly to the larva, via the mother's response to its movements in her uterus. If so, that would imply that the afternoon activity peak associated with parturition represents the larva's gating of its emergence (Fig. 5A), rather than a change in the circadian control of the mother's behavior.

On the other hand, the changes in activity pattern over the two preceding days seem more likely to represent real changes in the mother's circadian control, since nothing dramatic is happening to the larva at that time. Also, the low visual response through the day of larviposition suggests that as far as the circadian control is concerned, arousal is otherwise suppressed in much the same way as over the preceding 24 hr (Abdel Karim and Brady, 1984).

These changing diel patterns in response to incipient and actual larviposition are reminiscent of the changes in mosquitoes in response to oviposition. If fertilized female *Anopheles gambiae* are prevented from ovipositing for several days, they have a much higher early night peak and less midnight activity than normal (Jones and Gubbins, 1978); a similar situation occurs in *Aedes* (Jones, 1981). In mosquitoes, therefore, it is as if the pressure to oviposit raised the females' activity during the phase of normal oviposition behavior (postdusk) at the expense of the rest of the circadian pattern; and in tsetse flies, it is as if the comparable pressure to larviposit suppressed activity. Possibly this difference is associated with the mosquito's need to fly some distance to find water for egg-laying, whereas the tsetse may commonly be resting within a few meters of a larviposition site and have a greater need to conserve fuel (see Section II,A).

H. Toxic Chemicals

It has been apparent for some time—though rarely remarked upon—that although poisoning of insects by insecticides and other chemicals has obvious deleterious physiological effects, and exhibits markedly different strengths at different times of day (Brady, 1974b, p. 25), it has little effect on circadian rhythmicity per se. It is of interest in the present context that, apart from an initial excitation from DDT treatment, sublethal doses of several insecticides cause no obvious upset to either the diel activity pattern of *G. morsitans* (Kwan and Gatehouse, 1978; J. Nondo, personal communication) or the U-shaped probing pattern of *G. austeni*, even with acetylcholine-esterase inhibiting insecticides, and even though permethrin reduces the responsiveness fourfold (Chadd and Brady, 1982). Nor does irradiation at doses producing about 85% male sterility apparently have much effect (Langley *et al.*, 1974). In tsetse flies, therefore, in spite of the lability of the circadian behavioral timing, chemical poisoning seems to disturb the circadian system scarcely at all.

I. Summary of Effects That Modulate the Circadian Rhythm

One may conclude, at least for *G. morsitans*, that the cycle of the underlying circadian control system, as reflected in the free-running spontaneous activity of mature flies in constant darkness, is unimodal with a marked peak in the late subjective photophase, but that in driving the daily rhythm of behavior, this system (or its coupling to the centers with integrate behavior) is subject to much modulation. At least seven different factors have been found to affect its output. These, in order of the apparent magnitude of their effects, are as follows:

1. *Initial food intake and maturation.* This switches the phase-setting of the morning peak of the young unfed fly to the evening peak of the fed fly

and also greatly increases the amount of evening activity under entrainment to a light cycle.

2. *Entrainment to LD 12:12.* This generates the second peak in the cycle, driving it into its typical, bimodal U-pattern with morning and evening peaks.

3. *Pregnancy.* For 3 days before and during larval deposition, the female's activity pattern is radically altered, involving in particular an aberrant midafternoon peak when larviposition is imminent, a peak which moreover disconnects the otherwise closely coupled visual responsiveness and spontaneous activity.

4. *Starvation.* While raising the overall daily level of activity, this markedly changes the balance between the morning and evening peaks of the U, increasing the evening peak at least twice as fast as the morning peak. It also has a differential effect on a number of responses to external stimuli, leaving their U-pattern largely unchanged, with subequal peaks at all stages of starvation.

5. *Genotype.* The geographical separation of races, as with laboratory inbreeding, causes differences in activity level and in the shape of the pattern across the day.

6. *Temperature.* Unusually high or low temperatures both depress activity; when held constant, both change the balance between the morning and evening arms of the U, but do so differently, with low temperature leaving the morning peak untouched while virtually annihilating the evening peak, and high temperature substantially lowering both peaks.

7. *Insemination.* This alters the balance of the LD-entrained U-pattern in females, lowering their morning peak slightly and roughly trebling their evening peak.

## VIII. Changes in Responsiveness: Central or Peripheral?

Apart from the obvious implication of broad interbehavioral coupling, what do changes in responsiveness of the kind shown in Fig. 5 indicate about the circadian control of behavior? First, of course, they show that the fly's thresholds change cyclically across the photophase, so that its behaviors must be continuously modulated across time, rather than subject to daily pushbutton control. The latter may be involved in the gated, discrete-event rhythms of the eclosion/larviposition type, the control of which may be likened to the launch of a ballistic rocket, but the control of ongoing behavior must be more like flying an airplane.

An important neurobiological question is whether the daily modulation of these thresholds arises peripherally, in the sense organs, or in the CNS. In other words, do the behavioral thresholds change because sensitivity in the relevant receptors varies rhythmically, because central nervous excitability cyclically changes the levels of response to a *constant* sensory input, or both?

## A. CHEMORECEPTION

In insects, the question was asked originally in the different context of the control of "hunger" in blowflies (Dethier, 1976, p.418). Here, preliminary evidence clearly suggested that the flies' short-term arousal by sugar stimulation was due to central excitability: The labellar chemoreceptors did not change in their sensitivity. It has now been demonstrated that the blowflies' circadian rhythm of responsiveness to sugar is likewise due to central integration, since the tarsal receptors generate a constant number of spikes for a constant stimulus intensity at all times (Hall, 1980a,b; see Brady, 1981).

Until recently, it also seemed that the antennae provided a similar case of sense organ constancy. In *Trichoplusia ni* and in saturniids, there was clear evidence of circadian behavioral threshold changes to pheromone stimulation, but no parallel change in electro-antennogram sensitivity (Payne et al., 1970; Riddiford, 1974). That, indeed, seemed a sensible control strategy: To have variable sense-organ sensitivity would be like an engineer working with an elastic ruler. It is now becoming apparent, however, that chemoreceptors often *are* elastic rulers, at least in relation to noncircadian physiological inputs such as starvation and gonotrophic cycle.

The case of the blowfly sugar receptors may still be in dispute (see, e.g., Omand and Zabara, 1981, versus Rachman, 1979; Hall, 1980a; van der Molen, 1982), but other cases are not: Starvation changes the maxillary palp sensitivity of locusts (Abisgold and Simpson, 1988), mosquitoes change the sensitivity of their antennal lactic acid sensilla relative to their ovarian cycle (Davis, 1984), and the $CO_2$-evoked electro-antennogram of stable flies rises with starvation (Warnes and Finlayson, 1978). On the other hand, no such chemoreceptor change relative to the circadian cycle has yet been reported, and in the only places where it has been looked for it does not occur (Payne et al., 1970; Riddiford, 1974; Hall, 1980b).

## B. PHOTORECEPTION

Photoreceptors are another matter. It has long been apparent that daily rhythmicity in photoreceptor sensitivity is widespread, perhaps even universal. In arthropods it has been demonstrated in crabs (Aréchiga et al., 1974; Arikawa et al., 1987) crayfish (Fuentes-Pardo and Rubio, 1981), scorpions (Fleissner and Fleissner, 1978), king crabs (Kaplan and Barlow, 1980), spiders (Blest, 1978), beetles (Fleissner, 1982), locusts (Williams, 1983), bees (Kaiser and Steiner-Kaiser, 1983), moths (Bennet, 1983), and cockroaches (Wills *et al.*, 1985). It is also well known in vertebrates (e.g., in rats, LaVail, 1976, and rabbits, Brandenburg et al., 1983).

Unlike chemoreceptors, eyes have to cope with an entirely predictable daily change in stimulus instensity covering six or more log units; rhythmically programmed changes in photosensitivity might therefore be expected. How far these changes affect perception of movement, form, color, and contrast—and hence behavior—is less clear. An effect at least on visual acuity in compound eyes may be inevitable (Meyer-Rochow and Horridge, 1975), but in simple eyes that is not necessarily the case (Meyer-Rochow, 1974), and the relevant behavioral changes in visual responsiveness have not been tested, except at the very simplest level (Powers and Barlow, 1985). Even in the honeybee, where the measured rhythm is in the sensitivity of an optomotor interneuron to movement stimulation (Kaiser and Steiner-Kaiser, 1983), it is not reported whether the optomotor behavior varies rhythmically. But in any case, since it is an interneuron in which excitability changes, the control is, in effect, central. Indeed, changes in photoreceptor sensitivity are also often under efferent control from the CNS, as in scorpions, king crabs, and rabbits (Fleissner and Fleissner, 1978; Kaplan and Barlow, 1980; Brandenburg *et al.*, 1983; see reviews in Jacklet, 1985).

In tsetse flies, the rhythm in responsiveness to movement (Fig. 5F) seems likewise to arise centrally: the U-patterns of responsiveness run in parallel when measured at two widely different contrast intensities, implying a lack of change in the eye's sensitivity to movement (Brady, 1975b). As the threshold had to be estimated in populations of flies, not individuals, this interpretation is not firmly established, but there is other circumstantial support for the central hypothesis. The responsiveness to movement is also altered, independently, by starvation (Fig. 3). Were the rhythm to arise peripherally, one would thus have to suppose that the eyes' sensitivity is modulated not only by the time of day, but also by starvation, so that the eyes operate over a quite different daily range of sensitivity on the first day after a blood-meal from 4 or 5 days later. This appears both unnecessarily complicated, and unsuitably unadaptable.

## C. Mechanoreception

Mechanoreceptors have been little investigated (see Page, 1981a). It is not clear, for example, whether the rhythm in sensitivity to mechanical stimulation in crabs (Aréchiga *et al.*, 1974) arises in the receptors themselves or in the CNS. An interesting study concerns honeybees' gravity sensitivity. This is mediated by mechanoreceptor hair fields at the bee's "waist" and "neck," and Korall and Martin (1987) have shown that the response of these sensilla to a standard mechanical displacement varies across the 24 hours, closely in phase with the changes in the earth's magnetic field vectors. Honeybees' daily cycle of directional error in their waggle dances (*Missweisung*, Martin and Lindauer, 1977) may thus be due to this peripheral effect, driven by the geomagnetic input. It is, however, specifically not a circadian rhythm but an exogenous one, which is Korall and Martin's main point (see Brady, 1987b).

A quite different form of mechanoreceptor sensitivity rhythm occurs in male mosquitoes: In some species, the antennal hairs are erected in a circadian cycle coincident with the males' activity, giving rise to his responsiveness to the female flight tone (Charlwood and Jones, 1979). Like the photoreceptor rhythms, however, this rhythm is apparently generated by central efferent control (Beach, 1980), so whether it should be considered a receptor sensitivity rhythm, or a behavioral rhythm itself, is unclear.

D. Orientation Rhythms

Complex behavioral rhythms must arise centrally. Well-documented examples are the rhythms that occur in directed orientations (i.e., taxes), such as the tsetse's changing attraction to movement (Fig. 5K), geotaxis in pondskaters (Birukow, 1960), and the sun-compass navigation of sandhoppers (Enright, 1972), bees (von Frisch, 1967), beetles (Ercolini and Scapini, 1976), and birds (Hoffman, 1982). It is difficult to conceive how receptor changes could cause such orientational changes.

Simpler orientational rhythms also occur, but most of these may arise from receptor changes. For example, apparent phototactic and scototactic rhythms (e.g., Campan *et al.*, 1975; Forward, 1980; Edwards and Naylor, 1987; and perhaps Fig. 5J above) could in principle be due—as suggested by Forward—to the eyes' greater sensitivity to light at different times, as is apparently the case in *Daphnia* (Ringelberg and Servaas, 1971). Moreover, it is not always clear whether the rhythm is really in an orientationally directed response at all, or is merely in a nondirected kinesis, and hence due to parallel changes in the activity level (e.g., Birukow, 1964; Rensing, 1965; Kavaliers and Macvean, 1980). The same concerns exist with respect to thermo-orientation (e.g., Crawshaw, 1974; Kavaliers, 1981).

E. Conclusions

It is clear that the photsensitivity of eyes is commonly modulated by a circadian rhythm. But whether this change in sensitivity to light intensity affects rhythms in behavior is not at all clear, since the perception of movement, color, and form must be largely unaffected. Chemoreceptors evidently change their sensitivity in relation to long-term, noncircadian inputs such as the gonotrophic cycle, but the only evidence we have so far indicates no circadian changes in such sensitivity. Except for the exogenous effect on gravity sensitivity in bees (Korall and Martin, 1987), circadian rhythm effects on mechanoreception await direct investigation.

It looks, therefore, as if the circadian modulation of behavior—especially complex behavior—is due largely to changes in central nervous excitability or facilitation, rather than to peripheral changes in receptor sensitivity.

However, the latter cannot be ruled out, especially for certain aspects of photoreception.

## IX. THE OVERALL CIRCADIAN ORGANIZATION OF BEHAVIOR

### A. BASIC FEATURES

Circadian timing causes major changes in an animal's motivational state. This phenomenon is often labeled the *sleep-wakefulness cycle*, but it concerns much more than just that. The present analysis, based largely on a long study of tsetse fly behavior, indicates that the overall circadian organization of animal behavior involves at least the following nine features.

1. *Control is continuous.* Unlike the control of discrete, single-instance behavioral events such as hatching and adult emergence, circadian control of more typical, lifelong, daily-repeated behavior must be exerted continuously. This is suggested by the smooth-wave form of modulation of the periods of *in*activity in tsetse flies (Section II,B), by the fact that responsiveness must change via threshold changes and thresholds do not simply disappear at certain times (Section VIII); and also because of the ability of foraging bees and sun-compass orienting animals to "read" circadian time continuously (see Brady, 1979, p. 36, 1981; Walraff, 1981).

2. *Control is probabilistic.* Circadian behavioral control must also be exerted in a nonrigid manner since all that can be predicted at any one time is the probability of an element of behavior occurring (Section II,C). Even in highly active species such as cockroaches or rodents, activity is not continuous in the active phase, nor is rest totally uninterrupted. Behavior must be adaptive, allowing an animal to adjust to the changing exigencies of the environment (arrival of a predator, mate, food, etc.); circadian control therefore cannot be push-button or all-or-none.

3. *Rhythms occur around varying mean levels.* The 24-hr, circadian modulation of behavior is superimposed on changes in behavior that arise as a result of other factors. The rhythm of each behavior thus occurs around varying mean levels that are set by longer-term, noncircadian physiological inputs such as "hunger" and ambient temperature (Section VII, A,B, Figs. 3 and 6).

4. *Different behaviors cycle differently.* Even behaviors that change in close parallel across the 24 hours (6, below) may show differentially patterned rhythms in response to the same physiological input (Section VII,B, Figs. 3B,7).

5. *Rhythmicity arises centrally.* Rhythmicity in behavioral responsiveness is due mainly to changes in the central nervous system's processing and integration of afferent signals rather than to cyclical changes in receptor sensitivity. The latter also occurs, especially in photoreceptors, but this is often under

efferent CNS control, and there is no evidence that it affects anything other than the simplest levels of behavior (Section VIII,E).

6. *Many behaviors are modulated synchronously.* In each species, the circadian changes in many widely differing responses occur in phase with one another, whether the responses involve the same or quite different sensorimotor systems (Section VI,A, Fig. 5).

7. *Major phase changes may occur.* As a result of physiological changes associated with development, major retiming of behavior may occur (Section V,B, VII,D, Fig. 4). Presumably this involves the whole behavioral repertoire, but that possibility has not yet been tested.

8. *Some behaviors are modulated out of synchrony.* Not all behaviors run in parallel; some are mutually exclusive and are necessarily on average 180° out of phase with one another (e.g., activity and rest), while others adopt intermediate phase angles (Section VI,B).

9. *Circadian patterns change with physiological state.* Marked change occur in the typical pattern of activity across the day as a result of noncircadian inputs from maturation, pregnancy, genotype, starvation, temperature, and so on (Section VII, Figs. 8 and 9). Such pattern changes are quite distinct from the changes in mean level noted above.

B. The Control System

No model for the overall circadian control of animal behavior has yet been proposed. Models exist for circadian clock mechanisms, as they do for photoperiodism (see, e.g., Saunders, 1982), and much is known of the functional neuroanatomy of the circadian control of spontaneous activity in arthropods, molluscs, birds, and rodents (see, e.g., Follett and Follett, 1981; Jacklet, 1982, 1985). That topic, however, is not the subject of this review, which is the problem of how behavior as a whole is integrated across the 24 hours.

One initial general statement suggests itself: Although hormones are certainly involved in modulating behavior—especially in vertebrates and in relation to sex—simple circadian changes in hormone titre are unlikely to produce more than crude baseline changes in behavior level, perhaps along the lines of Point 3 above. For invertebrates there is, indeed, little evidence that hormonal rhythms play any important role in the circadian organization of behavior (see Brady, 1974b; Page, 1981a,b). And even for vertebrates, where melatonin plays a role in birds, its importance in driving behavioral rhythmicity is not fully resolved, and its involvement is different in different groups (see Menaker and Binkley, 1981; Menaker *et al.*, 1981; Jacklet, 1985). In any case, it is difficult to envisage how a daily cycle in hormone titre could control either the great multiplicity of in-phase and out-of-phase behavioral rhythms in the individual, or the subtle, second-by-second changes that behavior typically involves (Brady, 1981; Dreisig, 1984).

Because of the multiple, parallel rhythmicity of behavior (Point 6 above), and the fact that removal of the suprachiasmatic nuclei in rodents stops several rhythms, it has been tempting to look for a single circadian clock that controls behavior through the central control of excitability. The concept has been advanced (Brady, 1975b) that animals have an arousal center—such as the ascending reticular activating system (ARAS) in the vertebrate brain stem (see Thompson, 1975, p. 436)—which acts as a filter for incoming sensory information, facilitating the passage of signals to the relevant motor centers when central excitation is high, but attenuating or even blocking their passage when it is low. The level of excitation, it was proposed, is controlled by this arousal center being coupled to the circadian clock on the one hand, and to longer-term inputs such as hunger and sex on the other (Brady, 1975b). Different behaviors would thus change in parallel, on both circadian and noncircadian time scales (as in Figs. 5 and 6).

This hypothesis seems neatly to accommodate the first seven essential features listed above. They could be explained as the outcome of the control of central excitability by a single clock, with slight moderations on the output side to cover details such as Point 4. The hypothesis does not, however, cope well with either Point 8 or Point 9.

It is possible that the partially out-of-phase rhythms of Point 8 do arise as suggested (Section VI,B) from the interaction of changing arousal levels with the hierarchical organization of behavior. This hypothesis does not help to explain the common pattern changes of Point 9, however. These are difficult to reconcile with the central excitability model because they imply that as a result of noncircadian inputs such as maturation, insemination, pregnancy, and so on, the circadian clock's output to the arousal center is differentially altered across the day. Moreover, what is not known—because it has not been looked for—is whether behaviors that normally run in parallel are all similarly altered in the phasing of their patterns by such inputs. The differences between the effects of starvation or pregnancy on spontaneous activity and visual responsiveness (Figs. 3B and 9, inset) strongly suggest that they are not. This would, in fact, make good behavioral sense where new adaptive needs arose as a consequence of noncircadian inputs, for example, non-participation in mating swarms once inseminated, as in mosquitoes (Jones and Gubbins, 1978) and presumably also in tsetse flies (Vale, 1974, p. 583).

If this is the case, as appears likely, it virtually rules out the unitary arousal center proposal, because one response could not be increased without simultaneously increasing all others that are normally synchronous with it. There is, in addition, good evidence that the arousal system in vertebrates (the ARAS), though concerned with the control of sleep and wakefulness, is not directly involved in the circadian timing of behavior (Block and Zucker, 1976).

Furthermore, it is becoming clear that circadian systems in higher animals do involve multiple clocks (see Pittendrigh, 1981; Saunders, 1982, p. 114). Single CNS clocks such as the optic lobes of crickets and cockroaches (Page, 1984; Tomioka and Chiba, 1986) though not Diptera (Helfrich, 1986; Kasai and Chiba, 1987), and the suprachiasmatic nuclei (SCN) of rodents (Menaker *et al.*, 1981) seem primary in their role of driving behavior, but the effect of their removal has been tested only on locomotor activity or on locomotion-associated behaviors such as feeding and drinking (see Rusak and Zucker, 1979). Their role in driving the whole spectrum of the animal's behavioral rhythms has never been examined. And in any case, since different frequencies may appear in a single free-running rhythm (*frequency splitting*, Saunders, 1982, p. 116), at least two different clocks must be driving that particular behavior—as can arise from the uncoupling of a bilateral pair of driving clocks of the SCN or optic lobe type (e.g., Koehler and Fleissner, 1978).

A revised view of the central control of behavioral rhythms might propose, therefore, that there is not one clock and one arousal center, but many, each associated with one response or a group of closely related responses (i.e., like Moore-Ede and Sulzman's, 1981, Model III). Each behavioral center could then act as its own clock (as its cells must potentially be capable of doing, Brady, 1982, p. 138; Jacklet, 1982, 1985), but would also be linked with any master clock of the SCN type. These multiple clocks would thus be expected to keep generally in phase with each other by neural coupling as well as by entraining signals form the photoreceptors and/or the master clock. Any non-circadian inputs could then act on them independently, raising the excitability of one center without affecting others, so that circadian patterns of different behaviors would change differentially.

Behavioral control is based on the waxing and waning of excitation and inhibition as one behavior gives way to another (see, e.g., Kennedy, 1987; Barnard, 1983, p. 63). It is evident, therefore, that although the mean levels of different behaviors are subject to strong circadian control, this can only act by influencing complex and dynamic neural balances within the CNS. This process cannot be a deterministic turning on and off of a particular behavior; even at its strongest it is only going to be some kind of stochastic bias applied to the neural balances, a bias that surely must include changes in general excitability.

**Acknowledgments**

I thank Dr. Elfed Morgan for reading and making helpful comments on the manuscript. The work underlying this review was supported in part by the Overseas Development Administration of the Foreign and Commonwealth Office, London.

## References

Abdel Karim, E. I., and Brady, J. (1984). Changing visual responsiveness in pregnant and larvipositing tsetse flies, *Glossina morsitans*. *Physiol. Entomol.* **9**, 125–131.

Abisgold, J. D., and Simpson, S. J. (1988). The effect of dietary protein levels and haemolymph composition on the sensitivity of the maxillary palp chemoreceptors of locusts. *J. Exp. Biol.* **135**, 215–229.

Allemand, R. (1977). Influence de l'intensité d'éclairement sur l'expression du rythme journalier d'oviposition de *Drosophila melanogaster* en conditions lumineuses LD 12:12. *C. R. Acad. Sci. Paris, Ser. D* **284**, 1553–1556.

Allemand, R. (1983a). The circadian oviposition rhythm of *Drosophila melanogaster*. I. Influence of the laying substrate and of experimental conditions. *Biol. Behav.* **8**, 231–245.

Allemand, R. (1983b). The circadian oviposition rhythm of *Drosophila melanogaster*. II. Influence of biotic factors. *Biol. Behav.* **8**, 273–288.

Allemand, R., and David, J. R. (1984). Genetic analysis of the circadian oviposition rhythm in *Drosophila melanogaster*: Effects of drift in laboratory strains. *Behav. Genet.* **14**, 31–43.

Anderson, M., and Finlayson, L. H. (1978). Topography and electrical activity of peripheral neurons in the abdomen of the tsetse fly (*Glossina*) in relation to abdominal distension. *Physiol. Entomol.* **3**, 157–167.

Andrew, R. J. (1974). Arousal and the causation of behaviour. *Behaviour* **51**, 135–165.

Aréchiga, H., Huberman, A., and Naylor, E. (1974). Hormonal modulation of circadian neural activity in *Carcinus maenas* (L.). *Proc. R. Soc. London Ser. B* **187**, 299–313.

Arikawa, K., Kawamata, K., Suzuki, T., and Eguchi, E. (1987). Daily changes of structure, function and rhodopsin content in the compound eye of the crab *Hemigrapsus sanguineus*. *J. Comp. Physiol. A* **161**, 161–174.

Aschoff, J. (1982). Circadian rhythms in man. In "Biological Timekeeping" (J. Brady, ed.), Ch. 9, pp. 143–157. Cambridge Univ. Press, Cambridge.

Barnard, C. J. (1983). "Animal Behaviour—Ecology and Evolution." Croom Helm, London.

Barrass, R. (1962). The diurnal activity of the tsetse fly *Glossina pallidipes* Austen (Diptera, Muscidae). *Proc. Fed. Sci Congr., 1st, Salisbury, S. Rhodesia, 1960* pp. 287–290.

Barrass, R. (1970). The activity of *Glossina morsitans* Westwood (Diptera: Muscidae) in laboratory experiments. *Proc. R. Entomol. Soc. London Ser. A* **45**, 114–122.

Beach, R. (1980). Physiological change governing the onset of sexual receptivity in male mosquitoes. *J. Insect Physiol.* **26**, 245–252.

Bennet, R. R. (1983). Circadian rhythm of visual sensitivity in *Manduca sexta* and its development from an ultradian rhythm. *J. Comp. Physiol.* **150**, 165–174.

Birukow, G. (1960). Innate types of chronometry in insect orientation. *Cold Spring Harbor Symp. Quant. Biol.* **25**, 403–412.

Birukow, G. (1964). Aktivitäts- und Orientierungsrhythmik beim Kornkäfer (*Calandra granaria* L.). *Z. Tierpsychol.* **21**, 279–301.

Blest, A. D. (1978). The rapid synthesis and destruction of photoreceptor membrane by a dinopid spider: A daily cycle. *Proc. R. Soc. London, Ser. B* **200**, 463–483.

Block, M., and Zucker, I. (1976). Circadian rhythms of rat locomotor activity after lesions of the midbrain raphe nuclei. *J. Comp. Physiol.* **109**, 235–247.

Brady, J. (1970). Characteristics of spontaneous activity in tsetse flies. *Nature (London)* **228**, 286–287.

Brady, J. (1972a). Spontaneous, circadian components of tsetse fly activity. *J. Insect Physiol.* **18**, 471–484.

Brady, J. (1972b). The visual responsiveness of the tsetse fly *Glossina morsitans* Westw. (Glossinidae) to moving objects: The effects of hunger, sex, host odour and stimulus characteristics. *Bull. Entomol. Res.* **62**, 257–279.

Brady, J. (1973). Changes in the probing responsiveness of tsetse flies (*Glossina morsitans* Westw.) (Diptera, Glossinidae). *Bull. Entomol. Res.* **63**, 247-255.
Brady, J. (1974a). The pattern of spontaneous activity in the tsetse fly *Glossina morsitans* Westw. (Diptera, Glossinidae) at low temperatures. *Bull. Entomol. Res.* **63**, 441-444.
Brady, J. (1974b). The physiology of insect circadian rhythms. *Adv. Insect Physiol.* **10**, 1-115.
Brady, J. (1975a). 'Hunger' in the tsetse fly: The nutritional correlates of behaviour. *J. Insect Physiol.* **21**, 807-829.
Brady, J. (1975b). Circadian changes in central excitability—the origin of behavioural rhythms in tsetse flies and other animals? *J. Entomol. (A)* **50**, 79-95.
Brady, J. (1979). "Biological Clocks." *Stud. Biol.* **104**, Edward Arnold, London.
Brady, J. (1981). Behavioral rhythms in invertebrates. *In* "Handbook of Behavioral Neurobiology," Vol. 4, "Biological Rhythms" (J. Aschoff, ed.), Ch. 8, pp. 125-144, Plenum, New York.
Brady, J. (1982). Circadian rhythms in animal physiology. *In* "Circadian Timekeeping" (J. Brady, ed.), Ch. 8, pp. 121-142. Cambridge Univ. Press, London.
Brady, J. (1987a). The sunset activity of tsetse flies: A light threshold study on *Glossina morsitans*. *Physiol. Entomol.* **12**, 363-372.
Brady, J. (1987b). Circadian rhythms—endogenous of exogenous? *J. Comp. Physiol. A* **161**, 711-714.
Brady, J. (1988). Circadian ontogeny in the tsetse fly—a permanent major phase change after the first feed. *J. Insect Physiol.* **34**, in press.
Brady, J., and Crump, A. J. (1978). The control of circadian activity rhythms in tsetse flies: Environment or physiological clock? *Physiol. Entomol.* **3**, 177-190.
Brady, J., and Gibson, G. (1983). Activity patterns in pregnant tsetse flies, *Glossina morsitans*. *Physiol. Entomol.* **8**, 359-369.
Brandenburg, J., Bobbert, A. C., and Eggelmeyer, F. (1983). Circadian changes in the response of the rabbit's retina to flashes. *Behav. Brain Res.* **7**, 113-123.
Bursell, E. (1978). Quantitative aspects of proline utilization during flight in tsetse flies. *Physiol. Entomol.* **3**, 265-272.
Bursell, E., and Kuwengwa, T. (1972). The effect of flight on the development of flight musculature in the tsetse fly (*Glossina morsitans*). *Entomol. Exp. Appl.* **15**, 229-237.
Bursell, E., and Slack, E. (1969). Indications concerning the flight activity of tsetse flies (*Glossina morsitans* Westw.) in the field. *Bull. Entomol. Res.* **58**, 575-579.
Bursell, E., Billing, K. C., Hargrove, J. W., McCabe, C. T., and Slack, E. (1974). Metabolism of the bloodmeal in tsetse flies (a review). *Acta Trop.* **31**, 297-320.
Caldwell, R. L., and Rankin, M. A. (1974). Separation of migratory from feeding and reproductive behavior in *Oncopeltus fasciatus*. *J. Comp. Physiol.* **88**, 383-394.
Campan, R., Lacoste, G., and Morvan, R. (1975). Le rythme journalier de l'orientation scototactique chez le grillon des bois *Nemobius sylvestris* (Bosc): Approche de la signification biologique. *Monit. Zool. Ital. (N.S.)* **9**, 119-136.
Cardé, R. T., Comeau, A., Baker, T. C., and Roelofs, W. L. (1975). Moth mating periodicity: Temperature regulates the circadian gate. *Experientia* **31**, 46-48.
Chadd, E. M., and Brady, J. (1982). Sublethal insecticide effects on the probing responsiveness of tsetse flies and blowflies. *Physiol. Entomol.* **7**, 133-141.
Charlwood, J. D., and Jones, M. D. R. (1979). Mating behaviour in the mosquito, *Anopheles gambiae* s.l. I. Close range and contact behaviour. *Physiol. Entomol.* **4**, 111-120.
Chaudhry, M. A., and Morgan, E. (1983). Circadian variation in the behaviour and physiology of *Bulinus tropicus* (Gastropoda: Pulmonata). *Can. J. Zool.* **61**, 909-914.
Chiba, Y., Kubota, M., and Nakamura, Y. (1982). Differential effects of temperature upon evening and morning peaks in the circadian activity of mosquitoes, *Culex pipiens pallens* and *C. pipiens molestus*. *J. Interdisc. Cycle Res.* **13**, 55-60.
Chiba, Y., Shimizu, C., and Kasai, M. (1985). Modification of female mosquito circadian activity by a series of reproductive behaviors. *In* "Neurosecretion and the Biology of Neuropeptides" (H. Kobayashi *et al.*, eds.), pp. 497-503. Springer-Verlag, Berlin.

Clopton, J. R. (1984). Mosquito circadian and circa-bi-dian flight rhythms: A two oscillator model. *J. Comp. Physiol. A* **155**, 1-12.

Crawshaw, L. I. (1974). Temperature selection and activity in the crayfish, *Orconectes immunis*. *J. Comp. Physiol.* **95**, 315-322.

Crump, A. J., and Brady, J. (1979). Circadian activity patterns in three species of tsetse fly: *Glossina palpalis, austeni* and *morsitans*. *Physiol. Entomol.* **4**, 311-318.

Dann, S., and Aschoff, J. (1981). Short-term rhythms in activity. *In* "Handbook of Behavioral Neurobiology," Vol. 4, "Biological Rhythms" (J. Aschoff, ed.), Ch. 25, pp. 491-498. Plenum, New York.

Davis, E. E. (1984). Regulation of sensitivity in the peripheral chemoreceptor system for host-seeking behaviour by a haemolymph-borne factor in *Aedes aegypti*. *J. Insect Physiol.* **30**, 179-183.

Dean, G. J., Wilson, F., and Wortham, S. (1968). Some factors affecting eclosion of *Glossina morsitans* Westw. from pupae. *Bull. Entomol. Res.* **58**, 367-377.

Dean, G. J. W., Paget, J., and Wilson, F. (1969). Observations on the behaviour of tsetse flies (*Glossina morsitans orientalis* Vanderplank and *G. pallidipes* Austen) during an attempt to concentrate breeding around cattle. *J. Appl. Ecol.* **6**, 13-26.

Denlinger, D. L. (1983). Who controls the rhythm of tsetse parturition: mother or larva? *Physiol. Entomol.* **8**, 25-28.

Denlinger, D. L., and Ma, W-C. (1974). Dynamics of the pregnancy cycle in the tsetse *Glossina morsitans*. *J. Insect Physiol.* **20**, 1015-1026.

Dethier, V. G. (1976). "The Hungry Fly." Harvard Univ. Press, Cambridge, Mass.

Dreisig, H. (1980). The importance of illumination level in the daily onset of flight activity in nocturnal moths. *Physiol. Entomol.* **5**, 327-342.

Dreisig, H. (1986). Timing of daily activities in adult Lepidoptera. *Entomol. Gen.* **12**, 25-43.

Edwards, J. M., and Naylor, E. (1987). Endogenous circadian changes in orientational behaviour of *Talitrus saltator*. *J. Mar. Biol. Assoc. U.K.* **67**, 17-26.

Enright, J. T. (1972). When the beachhopper looks at the moon: the moon-compass hypothesis. *In* "Animal Orientation and Navigation" (S. R. Galler *et al.*, eds.), pp. 523-555. National Aeronautics and Space Administration, Washington, D.C.

Ercolini, A., and Scapini, F. (1976). Fototassia negativa e orientamento astronomico solare in due specie di stafilinidi ripari (*Paederus rubrothoracicus* Goeze e *Stenus bipunctatus* Erichson). *Redia* **59**, 135-153.

Fleissner, G. (1982). Isolation of an insect circadian clock. *J. Comp. Physiol.* **149**, 311-316.

Fleissner, G., and Fleissner, G. (1978). The optic nerve mediates the circadian pigment migration in the median eyes of the scorpion. *Comp. Biochem. Physiol. (A)* **61**, 69-71.

Follett, B. K., and Follett, D. E., eds. (1981). "Biological Clocks in Seasonal Reproductive Cycles." Scientechnica, Bristol.

Forward, R. B., Jr. (1980). Phototaxis of a sand-beach amphipod: Physiology and tidal rhythms. *J. Comp. Physiol.* **135**, 243-250.

Fuentes-Pardo, B., and Rubio, V. I. (1981). Correlation between motor and electroretinographic circadian rhythms in the crayfish *Procambarus bouvieri* (Ortmann). *Comp. Biochem. Physiol.* **68A**, 477-485.

Gee, J. D. (1975). The control of diuresis in the tsetse fly *Glossina austeni*: A preliminary investigation of the diuretic hormone. *J. Exp. Biol.* **63**, 391-401.

Glasgow, J. P. (1963). "The Distribution and Abundance of Tsetse." Pergamon, Oxford.

Hall, M. J. R. (1980a). Central control of tarsal thresholds for proboscis extension in the blowfly. *Physiol. Entomol.* **5**, 17-24.

Hall, M. J. R. (1980b). Circadian rhythm of proboscis extension responsiveness in the blowfly: Central control of threshold changes. *Physiol. Entomol.* **5**, 223-233.

Hargrove, J. W. (1975). The flight performance of tsetse flies. *J. Insect Physiol.* **21**, 1385-1395.

Helfrich, C. (1986). Role of the optic lobes in the regulation of the locomotor activity rhythm

of *Drosophila melanogaster*: behavioral analysis of neural mutants. *J. Neurogenet.* **3**, 321-343.
Hinde, R. A. (1970). "Animal Behaviour—a Synthesis of Ethology and Comparative Psychology," 2nd Ed. McGraw-Hill, New York.
Hoffmann, K. (1982). Time-compensated celestial orientation. *In* "Biological Timekeeping" (J. Brady, ed.), Ch. 4, pp. 49-62. Cambridge Univ. Press, Cambridge.
Huyton, P. M., and Brady, J. (1975). Some effects of light and heat on the feeding and resting behaviour of tsetse flies, *Glossina morsitans* Westwood. *J. Entomol. (A)* **50**, 23-30.
Jacklet, J. W. (1982). Circadian clock mechanisms. *In* "Biological Timekeeping" (J. Brady, ed.), Ch. 11, pp. 173-188. Cambridge Univ. Press, Cambridge.
Jacklet, J. W. (1985). Neurobiology of circadian rhythms generators. *Trends Neurosci.* **8**, 69-73.
Jones, M. D. R. (1981). The programming of circadian flight-activity in relation to mating and the gonotrophic cycle in the mosquito, *Aedes aegypti. Physiol. Entomol.* **6**, 307-313.
Jones, M. D. R., and Gubbins, S. J. (1978). Changes in the circadian flight activity of the mosquito *Anopheles gambiae* in relation to insemination, feeding and oviposition. *Physiol. Entomol.* **3**, 213-220.
Jones, M. D. R., Hill, M., and Hope, A. M. (1967). The circadian flight activity of the mosquito *Anopheles gambiae*: Phase setting by the light régime. *J. Exp. Biol.*, **47**, 503-511.
Jones, M. D. R., Gubbins, S. J., and Cubbin, C. M. (1974). Circadian flight activity in four sibling species of the *Anopheles gambiae* complex (Diptera, Culicidae). *Bull. Entomol. Res.* **64**, 241-246.
Jordan, A. M. (1974). Recent developments in the ecology and methods of control of tsetse flies (*Glossina* spp.) (Dipt., Glossinidae)—a review. *Bull. Entomol. Res.* **63**, 361-399.
Kaiser, W., and Steiner-Kaiser, J. (1983). Neuronal correlates of sleep, wakefulness and arousal in a diurnal insect. *Nature (London)* **301**, 707-709.
Kaplan, E., and Barlow, R. B., Jr. (1980). Circadian clock in *Limulus* brain increases response and decreases noise in retinal photoreceptors. *Nature (London)* **286**, 393-395.
Kasai, M., and Chiba, Y. (1987). Effects of optic lobe ablation on circadian activity in the mosquito, *Culex pipiens pallens. Physiol. Entomol.* **12**, 59-65.
Kavaliers, M. (1981). Rhythmic thermoregulation in larval cranefly (Diptera: Tipulidae). *Can. J. Zool.* **59**, 555-558.
Kavaliers, M., and Macvean, C. (1980). Effect of temperature and lunar phase on the phototactic responses of larvae of the wax moth, *Galleria mellonella* (Lepidoptera, Pyralidae). *Entomol. Exp. Appl.* **28**, 222-228.
Kennedy, J. S. (1987). Animal motivation: The beginning of the end? *In* "Perspectives in Chemoreception and Behavior" (R. F. Chapman, E. A. Bernays, and J. G. Stoffolano, Jr., eds.), pp. 17-31. Springer-Verlag, New York.
Koehler, W. K., and Fleissner, G. (1978). Internal desynchronization of bilaterally organized circadian oscillators in the visual system of insects. *Nature (London)* **274**, 708-710.
Kon, M. (1985). Activity patterns of *Chironomous yoshimatsui* (Diptera: Chironomidae). I. Effects of temperature conditions on the adult activity patterns. *J. Ethol.* **3**, 131-134.
Kon, M. (1986). Activity patterns of *Chironomous yoshimatsui* (Diptera: Chironomidae) II. Effect of temperature on the response of adults to light conditions. *Appl. Entomol. Zool.* **4**, 620-622.
Konopka, R. J. (1979). Genetic dissection of the *Drosophila* circadian system. *Fed. Proc., Fed. Am. Soc. Exp. Biol.* **38**, 2602-2605.
Konopka, R. J. (1981). Genetics and development of circadian rhythms in invertebrates. *In* "Handbook of Behavioral Neurobiology," Vol. 4, "Biological Rhythms" (J. Aschoff, ed.), Ch. 10, pp. 173-181. Plenum, New York.
Korall, H., and Martin, H. (1987). Responses of bristle field sensilla in *Apis mellifica* to geomagnetic and astrophysical fields. *J. Comp. Physiol. A* **161**, 1-22.
Kwan, W. H., and Gatehouse, A. G. (1978). The effects of low doses of three insecticides on activity, feeding, mating, reproductive performance and survival in *Glossina morsitans morsitans* (Glossinidae). *Entomol. Exp. Appl.* **23**, 201-221.

Langley, P. A. (1966). The control of digestion in the tsetse fly, *Glossina morsitans*. Enzyme activity in relation to the size and nature of the meal. *J. Insect Physiol.* **12**, 439-448.

Langley, P. A., Curtis, C. F., and Brady, J. (1974). The viability, fertility and behaviour of tsetse flies (*Glossina morsitans*) sterilized by irradiation under various conditions. *Entomol. Exp. Appl.* **17**, 97-111.

Lankinen, P., and Lumme, J. (1984). Genetic analysis of geographical variation in photoperiodic diapause and pupal eclosion rhythm in *Drosophila littoralis*. *Ciba Found. Symp.* **104**, 97-114.

LaVail, M. M. (1976). Rod outer segment disk shedding in rat retina: Relationship to cyclic lighting. *Science* **194**, 1071-1074.

Loher, W. (1979). Circadian rhythmicity of locomotor behavior and oviposition in female *Teleogryllus commodus*. *Behav. Ecol. Sociobiol.* **5**, 253-262.

Lohmann, M. (1967). Zur Bedeutung der lokomotorischen Aktivität in circadianen Systemen. *Z. Vergl. Physiol.* **55**, 307-332.

Martin, H., and Lindauer, M. (1977). Der Einfluss des Erdmagnetfeldes auf die Schwereorientierung der Honigbiene (*Apis mellifica*). *J. Comp. Physiol.* **122**, 145-187.

Menaker, M., and Binkley, S. (1981). Neural and endocrine control of circadian rhythms in the vertebrates. *In* "Handbook of Behavioral Neurobiology," Vol. 4, "Biological Rhythms" (J. Aschoff, ed.), Ch. 13, pp. 243-255. Plenum, New York.

Menaker, M., Hudson, D. J., and Takahashi, J. S. (1981). Neural and endocrine components of circadian clocks in birds. *In* "Biological Clocks in Seasonal Reproductive Cycles" (B. K. Follett and D. E. Follett, eds.), pp. 171-183. Scientechnica, Bristol.

Meyer-Rochow, V. B. (1974). Structure and function of the larval eye of the sawfly, *Perga*. *J. Insect Physiol.* **20**, 1565-1591.

Meyer-Rochow, V. B., and Horridge, G. A. (1975). The eye of *Anoplognathus* (Coleoptera, Scarabaeidae). *Proc. R. Soc. London Ser. B* **188**, 1-30.

Moore-Ede, M. C., and Sulzman, F. M. (1981). Internal temporal order. *In* "Handbook of Behavioral Neurobiology," Vol. 4, "Biological Rhythms" (J. Aschoff, ed.), Ch. 12, pp. 215-241. Plenum, New York.

Morgan, E., and Last, V. (1982). The behaviour of *Bulinus africanus*: A circadian profile. *Anim. Behav.* **39**, 557-567.

Neumann, D. (1976). Adaptations of chironomids to intertidal environments. *Annu. Rev. Entomol.* **21**, 387-414.

Nichols, P. (1979). "Behavioural Changes and Their Control During Starvation in the Tsetse Fly *Glossina morsitans*." Ph.D. thesis, University of London.

Nielsen, E. T. (1974). Activity patterns of *Eugaster* (Orthoptera: Ensifera). *Entomol. Exp. Appl.* **17**, 325-347.

Ollason, J. C., and Slater, P. J. B. (1973). Changes in the behaviour of the male zebra finch during a 12-hr day. *Anim. Behav.* **21**, 191-196.

Omand, E., and Zabara, J. (1981). Response reduction in dipteran chemoreceptors after sustained feeding or darkness. *Comp. Biochem. Physiol.* **70A**, 469-478.

Page, T. L. (1981a). Neural and endocrine control of circadian rhythmicity in invertebrates. *In* "Handbook of Behavioral Neurobiology," Vol. 4, "Biological Rhythms" (J. Aschoff, ed.), Ch. 9, pp. 145-172. Plenum, New York.

Page, T. L. (1981b). Localization of circadian pacemakers in insects. *In* "Biological Clocks in Seasonal Reproductive Cycles" (B. K. Follett and D. E. Follett, eds.), pp. 113-124. Scientechnica, Bristol.

Page, T. L. (1984). Neuronal organization of a circadian clock in the cockroach *Leucophaea maderae*. *Ciba Found. Symp.* **104**, 115-135.

Parker, A. H. (1962). Studies on the diurnal rhythms of the housefly, *Musca domestica* L., in a dry tropical environment. *Acta Trop.* **19**, 97-119.

Payne, T. L., Shorey, H. H., and Gaston, L. K. (1970). Sex pheromones of noctuid moths: Factors influencing antennal responsiveness in males of *Trichoplusia ni*. *J. Insect Physiol.* **16**, 1043-1055.

Peterson, E. L. (1980). The temporal pattern of mosquito flight activity. *Behaviour* **72**, 1-25.

Pilson, R. D., and Pilson, B. M. (1967). Behaviour studies of *Glossina morsitans* Westw. in the

field. *Bull. Entomol. Res.* **57**, 227-257.
Pittendrigh, C. S. (1981). Circadian systems: General perspective. In "Handbook of Behavioral Neurobiology," Vol. 4, "Biological Rhythms" (J. Aschoff, ed.), Ch. 5, pp. 57-80. Plenum, New York.
Powers, M. K., and Barlow, R. B., Jr. (1985). Behavioral correlates of circadian rhythms in the *Limulus* visual system. *Biol. Bull. Mar. Biol. Lab., Woods Hole* **169**, 578-591.
Rachman, N. J. (1979). The sensitivity to the labellar sugar receptors of *Phormia regina* in relation to feeding. *J. Insect Physiol.* **25**, 733-739.
Rensing, L. (1965). Tagesperiodik von Aktivität und Phototaxis bei *Corixa punctata* und *Anticorixa sahlbergi*. *Z. Vergl. Physiol.* **50**, 250-253.
Riddiford, L. M. (1974). The role of hormones in the reproductive behavior of female wild silkmoths. In "Experimental Analysis of Insect Behaviour" (L. Barton Browne, ed.), pp. 278-285. Springer-Verlag, Berlin.
Ringelberg, J., and Servaas, H. (1971). A circadian rhythm in *Daphnia magna*. *Oecologia* **6**, 289-292.
Rusak, B., and Zucker, I. (1979). Neural regulation of circadian rhythms. *Physiol. Rev.* **59**, 449-526.
Saini, R. K. (1981a). The pattern of sound production by the tsetse fly *Glossina morsitans morsitans* Westwood, 1850 (Diptera, Glossinidae). *Insect Sci. Appl.* **1**, 167-169.
Saini, R. K. (1981b). Effects of age and hunger on the pattern of sound production in the tsetse, *Glossina morsitans morsitans* Westwood, 1850 (Diptera, Glossinidae). *Insect Sci. Appl.* **1**, 393-397.
Saunders, D. S. (1982). "Insect Clocks" (2nd ed.). Pergamon, Oxford.
Slater, P. J. B. (1975). Temporal patterning and the causation of bird behaviour. In "Neural and Endocrine Aspects of Behaviour in Birds" (P. Wright, P. G. Caryl, and D. M. Vowles, eds.), pp. 11-33. Elsevier, Amsterdam.
Sokolove, P. G. (1975). Locomotory and stridulatory circadian rhythms in the cricket, *Teleogryllus commodus*. *J. Insect Physiol.* **21**, 537-558.
Thompson, R. F. (1975). "Introduction to Physiological Psychology." Harper & Row, New York.
Tomioka, K., and Chiba, Y. (1986). Circadian rhythm in the neurally isolated lamina-medulla complex of the cricket, *Gryllus bimaculatus*. *J. Insect Physiol.* **32**, 747-755.
Truman, J. W. (1973). Temperature sensitive programming of the silkmoth flight clock: A mechanism for adapting to the seasons. *Science* **182**, 727-729.
Tychsen, P. H. (1978). The effect of photoperiod on the circadian rhythm of mating responsiveness in the fruit fly, *Dacus tryoni*. *Physiol. Entomol.* **3**, 65-69.
Vale, G. A. (1971). Artificial refuges for tsetse flies (*Glossina* spp.). *Bull. Entomol. Res.* **61**, 331-350.
Vale, G. A. (1974). The responses of tsetse flies (Diptera, Glossinidae) to mobile and stationary baits. *Bull. Entomol. Res.* **64**, 545-588.
van der Molen, J. N. (1982). A direct comparison of electrophysiological and behavioural taste responses in the blowfly. *Chem. Senses* **7**, 117-127.
van Etten, J. (1982). Comparative studies on the diurnal activity pattern in two field and laboratory populations of *Glossina pallidipes*. *Entomol. Exp. Appl.* **32**, 38-45.
von Frisch, K. (1967). "The Dance Language and Orientation of Bees." Staples Press, London.
Wall, R. (1988). Analysis of the mating activity of male tsetse flies *Glossina m. morsitans* and *G. pallidipes* in the laboratory. *Physiol. Ent.* **13**, 103-110.
Wallraff, H. G. (1981). Clock-controlled orientation in space. In "Handbook of Behavioral Neurobiology," Vol. 4, "Biological Rhythms" (J. Aschoff, ed.), Ch. 16, pp. 299-309. Plenum, New York.
Warnes, M. L., and Finlayson, L. H. (1986). Electroantennogram responses of the stable fly, *Stomoxys calcitrans*, to carbon dioxide and other odours. *Physiol. Entomol.* **11**, 469-473.
Williams, D. S. (1983). Changes of photoreceptor performance associated with the daily turnover of photoreceptor membrane in locusts. *J. Comp. Physiol.* **150**, 509-519.
Wills, S. A., Page, T. L., and Colwell, C. S. (1985). Circadian rhythms in the electroretinogram of the cockroach. *J. Biol. Rhyth.* **1**, 25-37.

# Index

## A

*Aeshna*
  breathing cycles and, 106
  larvae
    breathing, 106-107
    foraging, 125
Aggression, song learning in zebra finch and, 27-28
Albatross
  insemination success and, 42
  sperm-storage duration and, 49
*Anax* larvae, oxygen pressure and, 105
*Aphelocheirus*
  breathing cycles and, 104
  larvae, breathing and, 106-107
Aquatic insects
  breathing and
    activity cycles, 104-106
    atmospheric air, 102-103
    foraging, 123-124
    postembryonic development, 106-108
    sequence, 103-104
  conflicting demands and, 127-128
  discussion of, 145-146
  environment and, 99-101
  light and, 110-111
  locomotory adaptation and
    foraging, 123-126
    general considerations, 111-113
    grooming, 124-125
    spatial distribution, 114-123
    time budget, 123-128
    variations in, 113-114
  oxygen and, 100, 101-102
  oxygen pressure and, 108, 110
  plastron and, 101, 102
    breathing cycles, 104
  postembryonic development and, 106-108
  predation risk and, 126-127
  respiratory constraints and, 101-102
  rest site and, 119-122
  surfacing mechanisms and, 108, 110-111
  terrestrial ambush predators vs.
    distance estimation, 132-134, 136, 137
    double strikes, 135-136
    general considerations, 129
    postmoult behavior, 141-145
    predatory behavior, 129-131
    size perception, 135
    target position, 134-135
    visual receptors, 136-139
Arthropods, circadian rhythm and, 179-180
Auditory template theory of song learning, 2-3, 14

## B

Bee-eater
  copulation period in, 40, 41
  insemination success of, 42
  paternity determination and, 37
*Belostoma flumineum*, breathing cycles and, 104
Belostomatidae
  light and, 110
  surfacing mechanisms in, 110
Bengalese finch, song learning and, 6, 15, 17-25
*Berosus*, respiration and, 103
Blackbird
  extrapair copulation and, 35
  paternity determination and, 37
Blowfly, circadian rhythm and, 168, 179
Bluebird, paternity determination and, 37
Bobolink, paternity determination and, 37
Bouting, tsetse fly and, 154-156
Breeding, song learning and, 6
Budgerigar, sperm-storage duration and, 47
*Buenoa*
  foraging and, 125
  larvae, 107

Bullfinch, song learning and, 30
Bunting
  copulation period in, 40, 41
  insemination success of, 42
  paternity determination and, 37
  sperm competition and, 62–63

## C

Call-note repertoire, zebra finch and, 14
*Chaoborus*
  foraging and, 126
  larvae, locomotor activity and, 113–114
Chicken
  fertilization window and, 41
  sperm precedence in, 51–58
  sperm-storage duration and, 46, 48–51, 53
Circadian organization of behavior, tsetse fly and
  basic features of, 182–183
  bouting of flight and, 154–156
  chemoreception and, 179
  control system for, 183–185
  eclosion and, 165–168
  entrainment of, 165
  general considerations for, 153–154
  in-phase behaviors and, 165–168
  laboratory conditions and
    bimodality, 161–162
    dusk activity, 164–165
    field behavior vs., 163–164
    phase-settings, 162, 163
  larviposition and, 165–168
  mechanoreception and, 180–181
  orientation rhythms and, 181
  out-of-phase behaviors and, 168
  photoreception and, 179–180
  physiological inputs and
    entrainment to LD, 164, 178
    genetics, 173–174, 178
    hunger, 168–171, 177–178
    insemination, 174, 178
    maturation, 171–172, 177–178
    pregnancy, 174–177, 178
    temperature, 173, 178
    toxic chemicals, 177
  temperature and, 157–160, 173, 178
  *zeitgeber* time and, 165

Cockatiel, sperm-storage duration and, 47
Coleoptera
  larvae, breathing and, 106–107
  respiration and, 102
Columbiformes, sperm-storage duration and, 50
Communication, aquatic insects and, 100
Copulation, future research and, 65
Copulation bout, birds and, 36
*Corixa dentipes*, breathing cycles and, 104
Corixidae
  light and, 110
  respiration and, 102–103
Cricket, circadian rhythm and, 168
Cuckolded males, sperm competition in birds and, 36

## D

*Daphnia*, circadian rhythm in, 181
DDT, circadian rhythm in insects and, 177
Dove, *see also* Ringdove
  copulation period in, 39–40
  sperm-storage duration and, 47, 49, 53
*Dytiscus marginalis*, respiration and, 102

## E

Eagle, sperm-storage duration and, 49
Egret
  copulation period in, 40, 41
  insemination success of, 42
*Eigenmannia*
  jamming avoidance response and, 78, 80
  neural mechanisms in, *see* Neural mechanisms, weakly electric fish and
Electric organ discharge (EOD), 74–77
Electrolocation, weakly electric fish and, 74–77
Electrophoresis, extrapair paternity and, 37, 38
Endocrine changes, song learning in zebra finch and, 30
EOD, 74–77
Extrapair copulations, sperm competition in birds and, 35–36

## F

Female-raised birds, song learning and, 12–14
Fertile period, sperm-storage duration and, 45, 47
Fertilization hypothesis, copulation frequency and, 44
Fertilization period, birds and
  copulation timing and, 39–43
  sperm-storage duration and, 45–51, 53
Fertilization window, birds and, 41
Finch, song learning in, *see* Song learning, zebra finch and
Flight patterns, tsetse fly and, 154–156
Flycatcher
  copulation period in, 40, 41
  insemination success of, 42
  paternity determination and, 37
Foraging, aquatic insects and
  breathing and, 123–124
  locomotor activity and, 125–126
  predation and, 127
Fulmar
  insemination success of, 42
  sperm-storage duration and, 49

## G

Galliformes, sperm-storage duration and, 50
Genetic factors, tsetse fly and, 173–174, 178
Genetic markers, extrapair paternity among birds and, 36–38
Goose
  copulation period in, 40, 41
  sperm-storage duration and, 46
Grasshopper, circadian rhythm and, 168
Great tit
  foraging and predation and, 128
  song learning and, 20
Grooming, aquatic insects and, 124–125
Guillemot, *see also* Seabird
  copulation period in, 40, 41
  insemination success of, 42
  paternity determination and, 38
  sperm competition and, 59–60
Guinea fowl, sperm-storage duration and, 46

## H

Heteroptera, respiration and, 102
Hormones
  circadian rhythm in insects and, 183–184
  song learning in zebra finch and, 30
Hunger, tsetse fly and, 170–171
*Hydrophilus*, respiration and, 102
Hygrometry, aquatic insects and, 100

## I

Ibis
  copulation period in, 40, 41
  insemination success of, 42
Insecticides, circadian rhythm in insects and, 177
Insemination, tsetse fly and, 174, 178
Irradiation, circadian rhythm in insects and, 177

## J

Jamming avoidance response (JAR), weakly electric fish and, 78–82
JAR, weakly electric fish and, 78–82

## K

Kestrel, sperm-storage duration and, 46, 49
Kinship, song learning in zebra finch and, 7, 30

## L

Larvae
  *Aeshna*, breathing and, 106–107
  *Anax*, oxygen pressure and, 105
  *Aphelocheirus*, breathing and, 106–107
  *Buenoa*, 107
  *Chaoborus*, locomotor activity and, 113–114

coleoptera, breathing and, 106–107
mayfly, oxygen pressure and, 105
straliomyidous, respiration and, 103
tsetse fly, 154
Larviposition, tsetse fly and, 175–177
*Lethocerus*, breathing cycles and, 104, 108
Light, aquatic insects and, 110–111
spatial distribution and, 116–119
Locomotor adaptation, aquatic insects and, *see* Aquatic insects, locomotor adaptation and

## M

Magpie, sperm competition and, 58–59
Mallard
copulation period in, 39–40
fertilization window and, 41
paternity determination and, 37
sperm precedence in, 51–58
sperm-storage duration and, 46, 53
Mantid vs. *Renatra*, *see* Aquatic insects, terrestrial ambush predators vs.
Marsh warbler, song learning and, 3
*Martarega*, foraging and, 125
Mate attraction, song learning and, 2
Mate choice, song learning and, 8
Maturation, tsetse fly and, 171–172
Mayfly larvae, oxygen pressure and, 105
Mechanoreceptor sensitivity, circadian rhythm in insects and, 180
Memorization, song learning in zebra finch and, 6–7
Monogamy, sperm competition in birds and, 35–36
Morphological correlates, extrapair paternity among birds and, 36–37
Morphological locomotory adaptations, aquatic insects and, 112
Mosquito, mechanoreceptor sensitivity in, 181
Murre, paternity determination and, 38

## N

*Nemotelus*, respiration and, 103
Nepidae
light and, 110
oxygen pressure and, 108, 110

Neural changes, song learning in zebra finch and, 30
Neural mechanisms, weakly electric fish and
ambiguity of messages and, 89–93
development of, 96
electrolocation and, 74–77
general considerations for, 73–74
jamming avoidance response and, 78–82
neuronal substrate for study of, 82–89
*Notiophilus*, visual receptors and, 138–139
*Notonecta*
foraging and, 125
respiration and, 103
rest sites of, 122

## O

Odonata, visual receptors and, 138–139
*Oncopeltus*, circadian rhythm in, 168
Ovulation, zebra finch song and, 4
Oxygen, aquatic insects and, 100–102
Oxygen pressure, aquatic insects and, 105, 108, 110

## P

Paternity determination methods, sperm competition in birds and, 36–38
Pheasant, sperm-storage duration and, 46
*Phormia regina*, foraging and, 125
Photoreceptor sensitivity, circadian rhythm in insects and, 179–180
Pigeon
copulation period in, 39–40
sperm-storage duration and, 46
Plastron, aquatic insects and, 101, 102, 104
Plumage, paternity determination and, 37, 38
Polyandry, sperm competition in birds and, 35–36
Postembryonic development, aquatic insects and, 106–108
predatory behavior and, 129–131
visual receptors and, 137–138
Poultry, paternity determination and, 37
Predation and foraging, aquatic insects and, 127

Predation hypothesis, copulation frequency and, 44
Pregnancy, tsetse fly and, 174–177, 178
Proactive interference, song learning in zebra finch and, 19–20
Proline, tsetse fly and, 154
Ptarmigan
  copulation period in, 39–40
  sperm-storage duration and, 46, 50
*Pyrrhosoma*
  breathing cycles and, 106
  foraging and, 126
  oxygen pressure and, 105

## Q

Quail, sperm-storage duration and, 46, 48–49, 53

## R

*Ranatra linearis*, behavioral adaptations of, *see* Aquatic insects
Rheas, sperm-storage duration and, 49
Ringdove, *see also* Dove
  sperm competition and, 61–62
  sperm precedence in, 51–58
  sperm-storage duration and, 47
Rival repulsion, songs for, 2
Rook, copulation period in, 40, 41

## S

Salt water insects, 99, *see also* Aquatic insects
Saturniid, circadian rhythm and, 179
Scaup
  copulation period in, 40, 41
  insemination success of, 42
Seabird, *see also* Guillemot
  sperm competition and, 59–60
  sperm-storage duration and, 49, 50
Sensitive phase theory of song learning, 3, 29
Sex differences, song learning in zebra finch and, 14

Sexual imprinting, song learning in zebra finch and, 19–21, 28, 29
Snail, circadian rhythm in, 167–168
Social bond hypothesis, copulation frequency in birds and, 44
Social factors, song learning in zebra finch and, 3, 14–15, 22, 27–28
Song learning, zebra finch and
  after adulthood, 7
  behavioral interaction and, 24–25
  call-note repertoire and, 14
  cross-fostering and, 16–17, 22–23
  endocrine changes and, 30
  father and, 6–11
  hormonal changes and, 30
  isolation and, 6–11
  kinship and, 30
  laboratory conditions and, 5
  mate choice and, 8, 28–29
  memorization and, 6–7, 30
  mixed species exposure and, 17–22
  neural changes and, 30
  own-species bias and, 22–25
  parents and, 6–11
  phrasing and, 10
  plumage and, 26–27
  proactive interference and, 19–20
  selectivity in, 8–9
  sequence of, 6–7
  sex differences in, 14
  sexual imprinting and, 19–21, 28, 29
  social factors and, 3, 14–15, 22, 27–28
  songs heard after 65 days and, 12–14
  species differences and, 1–2
  timing of, 15–22
  tutor selection and, 25–29
  updating and, 19–22
  visual contact and, 16–17, 24
  visual imprinting and, 26–27
  wild birds and, 8, 30
Song structure, own-species bias and, 23
Sound spectrograph, 1
Sparrow, song learning and, 6, 28
Species differences, vocal development and, 1–2
Sperm competition, birds and
  artificial vs. natural insemination in, 48, 54, 55, 58
  case studies of, 58
  guillemot, 59–60
  indigo bunting, 62–63

magpie, 58
ringdove, 60-61
swallow, 60-61
cuckolded males and, 36
extrapair copulations and, 35-36
extrapair paternity and, 36, 38-39
  detection methods for, 37
female resistance and, 43
fertilization hypothesis and, 44
future research and, 63-65
mechanisms of
  copulation frequency, 43-45
  fertilization period, 45-51
  sperm precedence, 51-58
  sperm-storage duration, 45-51, 53
  timing and success of copulation, 39-43
mixed paternity and, 36
monogamy and, 35-36
multiple paternity and, 36
paternity determination methods and, 36-38
polyandry and, 35-36
predation hypothesis and, 44
social bond hypothesis and, 44
sperm competition hypothesis and, 44
sperm precedence and, 35
Sperm competition hypothesis, copulation frequency in birds and, 44
Sperm precedence, birds and, 51-58
  future research and, 65
  sperm competition and, 35
Sperm-storage duration, birds and, 45-51, 53
  future research on, 64
Sperm-storage glands in birds, 55-56
Starvation, circadian rhythm in insects and, 179-180
Straliomyidous larvae, respiration and, 103
Surfacing mechanisms, aquatic insects and, 108, 110-111
Swallow
  copulation period in, 40, 41
  insemination success of, 42
  paternity determination and, 37
  sperm competition and, 60-61
Syrinx, song learning and, 3

## T

Temperature
  aquatic insects and, 99-100, 105-106
  spatial distributions, 123

circadian rhythm in tsetse fly and, 157-160, 173, 178
*Trichoplusia ni*, circadian rhythm and, 179
Tsetse fly, circadian organization of behavior and, *see* Circadian organization of behavior, tsetse fly and
Turkey
  sperm precedence in, 51-58
  sperm-storage duration and, 46, 48-51, 53
Tutor selection, song learning in zebra finch and, 25-29

## U

Updating, song learning in zebra finch and, 19-22

## V

Vasectomy, extrapair paternity and, 37, 38-39
*Velia*, visual receptors and, 138-139
Vision
  aquatic insects and, 100, 136-139
  predatory behavior, 131-134
  tsetse fly and, 179-181
Visual contact, song learning in zebra finch and, 16-17, 24
Visual imprinting, song learning in zebra finch and, 26-27
Vocal development, species differences in, 1-2

## W

Water environment, aquatic insects and, 99-100, *see also* Aquatic insects
Weakly electric fish, neural mechanisms in, *see* Neural mechanisms, weakly electric fish and
Wild birds
  copulation period in, 40, 41
  fertilization window and, 41

paternity determination and, 38
  song learning and, 8, 30
  sperm precedence in, 56–57
  sperm-storage duration and, 48–49
Woodpecker
  paternity determination and, 37
  sperm competition and, 36, 37

## Z

Zebra finch
  song learning and, *see* Song learning, zebra finch and
  sperm-storage duration and, 48–49
Zygoptera, oxygen pressure and, 105